WAR CRIMINALS

THEIR PROSECUTION

& PUNISHMENT

By Sheldon Glueck

Professor of Criminal Law and Criminology
Harvard University

NEW YORK

ALFRED A. KNOPF

1944

FIRST EDITION

TO THE MEMORY OF
A WISE AND KIND LADY
Anna B. Touroff

CONTENTS

PREFACE

☙❧

As THIS IS BEING WRITTEN, the impending doom of the Axis powers is patent to the whole world. Only the Nazis still shout defiance and speak of squeezing the perennial "last ounce of energy and fanaticism" out of the dazed German people. In three months the hard-hitting, brilliantly-generaled Russian armies, on a front stretching through almost the entire vertical diameter of Europe, have made such amazing progress that they are well on the way to Eastern Germany. In three months, the gallant American, English and Canadian troops, under superb military leadership, have not only pierced Hitler's impenetrable Atlantic Wall, but have swept across France, have liberated Paris, and are soon to take over the watch on the Rhine. In the Pacific, the dauntless and ingenious American troops have landed upon island after island in the ever-narrowing perimeter around Tokio. A number of Axis satellites, in addition to Italy, have given up the struggle; and some, at least, are turning on their German "friends." In the air, as well as upon land and sea, the mortal enemies of Nazism and Fascism have complete mastery, while the underground groups in all countries under Germany's heel have sprung to arms and crystallized into well-directed and militarily effective units.

With victory in sight, not the least perplexing question that will present itself to the United Nations is: What shall be done with the Nazi-Fascist war criminals?

The problems involved in answering this question are enormously complex. A rational and civilized approach to the issues presented must entail consideration of puzzling tangles of international and municipal law; of military and non-military law; of public policy on both national and international planes; of criminology and penology; of social psychology and social ethics.

An attempt to lay bare the major technical issues of law and polity involved in the development of even a fairly acceptable program for the treatment of war criminals ought in these times to be of social value. That is what this book purports to do.

It grew out of my membership (unfortunately, at a distance) on the Commission on Trial and Punishment of War Criminals of the London International Assembly, League of Nations Union, and out of a special Seminar which I conducted in the winter of 1942–43 at the Harvard Law School.

I am indebted to General Marcel deBaer, Chairman of the above-noted Commission and Belgian member of the United Nations Commission on the same subject, to my students, and to Mr. Louis Sohn for the opportunity of discussing with them some views and doubts regarding the problems involved. Naturally, however, responsibility for the arguments presented and conclusions arrived at is entirely my own.

Thanks are due to the editors of *Free World*, the *New Republic*, and the *Harvard Law Review* for permission to quote from my articles in those publications; to Mr. Kenneth G. Darling, for editorial suggestions; and to the Milton Fund and Clark Bequest of Harvard University for financial aid in assembling and translating some of the materials referred to in this volume.

My greatest thanks go out to my wife and daughter, whose constant encouragement contributed no little to the final completion of this work.

S. G.

Cambridge, Massachusetts,
September, 1944.

WAR CRIMINALS:
THEIR PROSECUTION AND
PUNISHMENT

"Now for my Part, being fully assured . . . that there is some Right common to all Nations, which takes Place both in the Preparations and in the Course of War, I . . . observed throughout the Christian World a Licentiousness in regard to War, which even barbarous Nations ought to be ashamed of: a Running to Arms upon very frivolous or rather no Occasions; which being once taken up, there remained no longer any Reverence for Right, either Divine or Human, just as if from that Time Men were authorized and firmly resolved to commit all manner of Crimes without Restraint. . . . But . . . far must we be from admitting the Conceit of some, that the Obligation of all Right ceases in War; nor when undertaken ought it to be carried on beyond the Bounds of Justice and Fidelity. . . ." Grotius, *De Jure Belli ac Pacis* (2d Ed., 1631), I, XXIX, xxvi.

". . . War is an element in the order of the world ordained by God. In it the noblest virtues of mankind are developed. . . . Without war the world would stagnate, and lose itself in materialism. . . . Every law presupposes an authority to superintend and direct its execution, and international conventions are supported by no such authority. What neutral States would ever take up arms for the sole reason that, two Powers being at war, the 'laws of war' had been violated by one or both of the belligerents? For offenses of that sort there is no earthly judge. . . ." Field-Marshal-General Count von Moltke in letter to Prof. J. K. Bluntschli, Dec. 11, 1880, Holland, *Letters on War and Neutrality*, 1914, p. 25.

". . . What we have in mind is the case of a conscious and deliberate violation of the laws of war as a matter of state policy. Now that these laws are being clearly defined and solemnly accepted by all states, the nation that could thus act must possess at once extreme unscrupulousness and enormous strength. It is just possible that now and again such a combination would occur. A ruler drunk with the consciousness of overwhelming power might venture to defy the moral sentiments of mankind, but only to discover by and by that outraged humanity avenges itself in unexpected ways. . . . Those, therefore, who imagine that a state is free to ignore because of the exigencies of the moment any rule to which it has subscribed its signature are as erroneous in their reasoning as they are anarchical in their sentiments. The laws of war are made to be obeyed, not to be set aside at pleasure." Lawrence, *The Principles of International Law* (7th Ed., 1923), 373-74.

CHAPTER I

INTRODUCTION *

☙

Not until the publication of the "March of Death" atrocities committed by the Japanese did the too complacent American public begin to realize that the Axis enemy is capable of the most abominable deeds against the laws of God and man. It was only then that the vials of wrath were fully poured out. This time it was not the smoking embers of some distant little Lidice, nor the anguished cries of anonymous Belgians, Czechs, Dutch, French, Greeks, Jews, Poles or Russians who were the victims of Fascist bestiality. This time it was the flower of American youth — our own heroes of Bataan and Corregidor. Now at last was the man in the street shockingly convinced that the press and radio accounts, which in their frequency and horror had so jaded his senses as to turn him into a tired skeptic, were not again those notorious "mere atrocity tales" which the Germans had so effectively exploited during the last world war to escape calumny and punishment.

The Nazis welcomed this sudden emphasis upon Japanese atrocities as turning the spotlight of condemnation from their own countless acts of torture, rapine and murder. But the later Nazis slaughter of imprisoned English aviators inside German prison camps and of surrendered American paratroopers in Normandy seem finally to have convinced most of the generous English and American peoples that the Germans, in their mad bid for world dominance, have committed deeds even more barbarous than those of the Japanese, and with far less excuse. For the Germans cannot be called, as the more lurid press has dubbed our far-Eastern enemies, "ape-men," "yellow devils," or savages. They have long regarded themselves as of the very cream of the cream of civilized men. They notoriously boast of

---

* The reference notes will be found in a separate section at the end of the book.

their advanced *Kultur* and of their God-favored status as the "Master Race." Yet this self-styled superior race has cold-bloodedly tortured and slaughtered not hundreds, nor thousands, but millions of helpless civilians, not to dwell at present on their brutal treatment of prisoners of war. On countless occasions this self-elected *Herrenvolk* has ruthlessly trampled upon most of the rules of legitimate warfare to be found in the lexicon of the law of nations and upon most of the principles of criminal law embodied in the penal codes of civilized States.

All is *not* fair in war; and the mere wearing of a uniform is neither justification nor excuse for criminalistic and gratuitously cruel practices, most of them wholly unconnected with military necessity. There are solemn conventions which the Axis powers, in common with member-states of the United Nations, have signed and ratified. These govern the legitimate ways of declaring war; the limitation of a State's resort to arms to a just (*i.e.*, a self-defensive) war; the permitted and the prohibited means of warfare; the minimal standards for the humane treatment of prisoners of war and the wounded; the rights of civilian populations in occupied territories, and other crucial matters. But even in the absence of such sacred international contracts, the permissible acts of warfare are, by the authority of long and common usage, strictly limited. The treaties entered into between members of the Family of Nations are but specific definitions and reenforcements of the general common law of nations, the "unwritten" rules of warfare, which for centuries have limited the method and manner of conducting wars. The common law of nations, by which all States are and must be bound, dictates that warfare shall be carried on only in accordance with basic considerations of humanity and chivalry.

These matters are of course well known to the German and Japanese war-lords and statesmen, as well as to their chief henchmen. They have long been convinced, however, that the governing "law" lacks the very life-juice of law: "sanctions." Without specific provisions for *punishing individual malefactors,* as well as States, the prohibitions of the law of nations in the domain of warfare are regarded by the Axis bullies as but empty threats; and considering the whole miserable era of servile appeasement it is no wonder that they are so regarded. The Axis powers, led by Nazified and militaristic Germany, set out determinedly to win World War II by hook or crook; and, winning it, they would most assuredly escape retribution for their wholesale deeds of theft, murder, rapine and enslavement. If they ever considered their losing this war as anything but a very remote contingency, they no doubt fondly recalled the softness of both heart and head displayed by the Allied and Associated Powers at the close of World War I which enabled the ex-Kaiser and his henchmen to escape punishment (see Chapter II). This would be a pleasant precedent for their own treatment by the United Nations if ever the day of reckoning for the second world war should arrive. The lesson for a possible third attempt to enslave the world is obvious. A saturnalia of blood and crime in which, win or lose, the guilty are not punished for the most flagrant violations of the rules is something that has a particularly intoxicating appeal to warlike peoples.

It is still not certain that most Axis malefactors will suffer punishment for their misdeeds. True, there have been numerous solemn pronouncements by leaders of the United Nations that retribution stalks close upon the heels of the Nazi and Japanese war criminals. But similar official pronouncements were made during the first world war; and thus far only Russia has acted as well as spoken. A tangle of misguided public opinion and outworn but still sacrosanct legal technicalities could easily bedevil the plan to punish those leading Axis war criminals who survive the falling out among thieves that must inevitably result in many murders and suicides of military and political personnel inside Germany and Japan.

Unfortunately, the program for coping with war criminals (particularly the German) has to be developed in an atmosphere of still divided American public and professional opinion. Russians, Poles, Greeks, Belgians and others who have somehow survived Nazi brutality are more united in their views. They know their Germans at first hand. In England, the latest surprise use of a weapon of indiscriminate killing — the "robot bomb" — is cementing the public attitude against Germany, although the generosity of the British people and the insistence of their lawyers upon the same technicalities in the prosecution of war criminals that they observe in the domestic administration of criminal justice may seriously weaken the program for coping with Nazi-Fascist malefactors. In the United States those who have expressed themselves on the problem of what to do with Axis war criminals appear to be in the greatest disagreement.

There are, first, the perpetual skeptics. Despite countless official as well as newspaper reports of atrocities that have stunned the world, these persons are not convinced. "Human beings simply don't do such things." These doubting Thomases recall that during the last war there was some mendacious propaganda about Germans chopping off the hands of children, and they therefore conclude that all reports of German atrocities during the past and present wars must be equally dubious. There is little that can be done with these chronic disbelievers. Even solemn proof in trials at law will not convince many of them. They will also not believe the brutal pronouncements of German military philosophy in such cynical handbooks for the guidance of officers as the *Kriegsbrauch im Landkriege* in which, although Germany has solemnly obligated itself to observe the provisions of the Hague Conventions regulating warfare, their humane tenets of international law are referred to as expressing degenerate "sentimentalism and flabby emotionalism" and are declared to be "in fundamental contradiction with the nature of war and its object"; and in which the German officer is sternly warned to "guard himself against exaggerated humanitarian ideas."

Opposed to the chronic skeptics are those who cry for indiscriminate vengeance. To them all the German and Japanese people are equally guilty. The survivors of atrocities and their relatives ought to be permitted to "take the law into their own hands" and give the Germans, Rumanians, Japanese and other brutal peoples a "good dose of their own medicine." In fact, so embittered have millions of victims of Nazi-Japanese hatred and blood-lust become that a major problem of the United Nations will be to police lands freed from Axis domination until such time as the thirst for indiscriminate mass-vengeance will have died down. Vengeance against the entire breed of Axis peoples, regardless of proof of individual guilt or innocence, is not likely to advance that regime of justice and decency which it is one of the principal aims of the United Nations to re-establish; nor is it likely, always, to punish those who most deserve it. It may not infrequently result in the shooting or hanging of many innocent persons who fought Nazism and militarism until forcibly silenced. In civilized justice, even the criminal taken *in flagrante delicto,* with a smoking revolver in his hand, is and should be given a fair trial to enable him to set up such defenses and matters of mitigation as he may have. The laws and traditions to which all decent States adhere require judicial proceedings as a basis for punishment; and this is true, also, of offenses against the laws of warfare which are usually triable by military tribunals. Even the most flagrant, obvious and hated war criminals ought therefore not be punished unless convicted upon impartial trials with opportunity to present such legally recognized defenses of justification, excuse or mitigation as are available to them.

Then there are those who are willing to admit the atrocities but who insist that the offenders should be magnanimously forgiven and told to go and sin no more. Representatives of this school not infrequently indulge in the annoying tactic of putting most other persons in the category of vengeance-thirsty sadists whilst they themselves bask in the sunshine of cheek-turning magnanimity. It is doubtful whether there is one among these noble-hearted religionists and moralists who has himself suffered torture at the hands of the Nazis or whose loved ones have undergone the foul indignities, brutalities or anguished death in the concentration camps, ghettos, charnel-houses or "murder-autos" of the Third Reich. To be sure, the "thirst for vengeance" is a low sentiment; but it ought not to be confused with the legitimate, commendable and morally virtuous desire of the survivors of Axis brutality to see that mankind's law and justice speak out, at long last, on their behalf.

Any program for coping with war criminals that concerns itself only or primarily with the effects upon the Nazis and other Fascists of a proposed course of action — particularly with placating them and bribing them to "be good" in the future — is not only degrading and unfair, but unrealistic. The effects on the victims of Nazi-Fascist crime, on world opinion generally, and on the future of the law of nations must also be taken into account. Yet the feelings of the survivors of Axis cruelty are utterly ignored by one branch of the magnanimity-to-the-Germans school. Their point is that if the Germans (they are often suspiciously silent about the Japanese) are treated generously, they will, with noble compensatory generosity, deign not to attack the peace-loving world again. This is of course simply the old appeasement policy all over again, an attitude which has proved so tragically bankrupt throughout the democracies' dealings with the Fascists. It amounts, simply, to the paying of blackmail to ruthless gangsters who have seized the reins of government in foreign lands. Is the world going to resume its fatuous genuflections toward Germany even after her defeat in the second world war brought on by herself despite the pleas and concessions of peaceful peoples? This, too, is not beyond the realm of possibility. It can be brought about by the most dangerous representatives of the soft-peace-for-Germany school, certain professors who have permitted their nostalgic reminiscences of student days at "good old Heidelberg" to becloud elementary common sense and the irrefutable evidence of German cruelties and crimes. By writings trimmed with the narcotic ideologies of quasi-disciplines that pass as "science," by the use of not altogether relevant analogies, by questionable emphases of various parts of the record of history, and by avoidance or under-emphasis of the evidence of deliberate mass murder of millions of non-offending men, women and children, these cognoscenti are able to lend a great show of "objectivity" and "scientific impartiality" and "justice" to views that ought to warm the cockles of Herr Goebbels's perfidious heart. Some of these learned appeasers come very close to suggesting that the United Nations are just as guilty as Germany, both in starting the war and in conducting it contrary to the laws and customs of permitted warfare. The success of their "arguments" would be once again to lay open the peaceful peoples of the world to the sworn enemies of peace; and this even in the face of evidence that the militarists of a Germany on the verge of thorough defeat are already casting about for ways and means to foster the truculent glories of the Fourth Reich.

History has of course abundantly demonstrated that appeasement of piratical States does not purchase security for the appeasing States; it only helps the former to wax stronger, until the tragic day when they can completely annihilate their too trusting victims. But nations and governments, like individuals, have short memories; and they are not always good interpreters of human motive in the making of history.

Another powerful source of opinion and policy-making in respect to war criminals will be the views of professional soldiers, especially Anglo-American. To their credit be it said that these gentlemen are distinguished by a highly developed sense of fair play and gallantry. But this very virtue might make them not like to contemplate the punishment of their "opposite numbers" for "merely doing their military duty." It may well appear that the trial and punishment of distinguished generals and admirals long after the occurrence of the alleged violations of the laws and customs of warfare is something distasteful, unchivalrous, reflecting, as it were, upon the profession of arms. Heartening to those who wish to see justice done are the several warnings issued by General Dwight D. Eisenhower to the Nazis in the various countries released from the German incubus that war criminals will be punished.

One must also consider the possibility of certain influential United Nations businessmen and bankers, interested in German cartels and friendly with German economists and industrial barons, intervening behind the scenes to save the precious necks of their colleagues.

Finally, German propaganda is already very active in this country and England to "soften up" the United Nations by circulating claims that only a very small number of Nazis are responsible for German atrocities, that most of the charges are propaganda anyway, and that somehow the saving of the skins of German criminals will strengthen Europe against the threadbare "Communist menace."

In addition to the points of view of non-lawyers, the attitudes of administrators of law and justice must of course also be considered in analyzing the currents of ideology and prejudice that make up American public opinion on the war criminals' problem.

There is a small group of lawyers and publicists who wish to see at least the major malefactors punished but who oppose resort to the elaborate processes of trial. Recognizing the significant fact that the victorious belligerent can impose upon the vanquished almost any terms he sees fit, they suggest that Hitler, Tojo, the other leaders in criminalism and their chief accomplices ought simply to be declared, by the armistice or treaty of peace, to be criminals and outlaws, and to be executed without the United Nations going through the time-consuming and expensive processes of prosecution, defense and judgment in courts of law. Trial by the United Nations in an international tribunal, they argue, would only give the Axis leaders a public platform from which they could continue to spread their propaganda and enhance their role as martyrs. Public trial, they claim, is essentially superfluous anyway, since it is a foregone conclusion that the vast majority of the accused would be found guilty. On October 4, 1944, Prime Minister Churchill intimated that some such action may be taken by the leaders of the United Nations, when he said "it should not be assumed that the procedure of trial will be necessarily adopted" for such war criminals as Hitler, Goering, Goebbels and Himmler.

At first blush there seems to be much in favor of these views. In the writer's opinion, however, a much more satisfactory program in the long run would be to prosecute ordinary offenders in the victims' domestic tribunals (military or civil, as locally provided) and leading culprits (Heads of State, members of general staffs and certain other high-placed classes discussed in the following pages) in an International Criminal Court to be established by the United Nations and such neutral States as wish to participate. For, in the first place, it should be emphasized that trials in courts constitute a necessary symbol of the re-establishment of the rule of law on a world plane; and, secondly, it can be shown that the advantages of such a plan far outweigh the disadvantages, while the dangers referred to above are more theoretical than practical.

The most influential group concerned with the war criminals' problem are, however, certain international lawyers of the traditional school. They are willing to grant that the chief violators of the laws and customs of warfare ought to be punished. But they insist that unfortunately international law is at present not such as to make trial and punishment possible save in exceptional cases. This is the school of thought represented by the American members of the Inter-Allied Commission on Responsibility at the close of the last war. And it is more than possible that the debacle of justice at the close of World War I has contributed a large share to the Nazi policy of brazen lawlessness in the conduct of the present conflict.

The bitter-end conceptualism to which the strict constructionist international lawyers adhered at Versailles, and to which certain American publicists still cling, can only lead to an annoying *impasse*. Their reasoning runs that the vast majority of Axis war criminals cannot be prosecuted and punished by the United Nations because, in the first place, to do so would violate the fundamental doctrine of criminal law which prohibits the giving of "retroactive" (*ex post facto*) effect to law; because, in the second place, the alleged offenses were "acts of State," for which only the German, Japanese and other Axis *nations* (the "collectivity of subjects") may be held responsible, not the individual officers, soldiers, sailors who committed the acts deemed atrocities. They insist, further, that only German courts have jurisdiction over German malefactors, especially for offenses committed on German territory. They say, also, that since practically all the offenders were only obeying the orders of their military superiors in committing the alleged war crimes, they are immune from responsibility. The absurd result is that none of the military and naval personnel, from ordinary soldiers or sailors up the ladder to and including the members of the Axis general staffs, could, "in strict legality," be prosecuted for war crimes, if they were only obeying the orders of their ultimate superior, the "Head of State." And, to cap the climax of this legalistic version of Alice in Wonderland, the "Head of State," the ultimate source of authority — Hitler, Mussolini, Hirohito or Tojo, for example — is also exempt from prosecution in a non-German or non-Italian or non-Japanese court (which in effect means exempt from punishment) because of the very fact that he holds this exalted sacred cow position of Head of State and has no superior!

Much of the present work is devoted to a critical examination of the alleged legal obstacles to the trial and punishment of war criminals; and to the development of a program of action that accords with the spirit and manner of law and justice yet is not shackled by technicalities of doubtful validity and relevancy. Most of the traditional writings on the branch of the law of nations concerned with legitimate and illegitimate methods of warfare seem largely to be affected with a sort of baffling ideologic *rigor mortis* in a field in which flexibility and realism are indispensable. Without these latter, there may be a triumph of strict legal logic; but it results in the impunity of the most flagrant wrongdoers while their hapless and law-abiding victims are without a remedy. If ever there was a domain to which Mr. Justice Holmes's illuminating dictum about a page of history being worth a volume of logic is applicable, it is that concerned with the war criminals' problem.

Critical examination of the arguments in support of the traditional views in this field will show them to involve two very questionable assumptions: First, that a victorious State is legally bound to observe all the technical niceties of local peacetime administration of justice in dealing with a vanquished State and its nationals, who have themselves played havoc with every civilized concept of law and justice; secondly, that international law is a fully developed and highly exact science. Such dogmas are not only extremely doubtful but their adoption as guiding lines to a United Nations policy will lead to the discrediting and weakening of the very international law they purport to protect. For they play directly into the hands of governments which, by their notorious flouting of the law, prove themselves to be but bands of international gangsters who, when finally brought to book, appeal hypocritically to the protection of the most devious technicalities of the very law they have done their utmost to destroy.

In respect to the first questionable assumption of the traditional approach to this problem, it should be emphasized that a victorious belligerent State *can* impose any terms it deems proper on the vanquished. It is simply a matter of power. Although duress may be a lawful ground for repudiation of an international contract entered into during a period of peaceful relationships between law-observing States, some compulsion is to be expected in a treaty of peace. It is frequently claimed that all treaties must be in conformity with international law; but it must not be forgotten that treaties also make international law. In the final analysis, the main considerations which limit the action of a victorious belligerent in imposing a treaty of *peace* are a decent respect for the judgment of history and fear of later reprisal. How Germany, Japan and satellites have dealt with their vanquished forms some of the foulest pages of contemporary history. The United Nations will most assuredly not descend to Nazi-Fascist conceptions of international law and justice. But the doing of justice in the matter of war criminals does not entail permitting flagrant violators of the laws and customs of warfare and of the most elementary principles of civilized criminal codes to escape punishment through blindly conceptualistic interpretations of doctrines that are themselves of doubtful validity. The law of nations has a long way to go before it can claim to be a coherent and fixed system. Its relevant tenets were developed under the presupposition that members of the Community of Nations are governed by self-imposed restraints in accordance with international law; but the emergence of States with a national policy of deliberate lawlessness and with their invention of "total war" in the service of a program of world enslavement, compels a realistic modification of inadequate doctrines and principles of law. Unless the United Nations are able reasonably to interpret legal doctrines with the resourcefulness and inventiveness necessary to bring about the desired result of punishing criminalism on an international plane, they will have failed in their duty both to international law and to the Family of Nations. For the doing of justice in the international field involves the taking into account of the injuries inflicted by a law-defying State not only upon the victimized belligerent and its nationals but upon the Society of Nations generally and upon the very substance of international law itself.

All this does not mean that traditional legal principle and method should or will be trampled underfoot in dealing with Axis war criminals. It is merely a recognition that not only the rights but the international duties of the victor State in an illegitimate war forced upon it by a ruthless and lawless aggressor State are among the data legitimately to be taken into account in reasoning about the application of the principles of law to the problem of war criminals.

The fact that the victorious United Nations could, if they chose, impose any conditions on the Axis States — including the surrender for execution *without trial* of a long list of leading militarists, politicians and industrialists believed to be involved in the murders, lootings and other crimes — is of basic importance. It is something that can legitimately be thrown into the scales whenever traditional conceptualistic argument or some unrealistic, outworn or basically irrelevant technicality inclines them against vindication of justice. In a relatively undeveloped and plastic field of law it is but following an historical process to blend "political" with legal concepts in stimulating the growth of standards and principles. Much of the law of nations has its roots in custom. Custom must have a beginning; and customary usages of States in the matter of national and personal liability for resort to prohibited methods of warfare and to wholesale criminalism have not been petrified for all time. "International Law was not crystallized in the seventeenth century, but is a living and expanding code."[1]

The second, and related, questionable assumption of some international lawyers of the strict school is that the law of nations is to be treated with the same type of legalistic technicality as lawyers apply to some such highly developed branch of jurisprudence as the law of wills or common law pleading. Thinking in terms of local, peacetime administration of criminal justice, those who hold this view insist upon applying all the familiar protections and technicalities appropriate in a domestic system of prosecution and trial to the special problem of coping with modern outlaw States and their criminalistic subjects. Thereby, such concept-intoxicated lawyers only succeed in arriving at the not very helpful conclusion that "legally" or "constitutionally" little or nothing can be done to prosecute and punish the wholesale violators of the laws of warfare and the common principles of penal law. If their views were to prevail, the military and political leaders of lawless aggressor nations would have the advantage of impunity regardless of the outcome of their aggressions: if they won an unlawful war, they would of course escape punishment for their crimes; and if they lost, they could count on technicalities and constitutional protections conveniently provided by the legal systems of their victims.

Nobody who has made a thorough study of the status of the branch of the law of nations involved in the war criminals' problem can adhere to the view that it is anywhere near as well developed or subject to the same techniques of rigorous "legal logic" as the more sophisticated branches of private law. The issues to be resolved entail, not finely-drawn spinnings out of inevitably one-sided conclusions from clearly defined and universally accepted principles of law resorted to generally by lawyers; they involve, rather, an exploration of the still wild borderland between the poorly developed field of the law of war and the public policy of civilized States conscious of their obligations as members of the Family of Nations. Debatable issues of a technical nature ought therefore always to be resolved, if this can reasonably be done, in favor of the right of the civilized world to punish those States, their governments and their military and political hirelings who have deliberately and scornfully flouted the most elementary principles of law and morals. The administration of justice is not some amiable little game of chess to be played forever according to the old rules though the heavens fall; it is rather a means to a socially and morally desirable end, and it must constantly be modified to achieve that end. In our day and age, one major aim of the administration of justice in international affairs is to demonstrate beyond doubt that lawlessness, whether indulged in by Heads of States, members of military general staffs, members of political cliques, or persons of lesser status, entails prosecution and punishment.

In the framing of a program of retribution for the atrocities committed by the Nazi-Japanese soldiers and politicians and their scavenger satellites, the United Nations should, therefore, be influenced but not shackled by legal principles traditional in the peacetime relation of law-abiding States and in the domestic administration of justice. Their program can derive from familiar concepts of fair play and still not be devitalized by the barren and unrealistic legalisms in which the books on international law traditionally embalm the subject of war crime. The legal principles and standards involved ought to be, and legitimately can be, adapted to the facts of life so brutally taught by the Axis war lords to a dangerously naive and morally shell-shocked world. The law of nations is capable of growth; and there has never been a better opportunity to shape it to the desirable end of enforcing respect for its tenets.

In analyzing the question whether the trial and punishment of Axis war criminals by an international tribunal would truly involve unfair "retroactivity"; in examining the problem whether the law of nations always and necessarily obligates only States and not their individual nationals; in evaluating the issue of "acts of State"; in estimating the principles of jurisdiction; in weighing the arguments involved in the defense of "superior orders"; in considering the types of tribunal best suited to try the accused; in exploring the question of sanctions, punishment and correction; in defining the very concept of war crimes itself, and indeed in considering any of the relevant issues there is an opportunity nowadays for the stimulation of creative growth in the law. The process of demonstrating how the resources of the law of nations can be made thoroughly adequate to the efficient enforcement of justice in the case of war criminals must entail departures that some international lawyers will not welcome. Yet if we look into realities and essences, instead of worshipping mere outer vestments or phraseologies, these departures will be seen not to do violence to the underlying principles of civilized justice. In fact, for not a few of them respectable precedents can be found.

But moulding the *law* to serve the ends of justice in our time is not the only task to be attacked. The problem of war criminals is highly complex; for our aims are multiple and not entirely consistent. We must guard against the Nazis and other Fascists leading us round by the nose as did the German military clique at the close of the last world cataclysm. (See Chapter II.) We must establish a vital symbol of the existence of the law of nations not merely in musty tomes but in the relations and behavior of States and their subjects. We must derive as much insurance as we possibly can against future war atrocities, through whatever deterrence there may be in the punishment of those who have defied the laws of legitimate warfare and of civilized penal codes. This point was stressed by Mr. Churchill when, on September 8, 1942, he assured the House of Commons that "those who are guilty of the Nazi crimes will have to stand up before tribunals in every land where their atrocities have been committed, in order that an indelible warning may be given to future ages and that successive generations of men may say, 'So perish all who do the like again.'" We must, at the same time, recognize that however true it be that millions of the doers of dark deeds were willing and even enthusiastic participants in the ruthless acts of enslavement, brutality, massacre, looting and receiving of stolen goods that are chargeable to the Axis peoples, many others were themselves but helpless victims of tyrannical political systems forced to participate in the crimes of their masters. This means that reformative programs, through correction, psychotherapy, education, religion and other devices of rehabilitation, ought not to be altogether excluded as United Nations' instruments of criminal justice. It also means that by publication of the plans to be pursued in dealing with war criminals, the United Nations can help to separate the more decent and hopeful elements in the Axis masses from their political misrulers and military castes. Yet, if it is to be realistic, the program to be developed for coping with war criminals must also take into account the understandable cry for retribution that rises from the anguished hearts of the countless victims of Nazi-Fascist bestiality.

Not an easy task, this; but one that is as important as any facing the United Nations. For the homes and factories of Europe and Asia laid waste by Axis aggression and greed are the least of the human possessions to be restored; the most precious thing to be salvaged from the ruins is man's hard-won heritage of justice through law.

As a basis for planning a specific program, certain vital questions — some of them involving technical issues of a legal nature, others concerned with more pervasive issues of public policy — must be considered:

(1) What type of acts can legitimately be denominated "war crimes"?

(2) Supposing the violation of the laws and usages of permissive warfare or of the criminal law of civilized nations, what can an injured belligerent State do about it? In addition to action which may be taken against the implicated State, is the injured nation legally justified in punishing individual subjects of that State? And if so, is this to be done under its own municipal law, under the law of the accused, or under the law of nations?

(3) Can Heads of State (e.g., Hitler) legitimately be subjected to trial and punishment by the United Nations; or are such high-placed malefactors exempt from legal liability and trial by a foreign jurisdiction?

(4) Are individuals liable for "acts of State"?

(5) What, if any, is the responsibility of subordinates, and how should an Axis soldier's defense that he committed atrocities only in obedience to orders of his Government or his military superior be treated?

(6) As a matter of high policy, by what courts should war offenders be tried? Is it advisable to prosecute the leading culprits in an international tribunal? If so, how would such a court be organized and staffed, and what system of law would it apply?

(7) How shall the accused be gotten hold of?

(8) How shall the guilty be punished? Is there room for corrective and therapeutic agencies in the penologic program?

Each of these questions is of the utmost significance in considering a plan of action for the United Nations. It is easy to say that all the Axis leaders and their principal assistants should be forthwith shot. But if the United Nations are to achieve their primary aim of re-establishing law and order in the world, they must proceed according to standards generally recognized as fair and decent. In order to do so, they must explore the issues just enumerated and arrive at reasonable and just solutions.

It will help us to understand the pitfalls to be avoided, if we postpone the consideration of these questions until we have studied the lesson of history by examining the record of the treatment of German war criminals at the close of the first world war.

CHAPTER II

THE RECORD OF HISTORY

⚖

THE HISTORY of the action taken against German war criminals under the Treaty of Versailles should serve as a warning of what must not happen again and as a basis for a realistic and just program for the United Nations.

On January 25, 1919, the Preliminary Peace Conference of World War I set up a Commission of Fifteen to inquire into and report upon violations of international law chargeable to Germany and her allies.[1] The Commission appointed sub-commissions to establish the facts regarding culpable conduct in the course of hostilities, to consider whether prosecution for such offenses could be instituted, and to indicate the persons deemed guilty and the courts in which they should be tried. In terms that would just as aptly describe Germany's crimes of the present, the World War I Commission summarized atrocity memoranda submitted by the various Allied Governments containing long lists of "breaches of the laws and customs of war committed by the forces of the German Empire and their allies on land, on sea, and in the air":

"In spite of the explicit regulations, of established customs, and of the clear dictates of humanity, Germany and her allies have piled outrage upon outrage. Additions are daily and continually being made. . . .

"It is impossible to imagine a list of cases so diverse and so painful. Violations of the rights of combatants, of the rights of civilians, and of the rights of both, are multiplied in this list of the most cruel practices which primitive barbarism, aided by all the resources of modern science, could devise for the execution of a system of terrorism carefully planned and carried out to the end. Not even prisoners, or wounded, or women, or children have been respected by belligerents who deliberately sought to strike terror into every heart for the purpose of repressing all resistance.

"Murders and massacres, tortures, shields formed of living human beings, collective penalties, the arrest and execution of hostages, the requisitioning of services for military purposes, the arbitrary destruction of public and private property, the aerial bombardment of open towns without there being any regular siege, the destruction of merchant ships without previous visit and without any precautions for the safety of passengers and crew, the massacre of prisoners, attacks on hospital ships, the poisoning of springs and of wells, outrages and profanations without regard for religion or the honor of the individuals, the issue of counterfeit money, . . . the methodical and deliberate destruction of industries with no other object than to promote German economic supremacy after the war, constitute the most striking list of crimes that has ever been drawn up to the eternal shame of those who committed them." [2]

The Commission recommended the setting up of a special commission to collect and classify systematically the information at hand or to be obtained, "in order to prepare as complete a list of facts as possible concerning the violations of the laws and customs of war committed by the forces of the German Empire and its Allies." A United Nations Commission with a similar object was established in London in the summer of 1943. Unfortunately, however, Russia is as yet (autumn of 1944) not a participant.

Speaking of liability, the World War I Commission was of opinion that "in the hierarchy of persons in authority, there is no reason why rank, however exalted, should in any circumstances protect the holder of it from responsibility when that responsibility has been established before a properly constituted tribunal." It expressly insisted that "all persons belonging to enemy countries, however high their position may have been, without distinction of rank, including chiefs of states, who have been guilty of offenses against the law and customs of war or the laws of humanity are liable to criminal prosecution." [3]

How, under Article 227 of the Treaty of Versailles, "William II of Hohenzollern, formerly German Emperor," was "publicly arraigned" for a "supreme offense against international morality and the sanctity of treaties," to be tried before a specially constituted tribunal; how the Government of The Netherlands, acting within its legal rights and long traditions, refused to surrender the Squire of Doorn for such an offense which was not among those listed in its extradition treaties with the Allies, and which it regarded as a non-extraditable political offense;[4] and how a distinguished bearded exile spent the rest of a long and prosperous life as the world's most illustrious wood-chopper — all this is well known. Not so well remembered is the tipsy dance of the Blindfolded Goddess with those malefactors less exalted than William II of Hohenzollern.

The Commission recognized that *international law permits a belligerent to try persons charged with offenses constituting violations of the laws and customs of war, once the accused are within its power, and it may for that purpose set up its own courts and procedure.* But four classes of charges seemed to the Commission to call for prosecution in an *international* tribunal: (a) offenses against civilians and soldiers of several Allied nations, such as outrages committed in prison camps housing prisoners of war of several countries; (b) offenses by "persons of authority" whose orders were "executed not only in one area or on one battle front, but affected the conduct of operations against several of the Allied armies"; (c) offenses by civil or military authorities, "without distinction of rank, who ordered, or abstained from preventing, violations of the laws or customs of war"; (d) charges against "such other persons belonging to enemy countries as, having regard to the character of the offense or the law of any belligerent country, it may be considered advisable not to proceed before a court other than the High Tribunal."[5]

The Moscow Declaration of November 1, 1943, solemnly proclaimed that at the time of the armistice the responsible German officers and officials who committed or assented to atrocities will be returned to the scenes of their crimes for trial and punishment by local courts, but that such disposal of war offenders "is without prejudice to the case of German criminals whose offenses have no particular geographical localization, and who will be punished by joint decision of the Governments of the Allies." Taking a leaf from the report of the Commission of the first World War, we may well conclude that the Moscow Declaration's statement regarding "German criminals whose offenses have no particular geographical localization and who will be punished by joint decision of the governments of the

Allies," pertains to very much the same types of cases as those embraced in the four classes noted above.

To conduct the trials in these four types of cases, the Versailles Commission recommended the setting up of a "High Tribunal," to be composed of three members appointed by each of the five chief Allied Governments, and one by each of the Governments of the lesser powers. This court was to apply *the principles of the law of nations as they result from the usages established among civilized peoples, from the laws of humanity and from the dictates of public conscience."* [6] It was empowered to determine its own procedure. Selection of cases for trial and direction of prosecutions were to be left to a five-member Prosecuting Commission to be appointed by the great powers. Upon a finding of guilty, the court could sentence to such punishment as could be imposed for the offense in question "by any court in any country represented on the tribunal or in the country of the convicted person." Conviction before an enemy court was to be no bar to trial and sentence by either the High Tribunal or a national court of one of the Allied Powers.

These, in brief, were the relevant recommendations of the "Commission on the Responsibility of the Authors of the War and on Enforcement of Penalties" to the Preliminary Peace Conference at the close of World War I. They were, however, not adopted, and the failure to adopt them resulted in one of the less satisfactory pages of history. In a "memorandum of reservations" the American representatives on the Versailles Commission differed from their colleagues regarding the means of accomplishing the common desire. In respect to the law to be applied, they pointed out that "the laws and customs of war are a standard certain to be found in books of authority and in the practice of nations. The laws and principles of humanity vary with the individual, which, if for no other reason, should exclude them from consideration in a court of justice, especially one charged with the administration of criminal law." [7]

In the Americans' opinion, also, the international tribunal, if established, "should be formed by the mere assemblage of the existing national military tribunals or commissions," which are "of admitted competence" in the matter, these military courts "bringing with them the law to be applied, namely, the laws and customs of war, and the procedure, namely, the procedure of the national commissions or courts."[8] The American members refused their assent to "creating an international criminal court for the trial of individuals, for which a precedent is lacking, and which appears to be unknown in the practice of nations."[9] They also denied assent to the "doctrine of negative criminality" (*i.e.*, criminal responsibility for failure *to prevent* violations of laws and customs of war and humanity), which the majority of the Commission insisted upon. The Japanese on the Commission (Japan was then one of the Allies) also presented reservations. They raised the basic question, among others, "whether international law recognizes a penal law as applicable to those who are guilty."[10] And it seemed to them "important to consider the consequences which would be created in the history of international law by the prosecution for breaches of the laws and customs of war of enemy heads of States before a tribunal constituted by the opposite party,"[11] an argument rejected in the Treaty.

The upshot of the matter was that, instead of the majority views of the Commission prevailing, there were inserted in the Treaty of Versailles the now almost completely forgotten "punitive" Articles 228, 229 and 230. By Article 228 the German government recognized "the right of the Allied and Associated Powers to bring before military tribunals persons accused of having committed acts in violation of the laws and customs of war."[12] The German Government was to "hand over" to one or all of the Allied and Associated Powers all such accused who were to be specified "by name or by the rank, office, or employment" which they held under the German authorities; and the guilty were to be sentenced to "punishments laid down by law." Article 229 provided for the trial of the accused in military tribunals of the power against whose nationals the alleged crimes were committed; and specified that "in every case the accused will be entitled to name his own counsel." By Article 230 the German Government undertook "to furnish all documents and information of every kind," the production of which might "be considered necessary to ensure the full knowledge of the incriminating acts, the discovery of offenders, and the just appreciation of responsibility."

In pursuance to Article 228, long lists of accused persons were prepared by the principal Allied Governments, from which a joint list was compiled and presented to the Germans on February 3, 1920, with the reservation that it did not comprise "all the authors of the innumerable crimes committed during the course of the war by the Germans." The list, which the Germans promptly dubbed "The Book of Hate," contained almost 900 names.[13]

France demanded the surrender of 334 persons, among them General Stenger, commander of the 58th Brigade and alleged author of the following orders dated August 26, 1914:

"(a) Beginning with today, no more prisoners will be taken. All prisoners, whether wounded or not, must be destroyed;

"(b) All prisoners are to be killed; the wounded whether armed or not, destroyed; even men captured in large organized units are to be put to death. Behind us no enemy must remain alive."

On a variety of grave charges including murder, many other high-ranking officers were requested for delivery, among them the Imperial Crown Prince, Count Bismarck, grandson of the "Iron Chancellor," and Marshal von Hindenburg.

The British claimed 97 Germans for trial, among them Grand Admiral von Tirpitz and Admiral Scheer, for having ordered unrestricted submarine warfare, twenty former commandants of German prison camps, for excessive cruelty, and (in a demand joined in by Belgium) von der Lancken, for shooting the famous Nurse Edith Cavell.

Belgium called for delivery of 334 Germans, including ex-Chancellor von Bethmann-Hollweg, for the notoriously lawless attack on Belgian sovereignty.

Poland, Rumania, Italy, and Yugoslavia also demanded the surrender of various high-placed criminals; for murders, arsons, thefts, pillage, wanton destruction of forests, bombardment of "open towns," etc. The United States submitted no names.

Though in signing the Peace Treaty the Germans had solemnly obligated themselves to deliver up the accused for trial, they soon reneged. In an article published in 1929, for the archives of German-made history, Baron von Lersner, President of the German Peace Delegation, pridefully recalls how, the Peace Treaty having been ratified by France in October, 1919, the head of the Peace Division of the German Foreign Office came to Paris early in November to help him "initiate diplomatic steps which would prevent the surrender of our 'war criminals.'" These two worthies informed the Allied diplomats that,

"the entire German Volk, without regard to class and party, is of the conviction that it is impossible to deliver up the so-called 'war criminals.' If, despite this, the Reich Government should attempt to carry out their extradition, it would encounter the strongest opposition. No German official would lend a hand to the arrest of a German in order to deliver him up to the justice of the Entente. The Government might of course discharge these officials, but it would be unable to find others willing to enforce the Allies' order. The mere proposal of an order of this kind would create such a storm of indignation that the entire peace structure would be gravely threatened." [14]

The German delegates emphasized the danger of a political and economic revolution, if the order for surrender of those on the Allied list were pressed.

In Germany, feelings ran high upon receipt of the list. Von Lersner proudly relates how mass meetings were held in churches and streets, and how everywhere "thousands upon thousands protested in the sharpest manner against the Auslieferungsforderung. Everywhere the surrender of the German 'war criminals' was refused. United and unanimously stood the whole German people, stood all parties together like one man." [15] The former Crown Prince wrote a note to President Wilson in which he magnanimously offered to immolate his noble self as a modest substitute for the hundreds of prospective martyrs on the hated list. [16]

Baron von Lersner indignantly returned President Millerand's Allied note containing the list of the accused. He then resigned in protest. He next called in representatives of the world press and apprised them of the entire progress of the extradition demands, his numerous diplomatic interventions in opposition ("10 times in writing and 13 times orally"), and the latest status of the matter. Baron von Lersner proudly records for German history that his statements were "printed almost literally in the press of the entire world." With injured innocence, irony and disdain — little justified by what the Germans have since done — he records for the German reader that, "the Entente Governments demanded the extradition and conviction of our greatest and best army leaders, statesmen, nobles, officers, under-officers and troops. Their judgment in the fort of Vincennes — according to the famous precedent of the shooting of the Duke of Enghien by Napoleon I — was out of the question. Despite all my pleas and remonstrances our war opponents demanded the extradition in order to demonstrate that the Germans are a criminal nation. Now, with the passing of judgment upon our leaders, they wanted to put the final seal on their Versailles polity; the 'moralistic' justification of the Draconian dictatorial determinations of Versailles should now be made known and demonstrated to the entire world. Against this it was necessary, without a moment's hesitation, to present an energetic front and leap into the breach." [17]

Von Lersner closes the account of his protest on a triumphant Wagnerian trumpet note:

"This first great demand which the Entente Government imposed on us by virtue of the *Diktat von Versailles* was shattered, like glass upon a stone, against the unity of the German people."

There is a lesson in all this which it would be foolish and tragic for the United Nations to ignore.

Shortly after von Lersner's defiant reply Millerand returned the list of accused to the new Chancellor of the German Republic, with a politely ironical comment:

"The powers have no doubt that M. Lersner's act was only a personal manifestation, not engaging the responsibility of the German Government. They have been unable to believe that in effect the latter is avoiding an obligation which it contracted in signing the Treaty of Versailles; . . . that less than a month after the Treaty has gone into effect, it refuses, of set purpose, to execute an essential stipulation." [18]

It is at this point that firmness and a show of force by the Allies might have turned the tide of history not only in the matter of the war criminals but as regards the subsequent sordid tale of the ridicule of international law and the reawakening of the not too soundly sleeping giant of German militarism which has led to World War II. But this is speculation. The "Allied and Associated Powers" early proved themselves inadequate to deal with the emergency, or, at any rate, eager to forget the entire sorry business and sink back into the narcotic sleep of "normalcy."

On January 25, 1920, before the list of wanted war criminals was presented, Germany had proposed, by way of "compromise," that all persons accused by the Allies of war crimes and misdemeanors should be tried before the Supreme Court of the Reich at Leipzig. "To this end Germany would make all conceivable guarantees for the impartial and firm execution of the proceedings, especially through the assistance of official representatives of the interested opposition States." As "new evidence of its earnest will to punish Germans guilty of a war crime or misdemeanor," it made known that on December 13, 1919, it had brought about the passage of a law for the prosecution of war offenders.[19] The Allies finally accepted the suggestion but without consenting to participate in the trials, "so as to leave full and complete responsibility with the German Government." They reminded Germany that the proposed trials at Leipzig could "in no case annul the dispositions of articles 228 to 230 of the Treaty"; and they expressly reserved the right to consider, as a result of these prosecutions, whether the German Government were sincerely resolved to administer justice in good faith. If not satisfied, the Allies would exercise the right to try the accused before their own tribunals, a right which the Germans acknowledged in their letter of reply.

On May 7, 1920, a sample "abridged list" of war criminals was delivered to the German Government for trial before the Supreme Court of Leipzig. How abridged this list was can be seen from the fact that while the Allies had cautioned that the 900 accused persons in the original list were themselves only a sample of all the actual offenders, this new "test list" contained only 45 names. To this list the British, for example, contributed only seven names. But having so easily obtained a major concession from the Allies, the Germans were not ready for trial even after receiving this abridged list. They informed the Allies that difficulties were being experienced in obtaining evidence against the accused, because much of the necessary proof was in possession of the Allied Governments. The Allies then arranged to assemble statements of the proof against the persons on the abridged list and transmit them to the *Oberreichsanwalt* (public prosecutor) in Leipzig. They prepared the evidence with commendable care. Preliminary examinations were made in France and Belgium; depositions were taken in London; witnesses were collected from across the seas and brought to Leipzig.

One matter which strictly limited the number of cases which the British would be prepared to bring to trial — and herein, also, there is a lesson not to be ignored by the United Nations — was their firm insistence upon proof according to English standards. Claud Mullins, who was present at the Leipzig trials as interpreter for the British Mission, and wrote a book on the subject, reminds us that "it is exceedingly difficult, if not impossible, for Englishmen to prove the conduct of ex-enemy Generals according to the standards of proof obtaining in British courts." With disarming simplicity, he adds that "the immediate result was that it was impossible to proceed against many of the worst offenders." [20] But why the highly technical rules of evidence and standards of proof required in Anglo-American jury trials were deemed necessary in view of the fact that the accused were to be tried in German courts, under German law, and before appraisers of facts who were not laymen but trained jurists, is not clear. Mullins himself points to the much looser trial procedure in German courts, the predominant role played by the judges in questioning witnesses and exploring the proof and, most important, the fact that "the German Court does not adhere to strict rules of evidence as do English Courts. Hearsay evidence seems to be given on both sides without objection and matters are considered which an English Court would consider irrelevant to the point at issue." [21]

The trial of the war criminals accused by the Allies began at long last in Leipzig on May 23, 1921, *two and a half years* after the fateful November 11, 1918 which had closed the war to make the world safe for democracy. But even then, instead of the seven defendants selected with such great care by the British, only *four* were tried, and these were unimportant underlings. The Germans claimed they were not in a position to bring U-boat Commander Patzig to trial, because, although he had an address in Danzig, his then whereabouts was unknown. It seemed that Lieutenant-Commander Werner was, unfortunately, now resident in Poland. However, Lieutenants Ludwig

Dithmar and John Boldt were put on trial, at the suggestion of the German Government, in connection with the *Llandovery Castle* atrocity for which Commander Patzig was unfortunately not available. The offenses involved were the sinking without warning of a British hospital ship and the firing on and sinking of the lifeboats containing the survivors, thereby converting them into death boats to the score of 234 persons.

The Criminal Senate of the Reich Court of Justice, before which the accused were tried, consisted of seven German judges. Admittedly, they had a most unenviable duty to perform, not made easier by the truculent chauvinism of the military caste. Mullins has painted a picture of the scene:

"The judges, who looked very dignified in their crimson robes and crimson berettas, sat around a horseshoe table. At the end of the table, at the president's left, sat the German State Attorney and his assistant. At the other end, on the judge's right, sat the clerk of the court. The witnesses gave their evidence inside the horseshoe, facing the Presiding Judge. At a separate table on the right, sat the accused and his defending counsel. Facing them, on the judge's left sat the British Mission (headed by the Solicitor General, Sir Ernest Pollock, K.B.E., K.C., M.P.) and, behind them, were a few representatives of the German Foreign Office and Ministry of Justice. The witnesses, both English and German, were called into the court at the opening of the trials; a roll-call was taken, and they were warned by the Presiding Judge that no feelings of prejudice or of national animosity must colour their evidence. They then left the Court and were called in one by one as the Presiding Judge determined. . . . Above the back of the hall, there was a gallery and, at moments when the trials were specially interesting, both this gallery and the seats for spectators in the body of the hall were crowded with people. Before the trials, an appeal had been issued to the German public by some patriotic organization that they should boycott the trials as they were held to be a humiliation to German pride. None the less, there was always a considerable audience, and at times the big hall was packed to suffocation." [22]

Limitations of space permit of the presentation of but one sample of the nature of the judicial reasoning at the Leipzig trials. The case was that of Captain Emil Müller, charged with maintaining atrociously bad conditions in a prison camp, from which hundreds of prisoners died; and with inflicting terrible cruelties on many prisoners. Despite numerous British witnesses to the contrary, the court found that the prison atrocities occurred after Müller was no longer in charge of the camp; hence he was not responsible. (But the officer who *was* responsible was not subjected to trial!) On some of the charges of personal brutality, the court found Müller guilty. While concluding that the English prisoners unfairly had a "preconceived idea that the accused was animated by feelings of spiteful malignity toward them," the court went on to say that "instead of earning the prisoners' confidence," the Captain, somehow, "got a reputation among them for being a tyrant and a nigger-driver."

Among the numerous instances of Müller's brutality found by the court to have been proved were, in its own words, the following:

"The accused admits that he liked, as soon as he appeared at roll-call, to ride quickly up to the ranks. He thought this was a suitable way of ensuring proper respect for himself and of making the prisoners attentive. According to the evidence of almost all the English, and also of some of the German witnesses, he frequently rode so far into the ranks that they were broken. The prisoners scattered on all sides and many who could not get out of the way quickly enough were thrown down by the horse. Such excesses when riding up to a body of men are altogether contrary to regulations and are to be condemned.

"The accused while on horseback struck a prisoner who was suffering from a bad foot. At roll-call this prisoner had raised his leg to show it to the accused, but the accused hit him across the leg with his riding cane. The man cried out, fell down and had to be carried into the barracks. . . .

"The accused once struck Drewcock at roll-call . . . across his wounded knee with his riding cane so hard that an abscess developed and later had to be cut. The accused could not have foreseen this, for the wounds on Drewcock's knee were not visible to him. But the blow must have been a heavy one. . . .

"According to the statement of the witness Lovegrove, the accused once saw two sick men lying down; they were so weak that they could not stand up before him and were groaning pitifully. But the accused is said to have got angry and impatient and to have kicked them. There is a possibility that the accused did not wish to hurt the men, whose sickness he apparently did not yet believe to be real, but that he only wished to secure that his order to get up was immediately obeyed. It is not clear that the kicking was particularly violent or painful. Clearly, however, in each instance this constituted a treatment of the sick contrary to regulations.

"There has been an accumulation of offenses which show an almost habitually harsh and contemptuous, and even a frankly brutal, treatment of prisoners entrusted to his care. His conduct has sometimes been unworthy of a human being." [23]

The court expressed its conviction that such conduct "dishonors the German Army." However, the very same paragraph of its opinion which ends with that statement, begins with this: "It must be emphasized that the accused has not acted dishonorably; that is to say, his honor both as a citizen and as an officer remains untarnished," and this though "his conduct has sometimes been unworthy of a human being"!

The defendant was held liable to punishment for crimes under the German Military Penal Code and the Reich Penal Code; and for the sixteen offenses in which it found him guilty, the court imposed a total sentence of six months' imprisonment.

Summarizing the outcome of the Leipzig trials, we get the following results:

Number of accused in original Allied list	896
Number included on abridged "test" list	45
Number actually tried (British charges — including 2 by Germans, 6; French, 5; Belgian, 1)	12
Number actually convicted (British-German charges, 5; French, 1; Belgian, 0)	6

The sentences imposed included: on British charges, two of six months and one of ten; on German charges, two of four years; and on French charges, one of two years. The French case [24] involved a German major, prosecuted for killing wounded French war prisoners and found guilty of homicide by negligence in allegedly misinterpreting General Stenger's actual orders. Stenger himself was acquitted despite much evidence by *German* witnesses that he had ordered the massacre of wounded war prisoners. Applause and bouquets followed his acquittal.[25] He received so many congratulatory letters on both his order to grant no quarter and his acquittal that he had to publish a notice in the press expressing his great regret that it was impossible for him to thank individually all who had written to him and begging them to accept the notice as expressing his gratitude. This too should serve as a lesson to be taken to heart by the United Nations.

The Allied mission sent to the Leipzig trials withdrew in protest at the outcome of the twelve test cases. The French, particularly, were both angered and saddened by the performance of the Leipzig Supreme Court. After recalling their representatives, they and the Belgians, who had suffered most from German atrocities during the first World War, indignantly withdrew the documents of accusation and proof. To them the goings-on at Leipzig were clearly a wholesale miscarriage of elementary justice. Certain prominent British observers of the Leipzig trials, on the other hand, concluded that the German court had done a fairly good job under great handicaps.[26] And here, too, is a lesson to be learned — regarding the durability of Allied solidarity; for the Germans were not slow to quote distinguished British apologists for the Leipzig proceedings.[27]

In January, 1922, a Commission of Allied jurists set up to inquire into the Leipzig trials unanimously recommended to the Supreme Council (of the Allied and Associated Powers) that it was useless to let the German court continue. The Committee concluded unanimously that "some of the accused who were acquitted should have been convicted and that in the case of those convicted the sentences were not adequate." It recommended that no new cases be sent to Leipzig and that the German Government be compelled to hand over accused persons for trial by the Allies in pursuance of Article 228. This only resulted in great indignation in Germany and in "looking toward England" as a familiar German tactic of dividing the Allies. Chauvinistic groups organized truculent protest meetings throughout Germany, at which high-ranking officers reminded the world that "250,000 national soldiers and the police of the *Reichswehr* are in alliance" to prevent the handing over of Germans to the "justice of the Entente." The Leipzig court proceeded with the trials in the absence of the Allied delegations;

and there followed a series of acquittals. Some 800 cases were disposed of without any trial, on the grounds that the defendants' "misdeeds were not covered by German law" or that there was "insufficient evidence."[28]

In August, 1922, Poincaré, on behalf of the Conference of Ambassadors, vigorously protested to the German Ambassador that the German Government "has not kept its promise to administer justice objectively and loyally," and that the Allies would "completely disregard the German proceedings taken by the Leipzig Court against future defendants," and would "resume and reserve to themselves all rights belonging to them by virtue of the Treaty of Versailles at present and in the future, in particular the right to prosecute the war criminals themselves, if necessary *in absentia*." The Germans, on the other hand, waxed indignant that "leading German personalities" including their idol, von Hindenburg, "continued to run the risk, if they set foot on French or Belgian soil, of being arrested and sentenced."[29]

A serio-comic turn rang down the curtain on the tawdry drama of the Leipzig trials. An item in the *Journal de Droit International*, appearing shortly after his imprisonment, carried the following tidings concerning one of the two officers who received the heaviest sentences for U-boat atrocities:

"The correspondent of the *Daily Mail* in Berlin telegraphed, on November 20, 1921:

"'Mystery still surrounds the circumstances of the escape of Lieut. Boldt, submarine commander, sentenced to four years' imprisonment by the tribunal of Leipzig for having torpedoed a hospital-ship. Lieut. Boldt escaped from the Holstenplatz house of detention at Hamburg. This prison serves only for those accused, and never for the convicted.

"'The director of the prison declared that Boldt had been authorized to wear civilian clothes. He had a private room and could communicate with the outside. At 3:30 a check-up established his presence; at 4:45 he had disappeared. The director of the prison believes that Boldt succeeded in reaching, by means of the ventilator shaft, a wing of the prison under repair. It is supposed that he passed, unnoticed, among the workmen.

"The police bloodhounds put on the trail lost the scent almost immediately. It is believed that Lieut. Boldt had prepared his escape for a long time and that his accessories, who had waited for him in an automobile, helped him to cross the Dutch frontier.'"

The other prisoner convicted of U-boat atrocities also somehow mysteriously "escaped." Great was the rejoicing in Germany at the flight of these "U-boat heroes."

Thus ended the tragi-comedy of the Leipzig trials, beginning with the German manipulation of the Allied statesmen for two and a half years, while the evidence of atrocities grew cold, accused and witnesses disappeared, and chauvinistic public opinion was whipped up inside Germany; and ending with the patriotic cooperation of those conveniently negligent bloodhounds! It is probable that chief reasons for the half-hearted efforts of the Allied and Associated Powers were war-weariness and eagerness to return to peacetime pursuits, the reliance upon the new German Republic, the hope that somehow the League of Nations would prevent future wars. But for the Allies to have made several solemn pronouncements that war criminals would be punished and then to have let the entire matter go by default was worse than if they had said nothing about war criminals. Unquestionably, the confidence in immunity from punishment contributed its share to the later effort of the German war lords.

What lessons can we learn from Versailles and Leipzig?

First, the United Nations must not again trust the Germans to do justice in the case of German war criminals. To the Germans, these men are heroes.

Secondly, surrender of the leading malefactors should be a condition precedent to the granting of an armistice, instead of being postponed until the peace treaty is signed. This basic lesson of Leipzig seems already to have been driven home; for President Roosevelt gave notice on October 7, 1942 that provisions for surrender of war criminals would be included in the armistice terms, a statement promptly seconded by the Lord Chancellor of England; and this policy has been approved by the other members of the United Nations. Whether it was followed in the case of Italy is unknown at the present writing, because the armistice terms for that country's surrender, though said by the Italian government to be extremely harsh, have not as yet been made public. However, the Allied-Rumanian and Allied-Finnish armistice agreements of September 12 and September 19, 1944 (articles 14 and 13, respectively) provide that the surrendering States undertake the obligation of collaborating with the Allied powers "in the task of the detention of persons accused of war crimes, and the trials of such persons."

Thirdly, the accused must be tried as soon as possible; otherwise, accused and witnesses will disappear, die off, or suffer losses of memory. Trials should begin as soon as the accused are seized, whether on United Nations territory or on German or other Axis territory. This means that tribunals and prosecuting staff for the purpose ought to be established as soon as possible.

Fourthly, the good faith of the government that succeeds the Hitlerian regime should be tested, among other things, by its cooperation in assembling the proof of German violations of the laws and customs of legitimate warfare and of the criminal law common to the civilized world; but most of the preparation for the trials should be by United Nations officials. Proof should be assembled at the earliest possible time. This should include the obtaining of sworn statements from enemy prisoners of war as well as from civilians and soldiers of countries victimized by the Axis.

Fifthly, fair and lawful, but not long-drawn-out, judicial proceedings should be provided. The United Nations should stand for no German bluster or chicanery; attempts to interfere with the orderly and efficient administration of justice should be severely punished.

Sixthly, German public opinion should be systematically prepared to recognize the justice of punishing leaders who are guilty of atrocities. Alleged heroes should be deflated by convincing proof of their barbarous actions. The fair and orderly United Nations proceedings against individual Germans accused of specific offenses should be contrasted with the indiscriminate mass-butcheries carried out upon orders of German military and political leaders against hundreds of thousands of innocent hostages. The just proceedings in United Nations courts should be contrasted with those brought against anti-Nazi Germans themselves, as well as conquered peoples, in the infamous Nazi "peoples' courts." It should be stressed that the

United Nations' prosecutions are directed more against the high-placed leaders and planners of atrocities than against the ordinary "*Hans Schmidts*" who, as common soldiers and citizens, were forced to execute their leaders' orders; and that punishments will be such as to take account of the difference in respect to freedom of action and to moral as well as legal responsibility between the position of the powerful and self-seeking leaders and that of ordinary, and especially of non-Nazi, Germans.

Lastly, the United Nations must *remain* united throughout the liquidation of the war criminals' problem and not be fooled, manipulated or intimidated by the chicanery or blandishments of the Germans or of their propagandists and apologists at home or abroad.

What is said above applies with equal validity to the trial and punishment of Japanese war criminals and those of the Axis satellites.

CHAPTER III

VIOLATIONS OF LAW BY AXIS NATIONALS

⚖

BEFORE going any farther, let us define *"war criminals."* Considering the Nazi conception of "total war,"[1] *we may legitimately define war criminals as persons — regardless of military or political rank — who, in connection with the military, political, economic or industrial preparation for or waging of war, have, in their official capacity, committed acts contrary to (a) the laws and customs of legitimate warfare or (b) the principles of criminal law generally observed in civilized States; or who have incited, ordered, procured, counseled, or conspired in the commission of such acts; or, having knowledge that such acts were about to be committed, and possessing the duty and power to prevent them, have failed to do so.*

Observe certain features of this definition:[2]

First, it is not intended to include the "crime" of flagrantly violating solemn treaty obligations or conducting a war of aggression. The Commission of Fifteen appointed by the Preliminary Peace Conference at the close of World War I to examine the responsibility for starting that war and for atrocities committed during its conduct, found former Kaiser Wilhelm II and other high-placed personages "guilty" of "gross outrages upon the law of nations and international good faith," but concluded that "no criminal charge" could be brought; although the outrages "should be the subject of a formal condemnation by the Conference."[3] They emphasized it to be "desirable that *for the future* penal sanctions should be provided for such grave outrages against the elementary principles of international law." But throughout the quarter-century between the two world wars nothing has been done by the nations of the world to implement this recommendation. The Kellogg-Briand Pact, signed in Paris in 1928, condemned recourse to war for the solution of international controversies, renounced it as an instrument of national policy, and bound the signatories to seek the settlement of all disputes by pacific means only. But that Pact too failed to make violations of its terms an international crime punishable either by national courts or some international tribunal. Therefore, the legal basis for prosecutions for violations of the Pact of Paris may be open to question,[4] though the moral grounds are crystal clear.

Besides, to prosecute Axis leaders for the crime of having initiated an unjust war, or having violated the "sanctity of treaties,"[5] would only drag a red herring across the trail and confuse the much clearer principle of liability for atrocities committed during the conduct of a war, be it a just or an unjust one. The Germans would surely argue that the Allies had first violated the Treaty of Versailles in not disarming;[6] and learned historians would insist, as they did at the close of World War I, that only lengthy historical and economic investigations could really fix responsibility for "causing" the war.

For these reasons, the origination of an unjust war ought, for the present, not to be included among the acts triable as "war crimes," however desirable it would be to establish judicially the principle involved.[7] The chief malefactors — Hitler, Tojo, Mussolini, their general staffs and the rest — can readily be prosecuted for violations of the laws and customs of legitimate warfare and of criminal law which they have committed during the course of the conflict.

Secondly, we do not include illegal acts by soldiers, sailors or marines in their private, non-official capacity, — i.e., ordinary crimes such as theft, rape, homicide committed by individuals on their own initiative and not connected with military operations. These are punishable by domestic tribunals (military or civil); but they are sporadic, they occur in any army, they are not acts officially sanctioned nor acts which public opinion recognizes as war atrocities. So, also, treason committed by a subject of one of the States comprising the United Nations (e.g., Quisling, Laval, Doriot, Degrelle), is a domestic crime cognizable by the courts of the injured State, and that country is best suited to deal with it. By "war criminals" we mean persons who, in the process of conducting "total" warfare, violated one or both of the sources of law specified in the definition.

Thirdly, we include those persons — usually high-placed officers or political personages — who, in the words of the Moscow Declaration of November 1, 1943,[8] "have taken a *consenting part* in the above atrocities, massacres and executions." It is legitimate, both in law and morals, to comprehend among the culpable persons who, with knowledge of impending atrocities and with power, authority, and duty to prevent them, refused to raise a hand in opposition, and thereby may be charged with consent to the dark deeds. This is particularly true of Heads of State (as in the case of the German Kaiser during the last war) who, whether or not they themselves directly ordered specific atrocities, either knew of their impending commission or approved them after they were accomplished.

Fourthly, we include not only military heads but *political* chieftains and henchmen, because in Germany's conception of "total warfare" there is little difference between the intimidating plottings and schemings of the von Ribbentrops, the von Papens, the Franks, or the cruelties and criminal responsibilities of the ruthless Gestapo, the notorious "S.S." (*Schutzstaffel*)[9] "elite guards" and "Death Head" guards at German concentration camps, or the leaders of the Japanese "Black Dragon," and those of the traditional military officers. Though some of the politicians may have been several steps removed from the actual bloody deeds, they were often, nonetheless, *participes criminis*.

Finally, we include high-ranking, policy-framing industrialists and bankers with political connections who more indirectly participated in or conspired to commit crimes (largely wholesale thefts and receipt of stolen goods) as part of a general scheme of economic conquest to go hand in hand with the military. This group includes particularly those who, by preconceived plan, profited by the looting of factories, plants and banks in the countries overrun by the militarists. These embrace officials of the *I. G. Farben* trust, the huge enterprises built up by Goering and other Nazi and Japanese politicians who stole their victims' property; the chief figures of the Thyssen and Krupp organizations and the Mannesmann concern;[10] the crooked economists and bankers whose machinations not only financed brutal aggressions upon peaceful neighbors, but gave a specious show of legality to the lootings committed under the guise of legitimate purchases; the Japanese business clans; and

others who more indirectly than, but just as surely as, the men
in uniform have waged illegitimate warfare and committed
crimes punishable under all civilized codes. As principals, accessories or conspirators these men ought to be subjected to
trial for specific larcenies, embezzlements and robberies undertaken as part of the Axis program of "total war." That their
crimes were committed on a huge scale and with governmental
sanction makes them no less crimes.

The acts enumerated in the last two paragraphs are of a kind
which might more appropriately and conveniently be tried in
the ordinary national courts of the victims; but some of these
crimes are of such a serious and widespread nature that they
ought to be prosecuted under the joint auspices of the United
Nations.

The kind of offenses involved in part (a) of the above definition of war crimes — *violations of the laws and customs of legitimate warfare* — have been briefly summarized on pages 86–87
of the *Rules of Land Warfare*, one of the basic field manuals
(FM 27–10) issued by the American War Department (1940).[11]
Section 347 of that manual reads:

"Offenses by armed forces. — The principal offenses of this class
are: Making use of poisoned and otherwise forbidden arms and ammunition; killing of the wounded; refusal of quarter; treacherous request for quarter; maltreatment of dead bodies on the battlefield; ill-
treatment of prisoners of war; breach of parole by prisoners of war;
firing on undefended localities; abuse of the flag of truce; firing on
the flag of truce; misuse of the Red Cross flag and emblem and other
violations of the Geneva Convention; use of civilian clothing by
troops to conceal their military character during battle; bombardment of hospitals and other privileged buildings; improper use of
privileged buildings for military purposes; poisoning of wells and
streams; pillage and purposeless destruction; ill-treatment of inhabitants in occupied territory."

The sources of the law involved in acts contrary to legitimate
warfare are given in the following opening statement of the
Army's *Rules of Land Warfare*:

"Among civilized nations the conduct of war is regulated by certain well-established rules known as the rules or laws of war. These

rules cover and regulate warfare both on land and sea. . . . Many of the rules of war have never yet been incorporated in any treaty or convention to which the United States is signatory. These are commonly called the unwritten rules or laws of war, although they are well established by the custom and usage of civilized nations."

The chief sources of *written* law governing the conduct of warfare which need to concern us are: (1) The Hague convention of 1899 relating to the laws and customs of war on land; (2) a revision and extension of this in Hague Convention No. IV (which issued from the second Hague peace conference in 1907), particularly its Annex which embodies detailed *Regulations* concerning land warfare; (3) a convention regulating the treatment of prisoners of war; and (4) another (Red Cross) convention ameliorating the condition of the wounded and ill of armies in the field, the last two signed in Geneva in 1929.[12]

It should be pointed out that the particular conventions referred to are generally deemed by international lawyers to obligate only *States* (the "High Contracting Parties") and not their individual nationals. Each of the States that is a party to such written agreements regulating warfare binds itself to see that its own troops observe its provisions and to punish them for violations. But according to the traditional theory, an injured State can take measures of recourse for violations (*e.g.,* reprisals) only against another *State* and not against that State's individual subjects. However, when a State has "implemented" its international obligations by *domestic* law (*i.e.,* statutes or, as in the case of the American *Rules of Land Warfare,* rules having the force of law), it has "converted" international law into municipal law; and, thereafter, violations of such domestic law by its own or enemy soldiers are punishable as offenses against its own sovereignty.[13]

The written agreements or conventions referred to are not the only sources of relevant international law. They are, in fact, but declaratory of a vast body of *unwritten* (customary or common) international law governing the usages and prohibitions of legitimate warfare.[14] It has been well said that "even if the entire body of modern international written law were completely obliterated, the common law of nations would still remain — a common law based on enlightened practice and ineradicable conceptions of humanity and justice." [15] And the framers of the Hague conventions, with commendable foresight, inserted in their preambles the *caveat* that it was not intended by the contracting States to leave matters not covered by those written agreements to the arbitrary will of military commanders. They therefore solemnly agreed that until a more comprehensive code of legitimate methods of warfare should be prepared, "inhabitants and belligerents should remain under the protection and the rule of the principles of the law of nations, as they result from the usages established among civilized peoples, from the laws of humanity, and the dictates of the public conscience."

Part of this unwritten law of warfare consists of the basic principles of *military necessity* [16] (which limits a belligerent's application of force to that needed to compel submission of the enemy with least possible loss of time, life and property), *humanity* (which prohibits employment of such kind or degree of violence as is not strictly necessary for the purpose of war), and *chivalry* (which prohibits dishonorable means, expedients or conduct). In fact the basic principles noted are the foundation of the entire structure. Says the War Department through its official *Rules of Land Warfare*:

"The unwritten rules are binding upon all civilized nations. They will be strictly observed by all forces, subject only to such exceptions as shall have been directed by competent authority by way of legitimate reprisals for illegal conduct of the enemy. . . . The written laws . . . are in large part but formal and specific applications of general principles of the unwritten rules. . . ." [17]

The American and English *Rules* implementing international law, like those of other civilized belligerents, contain prohibitions not only of acts mentioned in written conventions, but also of certain other acts not covered by the conventions but prohibited by long-standing customary usage having the force of law. [18]

So much for item (a) in our definition of war crimes as they ought to be conceived under the conditions of warfare imposed by the Axis.

As to item (b) — *acts contrary to the principles of criminal law generally observed in civilized States* — it will be seen from the quotation from the *Rules* listing "offenses by armed forces" that while some of the acts involved (*e.g.*, "abuse of a flag of truce") can by their very nature be only violations of the laws of war, others (*e.g.*, "ill treatment of inhabitants of occupied territory") have a dual aspect. From the point of view of military tribunals usually operating in wartime, they are essentially violations of the laws and customs of legitimate warfare; from the point of view of ordinary civil courts [19] which may operate after the conclusion of a war, the acts comprising such assaults upon the *law of nations* will frequently turn out to be also violations of the ordinary *domestic penal law* of the country involved (and of the vast majority of civilized States), comprising such familiar crimes as murder, robbery, larceny, and the like, which are punishable whether committed by soldiers or civilians. Even in military tribunals, while prohibited acts of warfare may be charged and prosecuted in general terms, as, for example, "ill-treatment of prisoners of war," if death results from such a violation of the laws of war, the act causing the death may be specifically charged as murder or manslaughter. [20] For even while a country is at war not all killings and appropriations of property are permitted. Although a soldier, in killing an enemy, is for obvious reasons usually exempt from responsibility for murder, [21] this rule of exemption nevertheless requires that the killing, even if done in warfare, be *lawful*. Soldiers, like civilians, are bound to act within the confines of the prevailing military and civil law. [22] As in the case of any other type of "justification" which cancels liability for acts otherwise criminal (*e.g.*, execution of a felon by the proper officer in a legitimate manner under a valid warrant following conviction and sentence for a capital crime), the indispensable prerequisites for exemption from liability must exist. And where an act normally prohibited (*e.g.*, killing) is committed by a soldier, even in the course of warfare, an indispensable condition for its justification is the lawfulness of the particular act of warfare involved. Were *all* acts of warfare lawful, mere proof that a killing was done by a soldier would be enough to exempt him from liability; but if, for example, the killing occurred after the victim, a surrendered enemy soldier, had laid down his arms, or after an armistice had been declared and notified to the accused, the killing would be unlawful. Now *lawfulness*, as was correctly held by the German Supreme Court in the Leipzig trials,[23] requires the acts of the soldier to be legitimate not only under domestic criminal law, but also under the law of nations, which all States and their agents are bound to obey. Stripped of the mantle of such legality, the act in question stands out starkly as an unjustifiable and inexcusable killing of a human being, something which, by all civilized military and civil penal codes, constitutes plain murder.[24]

While these considerations normally apply only to the sporadic crimes of individual soldiers acting on their own initiative — offenses for which the malefactors' own superiors are usually as eager to subject them to prosecution as are the officials of the enemy State whose nationals have been injured by the acts in question — the Axis nations, particularly Nazi Germany, have *officially* ordered and encouraged such crimes as part of a deliberate and calculated national policy. In fact, most of the atrocities committed by the Nazi-Fascist military and political personnel may legitimately be treated as ordinary crimes for purposes of prosecution in non-military tribunals if such a policy be deemed preferable to resort to military commissions. It has been well said "that a crime such as murder, or any serious offense against prisoners or civilians, is not the less a crime because it is also forbidden by International Conventions."[25] Murders are murders, whether committed by individual soldiers on their own initiative or by entire brigades or divisions of ordinary soldiers or political soldiers of the *Gestapo* or *Schutzstaffel* stripe on instructions of their government. No unilateral "legalization" of such acts is possible; because no member of the Family of Nations can be permitted to make its own rules of warfare justifying mass-murder when committed upon its own governmental order only and as an exclusive instrument of its national policy, thereby flagrantly violating its customary duties to all other States.[26] "It can be demonstrated that only with respect to new legislation does international law depend upon the will or consent of states, and that with respect to the great body of international law growing out of custom, the state is bound thereby as a condition of its admission to the family of nations, independently of its will or consent."[27] It is not the paranoid decrees of a lawless State that determine the criminal or non-criminal quality of the acts in question, but rather the general principles of law of civilized nations as embodied in and illustrated by the law of the State whose nationals have been slain. That mass murder and theft are committed under the plan and direction of a "sovereign State" or a "Head of State" does not render these acts any the less criminal in those who execute the State's or the *Fuehrer's* criminalistic program.

The Nazis have committed many hundreds of thousands of crimes, largely murders, *which have nothing to do with legitimate warfare.* The torture and slaughter of most of the Jewish victims of Nazi hatred and fanaticism, justified by the butchers simply on the ground that the victims belong to an allegedly sub-human race while their murderers have elected themselves as the "master race," would normally and might more appropriately have been put in the class of *ordinary, non-military crimes.* For even under the extreme German conception of "military necessity"[28] this mass-slaughter of innocents has not the remotest legitimate connection with the waging of war. In fact, a great many murders and other crimes against non-Germans were committed by the Nazis *before they declared war* on their hapless neighbors. In all these crimes involving extermination of innocent civilians there will therefore not even be need to examine the laws and customs of war on the point of possible justification of a soldier's acts of warfare. In these cases, it is not warfare that is involved but mass murder. The gruesome murders and greedy lootings are in this work designated "war crimes" only for convenience, since they were committed in preparation for or during the progress of a war upon helpless civilians in the clutches of ruthless military and political officials; and the miscreants could efficiently be tried for them by the same tribunals that will deal with violations of the laws and customs of warfare. This is particularly true of an International Criminal Court that might be set up by the United Nations to deal with more serious offenders and issues of a general interest to all civilized States.

In the following pages are presented some samples of the legal proscriptions together with illustrations of their violation by German and Japanese nationals in the present war. For reasons of convenience, the samples of the rules of law violated by the Axis powers are largely limited to extracts from the relevant written international law,—the Hague and Geneva conventions. However, many of the acts of the Germans and Japanese also run counter to the *unwritten* (common) international law of warfare and to the most elementary principles of civilized *criminal* law. Presentation of the details of the unwritten or common law of nations, and of the criminal law common to civilized States would require a large volume in itself. The unwritten law of nations respecting warfare are to be collected from the classic treatises, such as those by Belli, Gentili, Victoria, Grotius, Vattel, Wheaton, and the better modern works. Ascertainment of the specific provisions of criminal law commonly observed in civilized States but flagrantly violated by Axis officials and troops entails examination of the statutes, decisions of courts, and the criminal jurisprudence of Anglo-American and Continental States.[29]

We shall reserve for later discussion[30] the technical problems involved in establishing legal liability of individual persons (not merely States) for acts denominated war crimes. Here it need only be stressed that—apart from being violations of the prohibitions of any particular State's military or criminal law (triable in domestic courts)—the majority of the outrages committed by the Germans and Japanese[31] and their satellites are also contrary to the provisions of three bodies of law legitimately cognizable by an *international* tribunal: (a) conventional or "written" international (war) law, (b) common or "unwritten" international (war) law, (c) the prohibitions common to the great majority of civilized penal codes.

The illustrations of such violations are taken largely from the *Black Book of Poland*[32] (BBP), the *Polish White Book*[33] (PWB), *Soviet War Documents*[34] (SWD), and telegrams sent by Secretary of State Cordell Hull to the Japanese Government *via* the Swiss Legation[35] (SS). These are compilations of reports of authenticated atrocities committed by German and Japanese troops during the present war.[36] Many other reliable compilations of Axis-Fascist war atrocities exist which detail numerous violations of the laws and customs of legitimate warfare and sometimes involve even blacker crimes than those set out below; but limitations of space prohibit their use. Necessarily, only a very small proportion of atrocities and war crimes can be here recorded. The sample presented is however not atypical; if anything, it is rather an under than an over statement. There will doubtless be some who will insist that these illustrations are "mere atrocity tales" gleaned from sources unfriendly to the Germans and Japanese. They are welcome to their opinion; but one of the strongest reasons for the trial of Axis miscreants is to establish before all the world the truth or falsity of the charges against the Germans and Japanese, by familiar methods of proof in courts of law. The official United Nations Commission for the Investigation of War Crimes, established in London in 1943,[37] as well as each member of the United Nations separately, is collecting carefully documented evidence for use on the day of reckoning. As President Roosevelt has solemnly said, "when victory has been achieved, it is the purpose of the Government of the United States, as I know it is the purpose of each of the United Nations, to make appropriate use of the information and evidence in respect to these barbaric crimes of the invaders, in Europe and in Asia." [38]

In presenting the rules and standards involved, and instances of their flagrant violation, we first consider some *regulations pertaining to the duties of a belligerent State toward troops of the enemy*:

(1)

(*a*) *The rule of law*:

"It is especially forbidden . . . to kill or wound an enemy who, having laid down his arms, or having no longer means of defense, has surrendered at discretion." [39]

(*b*) *Violations of the rule of law*:

"After the capitulation of the fortress of Modlin, heroically defended until the moment of the surrender of Warsaw, the Germans in one sector of the front murdered a whole platoon of captured Polish soldiers. They ordered them to kneel down and raise their arms, then shot them all with machine guns. Several Polish officers who had been seized, were also shot in the same way. Others were transported to Sakroczym, where they were placed against the wall and shot." BBP, Pp. 116–117.

Excerpt from a report by Captain R. D. of the 76th Infantry Regiment: "On September 6th, 1939, the Germans shot in the fields around the village of Moryca nineteen officers of the 76th Infantry

Regiment who had been made prisoners. The rank and file prisoners were buried alive in the hut of the railway pointsman at Poryca and in one of the huts in Longinow. . . ." BBP, P. 117.

"The Soviet Military Command has established many instances in which captured and in most cases wounded Red Army men were brutally tortured, tormented and murdered by the German military command and by German army units. Red Army men taken prisoner have been tortured with red-hot irons, their eyes gouged out, their legs, arms, ears and noses cut off, their fingers hacked off and their stomachs ripped open. They have been tied to tanks and torn apart. . . .

"In July German troops captured groups of seriously wounded Red Army men near the Shumilino railway station and killed them on the spot. In the same month, near the town of Borisov in the Byelorussian Republic, Nazis captured 70 gravely wounded Red Army men and poisoned all of them with arsenic." SWD, Pp. 80–81.

". . . On June 8 (1944) near Pavie, in Calvados, Normandy, certain personnel of the Third Canadian Infantry Division who had been captured by the enemy were murdered by members of the German Army. A court of inquiry assembled at my request and composed of senior officers of the British, American and Canadian Armies has completed exhaustive inquiries and has examined all available evidence. It finds that on that date and place mentioned above nineteen Canadian soldiers, including one officer, were deliberately murdered by members of the Twelfth SS Panzer Division (Hitler Jugend) in clear violation of the well-recognized laws and usages of war." Notice published to troops by Lieut. Gen. H. D. G. Crerar, Canadian Army.

(2)

(a) *The rule of law*:

"It is especially forbidden . . . to declare that no quarter will be given." [40]

(b) *Violation of the rule of law*:

"On September 2nd and 3rd, 1939, between Rybwik and Wadzim, in Silesia, the Germans captured a detachment of the 12th Infantry Regiment. They took no prisoners, but threw the men to the ground, and drove over their bodies with tanks." BBP, P. 117.

(3)

(a) *The rules of law:*

"Prisoners of war . . . must at all times be treated with humanity and protected, particularly against acts of violence. . . . Measures of reprisal against them are prohibited." [41]

"Officers, soldiers, and other persons officially attached to armies who are wounded or sick shall be respected and protected under all circumstances; they shall be treated with humanity and cared for, without distinction of nationality, by the belligerent in whose power they are." [42]

(b) *Violations of the rules of law:*

"According to a deposition which has reached us from Lancut (Southern Poland), five thousand war prisoners were held in a country house park. A cold rain fell day and night. The men were forced to keep on their feet and were famished. . . . Their moans were heart-rending . . . this multitude . . . had not tasted anything for several days. Each morning the bodies of many who had succumbed to these hardships were removed." BBP, P. 118.

Report of the Red Cross Delegate at . . . dated January 29, 1940 (excerpt from affidavit): "During the first half of the month of January, 1940, a convoy of Polish prisoners of war liberated from the camps in East Prussia on account of their extreme exhaustion arrived at Warsaw. Of the 2,000 men in the convoy two hundred and eleven died of cold on the way. When the doors were unsealed and the cars opened, the prisoners who stumbled out seemed to have lost their reason. The journey had lasted eleven days and the soldiers had been packed fifty or seventy into an unheated car. When the men arrived at Warsaw they were not in a condition to take nourishment. They had to be fed for the first few days with liquid only." PWB, P. 226.

Excerpt from affidavit (supported by 14 concordant depositions): "Polish soldiers liberated from German prison camps are in most cases in a deplorable state. They look like walking corpses. Of 100 soldiers liberated it sometimes happens that one can only save a minority; the others die from the effects of cold and lack of food. Some of them lose their reason. Those who survive are so terrorized that they usually refuse to give their impressions." PWB, Pp. 226–227.

"Wounded and sick Red Army men in hospitals captured by the German invaders are systematically subjected to abominable outrages, tortures and brutal torments. There are innumerable instances of defenseless sick and wounded Red Army men in hospitals being bayoneted or shot by Nazi fiends.

"In the small town of Rudnya, in the Smolensk Region, Nazi units which captured a Soviet field hospital shot and wounded Red Army stretcher-bearers and nurses. Wounded Red Army men Shalamov and Azimov, Lieutenant Dileyev, Nurse Varya Boiko and others were killed. Many cases are known of the raping and outraging of nurses and women stretcher-bearers who fell into the hands of the Nazi invaders." SWD, P. 81.

"While prisoners are being marched to their destination those who weaken are shot on the spot. During a transfer of Soviet war prisoners from Khorol to Semenovka in the Ukraine, Red Army men were forced to run all the way. Those who fell from exhaustion were immediately shot." SWD, P. 82.

"Charge XVIII. Prisoners of war who were marched from Bataan to San Fernando in April, 1942, were brutally treated by Japanese guards. The guards clubbed prisoners who tried to get water, and one prisoner was hit on the head with a club for helping a fellow-prisoner who had been knocked down by a Japanese army truck. A colonel who pointed to a can of salmon by the side of the road and asked for food for the prisoners was struck on the side of his head with the can by a Japanese officer. The colonel's face was cut open. Another colonel who had found a sympathetic Filipino with a cart was horsewhipped in the face for trying to give transportation to persons unable to walk. . . . An American lieutenant-colonel was killed by a Japanese as he broke ranks to get a drink at a stream. . . .

"At Cabanatuan Lieut. Cols. Lloyd Biggs and Howard Breitung and Lieut. R. D. Gilbert, attempting to escape during September, 1942, were severely beaten about the legs and feet and then taken out of the camp and tied to posts, were stripped and kept tied up for two days. Their hands were tied behind their backs to the posts so that they could not sit down. Passing Filipinos were forced to beat them in the face with clubs. No food or water was given to them. After two days of torture they were taken away and, according to the statements of Japanese guards, they were killed, one of them decapitated. Other Americans were similarly tortured and shot without trial at Cabanatuan in June or July, 1942, because they endeavored to bring food into the camp. After being tied to a fence post inside the camp for two days they were shot. . . .

"At the Davao Penal Colony, about April 1, 1943, Sergeant McFee was shot and killed by a Japanese guard after catching a canteen full of water which had been thrown to him by another prisoner on the opposite side of the fence. . . . At about the same time and place an officer returning from a work detail tried to bring back some sugar cane for the men in the hospital. For this he was tied to a stake for twenty-four hours and severely beaten. . . ." SS.

(4)

(a) *The rules of law*:

"Belligerents shall be bound to take all sanitary measures necessary to assure the cleanliness and healthfulness of camps and to prevent epidemics.

"Prisoners of war shall have at their disposal, day and night, installations conforming to sanitary rules and constantly maintained in a state of cleanliness.

"Furthermore, in addition to baths and showers with which the camps shall be as well provided as possible, prisoners shall be furnished a sufficient quantity of water to permit of their bodily cleanliness. . . .

"Every camp shall have an infirmary, where prisoners of war shall receive every kind of attention they need. If necessary, isolation quarters shall be reserved for the sick affected with contagious diseases. . . .

"Medical inspections of prisoners of war shall be held at least once a month. Their purpose shall be to determine the general state of health and cleanliness, and to detect contagious diseases, particularly tuberculosis and venereal diseases." [43]

(b) *Violations of the rules of law*:

"Charge XII. The condition of health of prisoners of war in the Philippine Islands is deplorable. At San Fernando in April, 1942, American and Filipino prisoners were held in a barbed-wire enclosure so overcrowded that sleep and rest were impossible. So many of them were sick and so little care was given to the sick that human excrement covered the whole area. The enclosure at San Fernando was more than 100 kilometers from Bataan and the abominable treatment given to the prisoners there cannot be explained by battle conditions. The prisoners were forced to walk this distance in seven days under merciless driving. Many who were unable to keep up with the march were shot or bayoneted by the guards. . . . American and Filipino prisoners are known to have been buried alive along the roadside, and persistent reports have been received of men who tried to rise from their graves but were beaten down with shovels and buried alive.

"At Camp O'Donnell conditions were so bad that 2,200 Americans and more than 20,000 Filipinos are reliably reported to have died in the first few months of their detention. There is no doubt that a large number of these deaths could have been prevented had the Japanese authorities provided minimum medical care for the prisoners. The so-called hospital there was absolutely inadequate to meet the situation. Prisoners of war lay sick and naked on the floor, receiving no attention and too sick to move from their own excrement. The hospital was so overcrowded that Americans were laid on the ground outside in the heat of the blazing sun. The American doctors in the camp were given no medicine, and even had no water to wash the human waste from the bodies of patients. Eventually, when quinine was issued, there was only enough properly to take care of ten cases of malaria, while thousands of prisoners were suffering from the disease. Over two hundred out of three hundred prisoners from Camp O'Donnell died while they were on a work detail in Batangas. . . .

"It is reported that in the autumn of 1943 50 per cent of the American prisoners of war at Davao had a poor chance to live and that the detaining authorities had again cut the prisoners' food ration and had withdrawn all medical attention. . . ." SS.

"In German camps for war prisoners, sick and wounded Red Army men get no medical assistance and are doomed to death from typhus, dysentery, pneumonia and other diseases. . . .

"Captive Red Army men are starved and kept for weeks without food or on miserable rations of rotten bread or rotten potatoes. Refusing to supply Soviet war prisoners with food, the Nazis force them to search garbage cans and look for remnants of food thrown away by German soldiers or, as happened in several camps including the camp at Korma in the Byelorussian SSR, dead horses' carcasses are thrown over the wire fence to the Soviet prisoners.

"In the Vitebsk camp in Byelorussia, captive Red Army men received practically no food for four months. When a group of prisoners presented a written statement to the German command requesting food to keep them alive, a German officer demanded who had written the statement. Five Red Army men who affirmed that they had written it were shot on the spot. Similar instances of blatant arbitrariness and brutality occurred in other camps — Shytkovo, Demiansk and others.

, "Striving for mass extermination of Soviet war prisoners, German authorities and the German government instituted a bestial regime in prison camps. The German High Command and the Ministry of Food and Agriculture issued a decree establishing a ration for Soviet war prisoners inferior to the ration of war prisoners of other countries, both as to quality and quantity of food issued. The rations established by this decree — for instance, 600 grams of bread and 400 grams of meat per man per month — doom Soviet war prisoners to excruciating death by starvation." SWD, Pp. 82–83.

(5)

(*a*) *The rule of law:*

"Punishments other than those provided for the same acts for soldiers of the national armies may not be imposed on prisoners of war by the military authorities and courts of the detaining power. . . .

"Officers, noncommissioned officers, or soldiers who are prisoners of war undergoing disciplinary punishment shall not receive less favorable treatment than that provided in connection with the same punishment for those of equal rank in the army.

"Any corporal punishment, any imprisonment in quarters without daylight, and, in general, any form whatever of cruelty is forbidden.

"Collective punishment for individual acts is also forbidden." [44]

(*b*) *Violations of the rules of law:*

"Charge XVII. American personnel have suffered death and imprisonment for participating in military operations. Death and long-term imprisonment have been imposed for attempts to escape for which the maximum penalty under the Geneva convention is thirty days' arrest. Neither the American Government nor its protecting power has been informed in the manner provided by the convention of these cases or of many other instances when Americans were subjected to illegal punishment. . . ." SS.

"Beating and torturing the prisoners was a regular procedure, as well as punitive gymnastics on the slightest pretext. . . ." BBP, P. 120.

(6)

(*a*) *The rule of law*:

"Prisoners of war shall enjoy complete liberty in the exercise of their religion, including attendance at the services of whatever religion they may belong to, on the sole condition that they comply with the measures of order and police issued by the military authorities." [45]

(*b*) *Violations of the rule of law*:

"At Radom, the Germans made an antireligious demonstration about the beginning of November, 1939, by shutting up two thousand Polish prisoners of war in the Church of Our Lady, the largest in the city, and forbidding them to leave on any pretext whatsoever for forty-eight hours.

"In other localities also the prisoners were shut up in the churches often for several days without food or being allowed to relieve themselves, in order that the churches should suffer desecration." BBP, Pp. 117–118.

"Charge XIV. The Japanese Government has not permitted internees and prisoners of war freely to exercise their religion. For example, the internees at Camp John Hay were not allowed to hold religious services during the first several months of the camp's operation, and priests have not been allowed to minister to prisoners held by the Japanese in French Indo China." SS.

Here are some *rules enjoining duties toward the civilian population of occupied lands,* together with instances of their violation:

(7)

(*a*) *The rule of law*:

"No general penalty, pecuniary or otherwise, shall be inflicted upon the population on account of acts of individuals for which they cannot be regarded as jointly and severally responsible." [46]

"Hostages have been taken in war for the following purposes: To insure proper treatment of wounded and sick when left behind in hostile localities; to protect the lives of prisoners who have fallen into hands of irregular troops or whose lives have been threatened; to protect lines of communication by placing them on engines of trains in occupied territory; and to insure compliance with requisitions, contributions, etc. *When a hostage is accepted he is treated as a prisoner of war.*" [47]

"Hostages should not be put to death unless they have themselves done wrong."[48]

Note: Some modern authorities on international law have altogether repudiated the right of belligerents to take hostages; but the Nazis have raised hostage-taking to a diabolical fine art. In the German War Book, it is acknowledged that the civilian population of a territory occupied by a belligerent has certain rights which the occupant must observe, and that, reciprocally, the population owes obedience to the occupant. But the Germans have so completely ignored these rights that the reciprocal duty of obedience no longer exists. Hence the legal foundation for an occupant's right to take hostages has been destroyed by the occupant. Assuming that the Germans nevertheless have the right to take hostages, it will be seen from the above quotations that this right is limited both as to the purpose for which hostages are taken and as to the treatment to which they can be subjected. In both respects, the Germans have committed flagrant violations of international law. They have taken hostages for purposes of revengeful punishment for acts not previously prohibited, instead of preventive control; they have chosen as hostages the outstanding members of the population of every city, with the aim of deliberately exterminating its leaders; they have killed many hostages on the flimsiest pretexts and not by way of legitimate reprisal for illegal acts; they have employed hostages not only to control the civilian population but to influence the lawful military activities of the United Nations, as well as the conduct of the governments-in-exile; they have taken and have slain hostages who had not the remotest connection, either as to participation or geographic residence, with the community where the alleged hostile act against the occupant occurred; and they have on countless occasions butchered hostages in numbers out of all proportion to the number of Germans allegedly killed or the nature of other hostile acts allegedly done by the oppressed populations. The shootings of hostages by the hundreds of thousands has become so patent a fact of German policy that the practice might be taken "judicial notice" of without formal proof. It is difficult to select passages from the evidence in the compilations, because the Nazis have been so lavish in this form of cruelty that there is an embarrassment of tragic riches; the instances of slaying of innocent people for the alleged crimes of others about which and whom they knew absolutely nothing are far too numerous. However, here are a few taken at random:

(*b*) *Violations of the rule of law*:

". . . Statement by a local police officer at Zgierz: 'In 1939 after the murder of one German we shot 10 Poles; today for the death of every German 50 Poles die, and any further incident of this kind will entail the death of 100 Poles for one German. The sentences will not be carried out haphazardly, but will aim at exterminating the Polish intellectual class, which is your leading class.' " [49]

"The same day, people were hunted down in the town, on the pretext that an attempt had been made to fire at German soldiers from one of the houses. This was the same lie as was employed by the Germans in Belgium and at Kalisz, in Poland, in 1914, to justify their barbarous massacres.

"About sixty people were seized and shot. One of the houses in the Street of The Blessed Virgin Mary was set on fire by the Germans, after they had thrown hand grenades into it. There were many persons inside. It was forbidden to bury or to remove the bodies of those who had been shot, the object being to terrorize the inhabitants by the sight of these corpses. They were left unburied until two days later." BBP, P. 22.

"Reports reaching the Greek Government in Cairo from occupied Greece state that during the months of March, April and May, 1944, the Germans shot 4,100 Greek hostages. This figure is taken from official German communiques published by the press in occupied Greece." Greek Govt. Off. of Information, July 27, 1944.

"Official Announcement:

"In the course of the search for the murders of S. S. Obergruppenführer Heydrich unmistakable indications were discovered that the population of the commune of Lidice near Kladno afforded support and help to the set of culprits in question. Proofs were secured without the assistance of the local population, although enquiries were instituted among them. Their attitude towards the outrage which thus revealed itself was aggravated by further acts hostile to the Reich, such as the discovery of treasonable printed matter, of stores of arms and ammunition, of an illegal wireless sender, of an extremely large quantity of goods subject to rationing, as well as the circumstance that inhabitants of the commune are in the active service of the enemy abroad. As the inhabitants of this village through their activities and support to the murderers of S. S. Ober-gruppenführer Heydrich have most obviously offended against the promulgated laws, the male adults have been shot, the women taken to a concentration camp and the children sent away so that they may receive an appropriate education. The buildings of the village have been razed to the ground and its name erased from all public registers." [50]

The Germans have given the world other Lidices, notably the Greek village of Distomo, where even babes in arms were not spared in the slaughter of more than 1,000 Greeks and the burning down of a village in revenge for the death of 30 German soldiers in a battle with resistance groups.

"On June 24th, the commune of Ležáky near Louka (District Chrudim) was razed to the ground. The adult inhabitants of the place were shot under martial law. The inhabitants had given refuge to and attempted to hide from the police Czech agents dropped by parachute who played a leading part in the preparation of the mur-der of S. S. Obergruppenführer Heydrich. The official of the Protek-toratsgendarmerie responsible for the commune, who has assisted the criminals, committed suicide before he could be arrested." [51]

(8)

(a) *The rule of law*:

"[1] Family honor and rights, [2] the lives of persons . . . as well as [3] religious convictions and practice, must be respected." [52]

(b) *Violations of the rule of law*:

[1] "Excerpt from affidavit: Under pretense of arresting prosti-tutes, patrols of German soldiers organized regular raids to carry off young women. A patrol of the 228th regiment of German infantry organized such a raid in one of the quarters by the river early in 1940. Soldiers of the 7th anti-aircraft regiment did the same thing twice in the suburb of Kokotow. Women were taken not only in the streets but also from their homes. These young unfortunates were carried off to the barracks of the German soldiers and raped."

"Excerpt from affidavit: The German gendarmerie organized a raid in the streets of Lublin . . . and seized a certain number of young Polish girls and women. These unfortunate creatures were submitted to a medical examination and then, one after the other, raped by young German pilots who had just completed their train-ing course at the aerodrome of Swidnik."

"Base outrage of women and girls occurs everywhere in the occupied districts. . . . In Smolensk the German command opened a brothel for officers in a hotel, into which they drove hundreds of girls and women. These women were mercilessly dragged along the street by the hair.

"Everywhere the bestial German bandits break into houses, rape women and girls before the eyes of their relatives and children, torment their victims and brutally murder them on the spot. In Lvov 32 women workers of the Lvov clothing factory were raped and then killed by German storm troopers. Drunken German soldiers dragged Lvov girls and young women to Kosciusko Park and brutally raped them. When an old priest, V. L. Pomaznev, holding a crucifix in his hands, tried to prevent the rape of the girls, the fascists beat him, tore off his cassock, singed his beard and bayoneted him to death.

"Near the town of Borisov in Byelorussia, 75 women and girls who fled before the troops fell into the hands of the Hitlerites. The Germans raped and brutally murdered 36 women and girls. On orders of German officer Hummer, the soldiers took 16-year-old L. I. Melchukova into the forest and raped her. Later other women taken into the forest saw Melchukova impaled with bayonets to boards propped against a tree. Before the eyes of these other women, V. I. Alferenko and V. M. Bereznikova, the Germans hacked off the dying girl's breasts. . . .

"Reports of the vile outrages committed against women and girls, schoolgirls and small children by the Germans during their occupation are pouring in daily from villages and towns recently liberated from the German invaders, in particular various districts of the Moscow, Leningrad, Kalinin, Tula, Orel, Kursk, Voroshilovgrad, Stalino and Rostov Regions. In many cases the ravishers also murdered their victims." SWD, Pp. 95–96.

Excerpt from report received by the Polish Government on July 18, 1940: "In Polish Pomerania and in Posnania (February 1940), illegally annexed to the Reich, there have been numerous cases, how many it is impossible to say, of sterilization of young girls and boys. This measure has also been taken against older individuals expelled from these regions." PWB, Pp. 229–231.

In Holland, "several thousand Jews who were married to gentile women, were exempted from the general deportation measures when the Nazis, in September and October 1943, carried out the 'final' phase of the elimination of Jews from Holland's life. These remaining Jews were subjected to sterilization for the 'protection of the Nordic race,' and after having been kept in hospitals for a week, were given permission to go about without wearing the Star of David. But in true Nazi style, the occupation authorities have once more recanted a given promise. According to the underground newspaper *Vrije Nieuwscentrale*, these Jews are now being forced into the German 'foreign labor' service. The first group of 2,100, irrespective of age, were ordered to report last December to the Amsterdam Advisory Bureau — the organization responsible for assigning Dutchmen to work in foreign territories." [53]

[2] "The massacre of Poles in Bydgoszcz. . . . The Germans at once began to execute the Poles in a wholesale fashion, without trial, without even a shadow of pretext. People were conducted to the center of the town and mowed down with machine-guns, or were shot as they walked along the streets. Cases were known of entire Polish families being murdered in their own homes. . . . It is difficult to fix exactly the total number of Polish people murdered in Bydgoszcz. In any case, down to January 1, 1940, it exceeded 10,000 persons. The majority consisted of representatives of the Polish intellectual and middle classes: priests, officials, judges, professors, merchants, industrialists, although there were also many workmen, craftsmen, etc." BBP, P. 25.

Extract from a report by an Englishwoman, Miss Baker-Beall, who was present in Bydgoszcz during the events she recounts:

"From this time on life was a nightmare of horror. The Germans started the campaign of falsehood about the Polish atrocities on this so-called 'Bloody Sunday,' and almost the first victims of the campaign were a number of Boy Scouts, from twelve to sixteen years of age, who were set up in the market-place against a wall and shot. No reason was given. A devoted priest who rushed to administer the Last Sacrament was shot too. He received five wounds. A Pole said afterwards that the sight of those children lying dead was the most piteous of all the horrors he saw." BBP, P. 134.

The above events are, however, mere child's play compared to the colossal butcheries the Germans committed in extermination centers scientifically organized and staffed with true German efficiency. Two of the most appalling instances of wholesale torture and butchery are those of the Babi Yar ravine in Kiev and the concentration camp at Maidanek near Lublin, Poland. In the former, "even according to the obviously understated testimony of the accused (at the Kharkov trial late in 1943) lie 35;000 dead." As to the latter, American and English newspapermen who visited the 670 acre Maidanek camp late in August, 1944, reported to a shocked world the existence of a huge murder factory in which a million and a half innocent men, women and children from nearly every country in Europe were systematically "processed" to death during the past three years. The victims were first compelled to bathe in steam bathhouses in order to open their pores so that the lethal gas in store for them might take quicker effect. Scientifically built, hermetically sealed gas chambers were used to asphyxiate them with prussic acid gas, while their sadistic torturers watched their agonized death through small windows. The bodies were then carried in special steel stretchers to a series of equally efficient furnaces for mass cremation. Usually, the ashes from the crematories were, with true German economy, scattered as fertilizer for the cabbage-patch from which the murderers got their vegetables; but the ashes of some of the victims (and no guarantee was given that the ashes were those of any particular victim in question) were placed in urns and sold at high prices to the families of the victims. Other innocents were slaughtered in a variety of other diabolical ways, as was established by the huge mass graves which were opened for inspection of newspapermen at Krempitski near Maidanek. They were also shown huge warehouses containing the systematically classified belongings of the dead which were to be shipped, as in the past, for the enjoyment of the members of the master race back home in Germany. Newspapermen are traditionally "hard boiled"; they also possess an unusually sharp faculty for ferreting out the truth or falsity of a situation on the basis of the evidence. One correspondent, Mr. W. H. Lawrence of the New York Times, was moved to write: "After inspection of Maidanek, I am now prepared to believe any story of German atrocities, no matter how savage, cruel and depraved."

Despite the sufferings undergone by all the peoples of Europe at the hands of the Germans, no people has endured as much as the Jews. Here are but a few summaries of the enormous number of atrocities — largely cruelly inflicted murders — inflicted by the Nazis and their minions against the Jews of Europe:

A carefully prepared report of the murder of Jews by Axis barbarians up to the spring of 1943 concludes: "Some 3,000,000 Jews of Europe have perished since the war began four years ago. In the areas occupied or dominated by the Axis, there now remain a little over 3,300,000 Jews, compared to the former Jewish population of 8,300,000. . . . They have been destroyed by deliberate means; by planned starvation, forced labor, deportation, pogrom and methodical murder in the German-run extermination centers of Eastern Europe. . . . Some 1,700,000 were victims of organized massacres and pogroms, conducted for the most part under official German supervision, with the aid of satellite police and troops." [54]

A reliable report published in July, 1944,[55] by the Very Rev. Paul Vogt, head of the *Flüchtlingshilfe* of Zurich, a well known refugee organization, presents overwhelmingly strong proof that in two German "model extermination camps for Jews" in Upper Silesia, almost two million Jews were murdered and "disposed of," "without a hitch," during a two year period ending in April, 1944. Thirty percent of some 400,000 Hungarian Jews deported for extermination in German camps were accounted as "losses." The sadistic tortures to which the doomed were subjected before their "extermination" are too horrible to recount. The facts of these brutalities and large scale murders have been confirmed by the Ecumenical Refugee Commission of the International Church Movement, Geneva, and by British Foreign Secretary Anthony Eden in the House of Commons. Most of the deportations and murders occurred after solemn warnings by the United Nations that German and Hungarian instigators would be punished, and despite appeals by the Pope and the King of Sweden. As defeat approaches, the Germans and their puppets are becoming even more fanatically sadistic in their determination to exterminate Jews.

The following official account of mass-butcheries in Poland does not include the murders inside Warsaw nor the death of the heroic fighters in that city's ghetto:

"The Jewish situation is still worse. . . . In Lublin and the vicinity on the night of March 23 and 24, the Jewish population was simply driven out of their homes, and the sick and the infirm were killed on the spot. In the Jewish orphanage 108 children from the age of two to nine were taken outside the town together with their nurses, and murdered. Altogether that night, 2,500 people were massacred and the remaining 2,600 Jews in Lublin were removed to the concentration camps at Belzec and Trawniki. . . . In Belzec and Trawniki murder is carried out by means of poison gas. Mass murders occurred on such a large scale at Rawa Ruska and Bilgora, that Jewish communities have ceased to exist. In Wawalnica, near Kazimierz, on March 22 the Gestapo shot 120 Jews in the marketplace and an unknown number of Jews was led out of town and slaughtered. On March 30 Jews were driven from Opol to Naleczow. Three hundred and fifty were killed on the way and the rest were put into freight trucks which were sealed and deported to an unknown destination. In Mielec about 1,300 Jews were slaughtered on March 9; in Mir 2,000 Jews were killed; in Nowogrodek, 2,500; in Wolozyn, 1,800; in Kajdanow 4,000 were killed. Thirty thousand Jews from Haburg were deported to Minsk where they were all murdered. Jews slaughtered in Lwow amount to 30,000; in Wilno to 60,000; in Stanislawow 15,000; in Tarnopol 5,000; Zloczow 2,000; and Brzesany 4,000. Reports have been received that Jews have been murdered in Tarnow, Radom, Zborow, Kolomyja, Sambor, Stryj, Drohobycz, Zbaraz, Brody, Przemysl, Kolo and Dab. They are forced to dig their own graves and then are mown down with machine guns and hand grenades, and are poisoned with gas. These are methods daily applied to annihilate the Jewish population. In Lwow the Jewish Council had to provide victims themselves." BBP, P. 579.

Both the policy of extermination and the diabolical methods used were conducted as a calculated, official, governmental policy. Speaking of the Kharkov trial, an editorial in *Pravda* quotes some of the testimony of Retslaw, one of the German defendants:

"Wholesale executions by hanging and shooting . . . seemed to the German command too troublesome and slow a means for the accomplishment of the tasks assigned to the punitive organs, and therefore more simple methods had to be devised for the extermination of the population. It must be said that these methods were found." [56] Colonel Heinisch, Hess's assistant Chief of Staff, "told the court [during the Kharkov trial] that in the autumn of 1942 there was a conference between Hitler, Himmler and the Chief of the SD, Kaltenbrunner, at which it was decided to proceed to exterminate the superfluous part of the population of the German-occupied regions. It was then that the wide-scale employment of the 'murder cars' began, as an easy and perfected method of wholesale extermination. The Germans also began to asphyxiate people in special bathhouses to which they were sent supposedly to bathe and have their clothing disinfected. They were stripped naked in one building and passed into another — the bathhouse proper. But there was no hot water or steam; instead, poison gas was injected into the room. The asphyxiated people were then dragged to a third house and burned in specially constructed furnaces accommodating 200 bodies each. Such bathhouses were built in concentration camps in Germany and also in the Ukraine." [57]

Even under the Nazi conception of "military necessity," this mass-slaughter of innocents has not the remotest connection with waging war. It is simply a cold-blooded and premeditated policy of extermination of millions of human beings, in order to seize their land and possessions. The Germans have felt secure in this diabolical program because they know that civilized nations would hesitate to indulge in similar mass butcheries by way of reprisal.

That heartless brutality has pervaded even the German medical corps is seen by the following extract from a report received by Science Service from the Soviet Scientists' Anti-Fascist Committee: "At the village of Gastogayevskaya in the Krasnodar district, the German police detained forty children, all of them under 13 years. The children were taken to a German Army hospital at Starotitarov-skaya where all the blood was pumped out of them. All forty children died. German doctors used Soviet citizens as guinea pigs for their experiments with poisonous substances and for experimental operations. In the city of Orel a medical commission headed by Academician Nikolai Burdenko established the fact that the Germans deliberately poisoned seventeen workers from a sheet metal shop with mustard gas and then placed them in a German hospital for detailed clinical and laboratory examination. The victims were frequently photographed and demonstrated to German doctors who passed through the town. All this was done for testing the efficacy of some medicines." [58]

"It was established that between August 5 and 10, 1942, some German soldiers from the SS Kommandatur, with Obersergeant Major Goering and Sergeant Major Schmidt at the head, took out of the Stavropol Psychiatric Hospital and killed in these vans with carbon monoxide 660 patients." SWD, Pp. 172–173.

[3] "At Bydgoszca (Bromberg) at Dziewierzewno, at Peplin, at Tarnow and in other places religious edifices have been destroyed or burned down, or else used as warehouses, garages or stables. (Cf. Reports of His Eminence Cardinal Hlond to the Holy See.)

Synagogues were burned down at Czestochowa, Wloclawek, Lodz, etc. The German controlled press of the occupied regions often comments on these events in the same strain as it employed toward similar happenings in Germany at the time of the rise of the national socialist movement there." PWB, Pp. 32, 36.

The legal prohibitions set forth above are but a small segment of the net-work of customary and conventional international law, and the illustrations presented are but a minimal sample of atrocities that violate both the laws of warfare and the prohibitions common to the vast majority of civilized penal codes. Not only are thousands of instances of brutal treatment of both prisoners of war and civilians not included, but many hundreds of instances of the lootings of shops, factories, banks, museums, or of the wanton destruction of historic monuments, works of art and literary treasures, are not set forth.

Finally, to include even a few samples of German *use of prohibited methods of warfare* would have necessitated another long chapter. The surprise employment of "robot bombs" is but one illustration. These cannot be aimed at military objectives. Their point of target-contact is indiscriminate; and their employment shows a deliberate determination to violate all conventional and customary laws of warfare that protect Red Cross and hospital installations, churches, schools, art centers, undefended towns, and the like. (Hague Regulations, Articles 22, 25, 27; American *Rules*, Paragraphs 26, 45, 58.) The true measure of the Axis crimes is so monstrous as to call forth the very reaction Hitler and his fellow-murders anticipated — amazed skepticism leading to disbelief. But nobody who has examined even a small quantity of the official compilations authenticated by sworn eye-witness accounts, documents, photographs, and pathologic examinations of disinterred bodies can doubt the verity of the bloody catalogue. That these heartless slaughterings were executed as a carefully planned program of extermination is incontestably proved by the Axis legislation, decrees, regulations, official orders and other documents, as well as by that diatribe of pathologic hatred, Hitler's *"Mein Kampf."*

Numerous German army orders (Japanese are not as readily available) attest to the premeditated policy of ruthless inhumanity. Thus Paragraph 2 of an order of the German army on January 14, 1942, in the name of Hitler as commander-in-chief, expresses this policy: "Any leniency or humane treatment to a prisoner is to be strictly discouraged. A German soldier must always make a prisoner feel his superiority. . . . Any hesitation in the use of arms on a prisoner is dangerous. The commander-in-chief trusts that this order will be fully carried out." [59] Order No. 166–41 sent to the 60th Motorized Infantry Division rewards bravery in battle in defense of one's motherland as follows: "Russian soldiers and minor officers are very determined in battle and even the smallest unit always resists attack. Therefore, any humane treatment of prisoners cannot be allowed. Extermination of the enemy by fire or cold weapons must be continued until he is rendered completely harmless. . . ." [60] And Order No. 1–3058 of the German command shows Germany's premeditated policy of not observing its solemn obligations with respect to prisoners of war, under the Geneva convention and common international law: "The slightest sign of insubordination must be met in an energetic and direct way. Arms are to be used without mercy and sticks, canes and whips should not be used. Softness, even toward an obedient and industrious prisoner, only displays weakness and it should not be practiced. . . ." [61]

Yet there are those who seriously urge that the planners and executors of the blackest list of cruelties to be found in recorded history be permitted to escape the judgment of law. [62] To allow this would be to deal an almost fatal blow to the administration of justice in the affairs of men, and to lend encouragement to the protean forces of evil which have almost succeeded in turning the world into a slave-pen and charnel-house. It is to be hoped that the member states of the United Nations will never subscribe to such a fatuous policy; that they will rather wait until the chief miscreants have fallen into their hands; and, as nations dedicated to civilized standards of justice, will not punish indiscriminately, as the Nazis have done, but on the basis of a trial of each of the accused. This is necessary not only because one of the chief aims of the United Nations is to reestablish a regime of law and decency, but because under the influence of prejudice and propaganda many persons will regard the unspeakable brutalities chargeable to the Germans (not so much those attributable to the Japanese) as "mere atrocity tales." History is repeating itself; and just as proof that a few of the tales of German cruelties during the first world war were circulated as Allied propaganda made too many Americans and English believe that the Germans were innocent of all wrongdoing, so during the present war, despite the anguished cries of the innocent victims of Lidice, the Warsaw ghetto, and the Babi Yar in Kiev, there are still too many who babble that reports of Nazi cruelties beyond the reach of civilized imagination are but the imaginative figments of anti-German and anti-Japanese propagandists.

"In all wars many shocking and outrageous acts must be expected, for in every large army there must be a proportion of men of criminal instincts whose worst passions are unloosed by the immunity which the conditions of warfare afford. . . .

"In the present war, however — and this is the gravest charge against the German army — the evidence shows that the killing of noncombatants was carried out to an extent for which no previous war between nations claiming to be civilized (for such cases as the atrocities perpetrated by the Turks on the Bulgarian Christians in 1876, and on the Armenian Christians in 1895 and 1896, do not belong to that category) furnishes any precedent. That this killing was done as part of a deliberate plan is clear from the facts hereinbefore set forth regarding Louvain, Aerschot, Dinant, and other towns. The killing was done under orders in each place. It began at certain fixed dates, and stopped (with some few exceptions) at another fixed date. Some of the officers who carried out the work did it reluctantly, and said they were obeying directions from their chiefs. The same remarks apply to the destruction of property. House burning was part of the programme; and villages, even large parts of a city, were given to the flames as part of the terrorizing policy.

"Citizens of neutral states who visited Belgium in December and January report that the German authorities do not deny that noncombatants were systematically killed in large numbers during the first weeks of the invasion, and this, so far as we know, has never been officially denied. If it were denied, the flight and continued voluntary exile of thousands of Belgian refugees would go far to contradict a denial, for there is no historical parallel in modern times for the flight of a large part of a nation before an invader.

"The German Government have, however, sought to justify their severities on the grounds of military necessity, and have excused them as retaliation for cases in which civilians fired on German troops. There may have been cases in which such firing occurred, but no proof has ever been given, or, to our knowledge, attempted to be given, of such cases, nor of the stories of shocking outrages perpetrated by Belgian men and women on German soldiers.

"The inherent improbability of the German contention is shown by the fact that after the first few days of the invasion every possible precaution had been taken by the Belgian authorities, by way of placards and hand-bills, to warn the civilian population not to intervene in hostilities. Throughout Belgium steps had been taken to secure the handing over of all firearms in the possession of civilians before the German army arrived. These steps were sometimes taken by the police and sometimes by the military authorities. . . .

"That these acts should have been perpetrated on the peaceful population of an unoffending country which was not at war with its invaders but merely defending its own neutrality, guaranteed by the invading Power, may excite amazement and even incredulity. It was with amazement and almost with incredulity that the Committee first read the depositions relating to such acts. But when the evidence regarding Liége was followed by that regarding Aerschot, Louvain, Andenne, Dinant, and the other towns and villages, the cumulative effect of such a mass of concurrent testimony became irresistible, and we were driven to the conclusion that the things described had really happened. . . . The excesses . . . committed in Belgium were, moreover, too widespread and too uniform in their character to be mere sporadic outbursts of passion or rapacity.

"The explanation seems to be that these excesses were committed — in some cases ordered, in others allowed — on a system and in pursuance of a set purpose. That purpose was to strike terror into the civil population and dishearten the Belgian troops, so as to crush down resistance and extinguish the very spirit of self-defense. The pretext that civilians had fired upon the invading troops was used to justify not merely the shooting of individual francs-tireurs, but the murder of large numbers of innocent civilians, an act absolutely forbidden by the rules of civilized warfare.

"It is proved:

(*i*) *That there were in many parts of Belgium deliberate and systematically organized massacres of the civil population, accompanied by many isolated murders and other outrages.*

(*ii*) *That in the conduct of the war generally innocent civilians, both men and women, were murdered in large numbers, women violated, and children murdered.*

(*iii*) *That looting, house burning, and the wanton destruction of property were ordered and countenanced by the officers of the German Army, that elaborate provision had been made for systematic incendiarism at the very outbreak of the war, and that the burnings and destruction were frequent where no military necessity could be alleged, being indeed part of a system of general terrorization.*

(*iv*) *That the rules and usages of war were frequently broken, particularly by the using of civilians, including women and children, as a shield for advancing forces exposed to fire, to a less degree by killing the wounded and prisoners, and in the frequent abuse of the Red Cross and the White Flag.*

"Sensible as they are of the gravity of these conclusions, the Committee conceive that they would be doing less than their duty if they failed to record them as fully established by the evidence. Murder, lust, and pillage prevailed over many parts of Belgium on a scale unparalleled in any war between civilized nations during the last three centuries.

"Our function is ended when we have stated what the evidence establishes, but we may be permitted to express our belief that these disclosures will not have been made in vain if they touch and rouse the conscience of mankind, and we venture to hope that as soon as the present war is over, the nations of the world in council will consider what means can be provided and sanctions devised to prevent the recurrence of such horrors as our generation is now witnessing."[63]

The above quotation is from the report of the Committee headed by Lord Bryce, setting forth evidence of German atrocities during the last world war. At that time, even investigators, scholars and statesmen of the stamp of Lord Bryce and Sir Frederick Pollock (another distinguished member of the British committee) were accused of circulating "atrocity tales." One may be pardoned for suggesting that perhaps the undeniable mass of atrocities committed by the German military hordes during the present war shed an illuminative backward light on the question of alleged German atrocities during the first world war. At that time, the malefactors not only went unwhipped of justice but were vociferously championed by strong elements of English and American public opinion. This wrapping of the mantle of injured innocence about the Germans did not in the slightest restrain them from again attacking their peaceful neighbors in treacherous breach of treaties, nor from committing even greater atrocities during the conduct of the second world war.

Will the history of unpunished lawlessness once more repeat itself?

CHAPTER IV

LEGAL LIABILITY FOR ATROCITIES

⚖

SUPPOSING the violation of the laws and customs of warfare, what steps may an injured nation take to enforce respect for the rules of the grim game?

The remedies fall into two classes: those against a belligerent State and those against its individual nationals.

As to measures affecting an implicated *State,* Article 345 of the American *Rules of Land Warfare,* following international law, provides that "the injured Party may legally resort to such remedial action as may be deemed appropriate and necessary within the following classes:

a. Publication of the facts, with a view to influencing public opinion against the offending belligerent.

b. Protest and demand for punishment of individual offenders, sent to the offending belligerent through neutral diplomatic channels, or by parlementaire direct to the commander of the offending forces. . . .

c. Reprisals."

In addition to these remedies, Article 3 of the Hague Convention No. IV. (1907) provides a fourth line of action which may be taken against a lawless State after the close of a war: A belligerent party which violates the provisions of the *Regulations* annexed to that Convention, "shall, if the case demands, be liable to pay compensation. It shall be responsible for all acts committed by persons forming part of its armed forces."

Examination of these remedies available against a State soon reveals their inadequacy in dealing with nations that have run amuck.

The first—*publication of the facts*—has frequently been resorted to by leaders of the United Nations. Numerous compilations of authenticated atrocities have been published by the governments in exile and by the Untied States, Great Britain, Soviet Russia and China. President Roosevelt, Premier Churchill, Marshal Stalin and the respective foreign offices and legislative bodies of many of the United Nations have publicly condemned the atrocities committed by the Axis powers led by Germany and Japan. It is a notorious fact, however, that such attempts to influence public opinion have not had much practical effect on the few remaining neutral States and have fallen on deaf ears so far as the enemy countries are concerned. Indeed, publication of the facts of atrocities seems to have resulted only in increased and more flagrant Axis violations of the laws and customs of legitimate warfare and of the principles governing the criminal law of civilized lands.

The second remedy — *protest and demand for punishment of individual offenders* communicated through diplomatic channels — is illustrated in the previous chapter by the extracts from the communication sent through Switzerland by Secretary Hull to the Japanese Government. This, too, has proved worse than abortive; the cynical Japanese and German militarists continue to ignore protests against their acts of barbarism, and there is no indication of an early change of practice on their part.[1] We may indeed expect that the more panicky they become with the closer approach of the day of reckoning the more unrestrained will their behavior become and the less inclined will they be to punish their own violators of the laws and customs of warfare. This is demonstrated by Goebbels' deliberate egging on of the German population to lynch American fliers who parachute on German soil and the probability that such murders have been perpetrated. Perhaps the governments which immediately succeed the present German and Japanese war lords and political leaders will seek to curry favor with the United Nations by a few well-advertised trials of a number of their own military scapegoats. But even this is doubtful, in view of the experience at the close of the last world war which culminated in the Leipzig trials.

The third remedy against guilty States for violations of the laws of warfare — *reprisals* — also has many disadvantages. It is hard to administer fairly. "The right to exercise reprisals carries with it great danger of arbitrariness, for often the alleged facts which make belligerents resort to them are not sufficiently verified; sometimes the rules of war which they consider the enemy to have violated are not generally recognized; often the act of reprisal performed is excessive compared with the precedent act of illegitimate warfare."[2] Still worse is the fact that reprisals invariably lead to counter-reprisals (retaliations), and these to counter-counter-reprisals; and in this game the more brutal and militaristic nations must, because of their cynical unscrupulousness, inevitably be the winners.

The fourth recourse — *post-war compensation* by the guilty belligerent State to the injured belligerent State for violations of the laws of war — is also, for a number of cogent reasons, an inadequate remedy: While the war is in progress, it is not deterrent to the leaders of a ruthless nation, because they firmly believe their State is going to win the war. It is perhaps for this reason that post-war indemnification was so generously proposed by the German delegation to the Hague Peace Conference as a means of compelling observance of the *Regulations* annexed to the Convention governing land warfare. Ironically enough, it became the legal foundation for the Allied imposition of an indemnity on Germany for the injuries committed by her during the first world war; and it may be resorted to again at the close of the present struggle. Post-war indemnification is, however, not deterrent to officers and men, because the remote possibility of a guilty State having to pay a monetary compensation at the close of a war it expects to win is a too vague and generalized prospective punishment; therefore not the sort of threat which is psychologically likely to influence the behavior of individual offenders. Besides, a monetary payment can never be an adequate moral and psychologic requital for the injuries inflicted by the Nazi-Fascist militarists; not all the money in the world can possibly compensate for their atrocities that have taken millions of lives. Finally, it is hard to establish the guilt of an entire people without historical investigation, even in the case of the Germans.

This analysis would suggest that the most effective remedy immediately available is not to be found in action against States but rather in the punishment, both during and after a war, of *individual violators* of the laws and customs of legitimate warfare and of the tenets of civilized criminal law. There is little sound basis for the view of some publicists that resort to the other remedies — those against the offending *State* — necessarily rules out the trial and punishment of individual malefactors.[3] Nevertheless, there has long been much legalistic debate upon this fundamental means of making the laws and customs of legitimate warfare effective.

Despite considerable and long-standing precedent,[4] there is still some difference of opinion regarding the right of a belligerent to prosecute individual enemy violators of the laws and customs of warfare; more debate about its right to do so after the legal reestablishment of a status of peace; its right to do so in civil, as opposed to military, tribunals; and, more recently, the right of a group of nations to do so through a joint or an international tribunal.[5] Some of these questions will be discussed in the present chapter; others may more appropriately be considered later.

Can a State lawfully try individual enemy violators of the laws and customs of legitimate warfare and of its criminal laws, in its own tribunals?

It was long contended that acts of enemy soldiers constituting crimes or violations of the laws and customs of warfare could not be prosecuted in the courts of an occupied country, because under a general rule of international law members of the occupying army are subject only to the jurisdiction of their *own* tribunals and exempt from the normal criminal jurisdiction of the invaded country.[6] However, to limit the right of trial to the courts of the enemy State easily leads to abuse. Such a nation could defeat justice by simply refusing to proceed against its own violators of the laws and customs of warfare and the criminal law of civilized States as represented by the code of the occupied country. If, after its defeat and under pressure of the victorious State or of neutrals, the defeated belligerent did prosecute its own nationals, the outcome would tend to be unsatisfactory, as was demonstrated by the Leipzig trials. Bold and arrogant States would have the advantage over easygoing, "live-and-let-live" members of the Family of Nations.

The better view nowadays is, that by virtue of the common law of war as gleaned from the practice of many countries over a long period, as well as conventions entered into by them at various times, there is a *concurrent* jurisdiction of both belligerents — the injured State as well as the State to which the accused belongs — in the trial and punishment of violators of the laws and customs of warfare.[7] All nations are obligated to see that international law — including that branch of it which concerns prohibited methods of warfare — is enforced. While it is true that the armed forces of a belligerent are normally exempted from the criminal jurisdiction of the non-military courts of the State they have occupied, such a privilege is limited to acts of *lawful warfare*. Moreover, ordinary crimes that have nothing to do with warfare or military necessity are contrary to the elementary principles of criminal law common to all civilized States and are specific violations of the injured State's own penal code which reflects such principles. They are therefore assuredly triable in the injured State's own courts. "Beyond this, the occupying power may in fact be able to suspend the exercise of the sovereign rights of the occupied State, but, in law, it cannot claim exemption for acts which are contrary to the selfsame International Law on which its claim to the extraterritoriality of its army is based."[8] Therefore a captured enemy soldier who is prosecuted cannot legitimately argue that since he was part of the armed forces of his own country when he committed the alleged violation, he was subject exclusively to its laws and can be tried only by its tribunals. Certainly, while a war was still in progress, the United States, Great Britain, France, Germany and other belligerents have in the past found no serious legal obstacle in the way of subjecting to trial and punishment prisoners of war charged with having violated the laws and customs of legitimate warfare;[9] the American *Rules of Land Warfare* (Sec. 347 c), following the British rules, provide among the remedies open for the control of enemy conduct of warfare, the "punishment of captured individual offenders."

Nor can such offenders choose the tribunal before which they are to be tried; this is a matter of the internal polity of the injured State, not a right of the accused under international law.[10]

But can the United Nations lawfully assume a *post-bellum* jurisdiction to prosecute flagrant violaters of the laws and customs of warfare who are in their hands or who may be turned over to them under the terms of "unconditional surrender"? At the close of the last world war, the Germans strenuously objected to the trial of German war criminals by the Allies after the Peace Treaty had been signed. They insisted that past practice had permitted *postwar* trials of war criminals only by their own nation. They took it for granted that under international law based on custom a treaty of peace invariably operates as an amnesty; and that the most the Allies could therefore ask was that Germany should herself prosecute her nationals accused of violations of the laws and customs of warfare. The Allies, on the other hand, assumed that the amnesty rule of international law is not universal, but dependent upon the contractual terms of the particular treaty of peace.[11] They consequently compelled Germany and the other Central Powers to accept the penal clauses of the Treaty of Versailles. Under these, the Central Powers waived exclusive *post-bellum* jurisdiction over German war criminals regardless of whether the acts complained of had taken place inside Germany or in the lands the German armies had previously occupied. Germany and the other Central Powers consented, "notwithstanding [the fact that] peace may have been declared,"[12] to deliver up the accused for trial in Allied military tribunals. This significant precedent thus acknowledges[13] the right of the belligerents to subject enemy violators of the laws and customs of warfare[14] to trial and punishment, even after the official termination of a war. The Treaty of Versailles is apparently the first peace pact in which the victorious belligerent, with good grounds for not trusting the defeated belligerent to punish its subjects for violating the injunctions of international law in regard to methods of warfare, enforced the principle of individual responsibility after the termination of the war.[15]

The defeated Germans will doubtless claim, as they did previously, that, at least as to crimes committed on German territory, their own law must govern and that violations of that law should be prosecuted only in German courts. But in the absence of an *international* criminal tribunal armed with adequate enforcing power — a court representing all or most of the civilized nations of the world, including neutrals — there is no other way than that of Versailles to vindicate the branch of the law of nations in question when dealing with a State that has flagrantly trampled on both municipal and international law. The justifications for such a *post-bellum* right on the part of the victor is amply shown by Germany's failure, when left to her own devices, to punish her war criminals at the end of the last war. The justice or injustice of the proceedings in a victorious nation's tribunals is a matter to be left to the conscience and legal training of its judges and prosecutors; it is open to the scrutiny of neutrals, and subject to the judgment of history.

It is however not very probable that at the conclusion of the present hostilities this question of postwar jurisdiction over war criminals will be more than an academic one. From all reports, it seems to be the plan of the United Nations to postpone the signing of a peace treaty with the Axis powers for a considerable time beyond their unconditional surrender. During that period — legally still a period of *war* — there ought to be adequate time to dispose of the war criminals' problem. Undue delay will only result in the deterioration of the proof, disappearance of witnesses, loss of interest on the part of the prosecuting States. If, on the other hand, an early treaty of peace is envisaged, that treaty (as did the Versailles agreement), or preferably, the armistice terms as well as the treaty of peace,[16] can provide for the *post-bellum* trial of specified classes of war criminals, such as those embraced in the definition analyzed in the prior chapter.

CHAPTER V

COURTS FOR THE TRIAL OF WAR CRIMINALS

⚖

B Y *what type of tribunal ought war criminals to be tried?*
Before exploring this technical question, one ought to consider whether trials — at least of the leading malefactors — are
necessary and desirable. On the basis of available information,
the United Nations, as victorious belligerents, could simply
declare Hitler, Tojo (or Hirohito), Mussolini and other heads
of State as well as their chief henchmen to be guilty of various
crimes, without subjecting them to trial. The fact that they
ordered or executed numerous acts contrary to the laws and
customs of warfare and to the basic principles of civilized
criminal law is notorious. By proclaiming them to be criminals
and outlaws, they would be put in the position of fugitives from
justice, and subject to summary execution when captured or
surrendered. This was essentially the way the case of Napoleon
was treated, although he was exiled instead of being executed.[1]

As was stressed at the outset, there is very little limitation on
what a victorious nation can do with a vanquished State at the
close of a war. One shudders to think what Germany and Japan
would do if they were the victors! But the common law of
nations probably requires a fair trial of offenders against war
law as a prerequisite to punishment for alleged offenses;[2] and
the Geneva Convention[3] so prescribes in the case of prisoners of
war.[4] But in the final analysis, a decent respect for the opinion
of mankind and the judgment of history is, in effect, a victorious
belligerent's main limitation on its treatment of the surrendered
at the close of a war; and this is self-imposed. The United
Nations are solemnly committed to vindication of the rule of
law which has been so ruthlessly destroyed by the Nazis and
Japanese. "Formalized vengeance can bring only an ephemeral
satisfaction, with every probability of ultimate regret; but
vindication of law through legal processes may contribute sub-

stantially to the re-establishment of order and decency in international relations."[5] Centuries of civilization stretch between the summary slaying of the defeated in a war, and the employment of familiar processes and protections of justice according to law to determine the extent and nature of individual guilt. Proof in a tribunal, under the auspices of judges trained in the conduct of fair trials, is more solemn and convincing than proof by private methods. And in the civilized administration of justice even the most loathsome criminal caught red-handed must be given his day in court and an opportunity to interpose such defenses as he may have. Besides, solemn proof of guilt in an international court of justice will establish once and for all that violations of various specific laws of legitimate warfare or of the prohibitions of civilized penal codes are crimes punishable not only by the injured State but by the Family of Nations in its *collective capacity*. The trial of Hitler, Tojo, Mussolini and their leading military and political henchmen in an International Criminal Court would be a significant symbol of the growing unity of the nations of the world. It would demonstrate vividly that all peoples have a common interest in the prevention of crime, and that the mere fact that wholesale crime has been clothed in a mantle of warfare, or ordered by a government in the name of a sovereign State, is no defense but rather a circumstance of aggravation. Thus can that which could be an arbitrary and one-sided political act of force by the victorious belligerent be transmuted into a solemn judicial proceeding.

The fear that the Axis war criminals can turn the trials into a forum for the propagation of their stupid and inhumane "philosophy" is not justified. Strong judges not only can prevent this by ruling on the relevancy of the offered proof, but can bring home to the entire world the unscientific, immoral and absurd basis of the Nazi racial propaganda. Surely no civilized system of criminal law and no ordinary judge would permit an argument in justification or excuse based on the view that human beings believed by the accused to belong to an inferior race can be murdered with impunity. The very offer of such a defense would give a court the opportunity to brand it before all the world as not only nonsensical but contrary to the very rudiments of civilized criminals justice.

It being desirable, then, to subject Axis war criminals to

trial, at least five different types of tribunal might be resorted to: *(1) the ordinary domestic criminal courts of each of the injured States; (2) their military commissions or other tribunals enforcing military law; (3) the military or ordinary criminal courts of the defendant's State; (4) a joint ("mixed") multinational military tribunal combining the separate military codes and procedures of the various States comprising the United Nations; (5) an international criminal court set up for the specific purpose of trying violators of the laws and customs of legitimate warfare and of the principles of criminal law common to practically all civilized States.*

(1, 2) According to a number of official pronouncements by United Nations' statesmen, the vast majority of offenders will be tried in the domestic criminal or military tribunals of the injured nations. Thus on August 21, 1942, President Roosevelt, in condemning the crimes committed against the civil population in occupied lands, solemnly announced that "the time will come when" the criminals "will have to stand in courts of law in the very countries which they are now oppressing, and to answer for their acts."[6] On September 8, 1942, Mr. Churchill promised that "those who are guilty of the Nazi crimes will have to stand up before tribunals in every land where the atrocities have been committed."[7] The Moscow Declaration of November 1, 1943 sternly warned that "at the time of granting of any armistice to any government which may be set up in Germany, those German officers and men and members of the Nazi party who have been responsible for or have taken a consenting part (in the various) atrocities, massacres and executions will be sent back to the countries in which their abominable deeds were done in order that they may be judged and punished according to the laws of these liberated countries and of the free governments which will be erected therein," and that "the Allied Powers will pursue them to the uttermost ends of the earth and will deliver them to the accusers in order that justice may be done."[8]

Thus, under the varying domestic constitutional and legal systems of the States comprising the United Nations, some of the enemy offenders may be tried in ordinary criminal courts for violating provisions of the penal law of the land; most of them will probably be prosecuted in military tribunals for violating the laws and customs of legitimate warfare as reflected and amplified in the domestic Army's rules of warfare, or in local legislation. The recent Kharkov trial, in which three German officers and a Russian traitor were expeditiously but fairly dealt with by a Russian military tribunal, and were convicted and hanged for atrocities, is an illustration of the use of domestic courts.[9] In case of offenses and crimes against Americans, prosecutions can be conducted in military commissions to be set up in European or Asiatic territory or wherever else the unlawful acts occurred. There is ample precedent for the employment of such tribunals; they are efficient but fair; their jurisdiction is not dependent upon whether or not the offense or crime was committed on American soil, but extends to wherever it occurred.[10] Employment of non-military courts — either the Federal district courts or special tribunals created by Congress for the purpose — would entail too many practical and constitutional difficulties.[11]

It is appropriate that the vast majority of war criminals should be tried in the countries in which they committed their outrages. Their deeds have violated not only the laws and customs of legitimate warfare — part of the law of nations — but also the military and penal law of local sovereignties; the proof of their misdeeds can best be assembled at the places in which they occurred; the trial procedures are familiar; the local community's outraged feelings can best be satisfied by proceedings against the malefactors in domestic courts.

In the vast majority of war criminals' cases, trials in domestic courts can therefore proceed fairly and expeditiously under local military or criminal law, which defines the offenses and specifies the punishments. However, in the employment of domestic courts — especially non-military tribunals — we run into a technicality involving the problem of the *territoriality* of jurisdiction, a matter particularly dear to Anglo-American jurists.[12] According to this doctrine courts cannot take jurisdiction for the trial of crimes which were not committed within their national geographic bounds. Yet a great many atrocities have occurred inside Germany, where there are millions of war prisoners and forced laborers. Should the territorial theory of jurisdiction bar trials in all these cases by the courts of the injured nations? Here, as in the case of "acts of State" and the defense of obedience to the military orders of a superior, to be considered later,[13] the rule of practical reason should take precedence over the rule of abstruse conceptualism. While the territorial principle is fundamental to jurisdiction in ordinary situations, there already exist exceptions in the law of many nations based largely on necessity and realism. Thus crimes threatening the security of a State, or interfering with the functioning of its public agencies and instrumentalities, or committed against its nationals, are frequently and ought reasonably to be punishable by the injured State no matter where or by whom they are committed.[14]

The reasoning used to justify such invasion of the pristine doctrine of the territoriality of jurisdiction in the case of war crimes is even more persuasive than that used to justify existing exceptions to the doctrine in the case of ordinary crimes. The very fact that many States, including Germany,[15] have seen fit to modify the absoluteness of the doctrine of territoriality shows that this technicality, based largely on strict notions of sovereignty, ought not to be permitted to rule out prosecutions of war criminals for numerous offenses committed inside Germany, Japan and other enemy countries. The ordinary reasons for the strictly territorial basis of jurisdiction are not very cogent when it comes to the trial of war criminals. It must be remembered that the laws and customs of legitimate warfare are binding on *all* civilized nations and their peoples. So also, the basic principles of penal law governing the more serious crimes are to be found in practically all civilized legal systems. Moreover, the protections of the accused in connection with trials are very much alike in all civilized systems. Certainly, the trial procedures in United Nations courts afford just as much protection to the accused as they would receive in German courts, if not more. Consequently, it cannot be claimed that some strange new law or unfair procedure would be applied were the accused to be prosecuted in foreign courts.

Nor can it be legitimately claimed that difficulties of assembling witnesses and proof make it wholly impractical to prosecute Germans or Japanese outside their own countries. Despite the fact that the Allies had consented to the Germans' trial of German war criminals in their own court at Leipzig, the Germans threw upon the Allies the burden of assembling the proof at the close of the last world war. Allied military governments will be on the ground and can readily assemble the necessary witnesses and proof, whether the accused are to be tried on Axis territory or outside such territory.

There is, besides, a serious question whether *military* crimes, at least if tried while the status of war still exists, are altogether subject to the traditional notions of jurisdiction prevailing in peacetime between friendly nations.[16] To cite but one precedent, a United States court convened in Texas found no difficulty in trying and convicting an officer charged with a drunken exhibition in a public hall in Mexico, giving as the reason the view that the military jurisdiction "does not recognize territoriality as an essential element of military offenses but extends to the same wherever committed."[17] While this involved an American defendant, there is some precedent and much reason to believe that the same rule prevails in the trial of enemy offenders as well, at least before the legal status of peace has been restored.[18]

Despite such arguments, however, some members of the United Nations will hesitate to depart from the doctrine of the territoriality of jurisdiction; but even in such States (*e.g.*, Great Britain, the United States — in non-military courts — France, Belgium) there ought to be no difficulty in enacting legislation which expands the jurisdictional basis but strictly limits such expansion to carefully specified war crimes committed against their nationals. Crimes committed by enemy subjects inside Axis countries against *"Heimatlose"* (*i.e.*, stateless persons), such as Jews denationalized by Germany, can appropriately be dealt with by an international tribunal.

(3) One lesson the Leipzig trials has taught is that it would be folly to permit the immediate successor to the German government now in power to try German violators of the laws and customs of warfare; and this even in the case of atrocities committed inside Germany. To turn the task over to the Germans would very probably result in another Leipzig debacle. True, the situation at the close of the present war will be different from that following Versailles, in that an anti-totalitarian attitude may perhaps be expected on the part of German survivors of Nazi brutalities. But even so, fascistic and militaristic indoctrination of the young has been so thorough and wide-

spread that it is doubtful whether — left to their own devices —
the Germans will be any more willing to convict and punish
their glorified leaders at the close of the present conflict than
they were at the end of World War I. So also the Japanese
militarists and industrialists enjoy too favored a place in the
imagination of their peoples to be prosecuted by them in Japanese courts. Even impartial native judges will find it very difficult, in an atmosphere of defeat, hatred and misery, to do
more than was done by the German judges at the Leipzig
trials.

Moreover, as soon as one considers the law to be applied,
the impracticability of a proposal to permit the Germans (or
Japanese) to proceed against their own war criminals becomes
glaringly evident. What law would their courts apply? If, for
example, German courts were to resort to the statutes and
decrees of the Third Reich, the United Nations would indirectly
be subscribing to such perverted Nazi inventions as the grossly
unfair racial discriminations in German legislation, the flagrant
and real (not merely formal) *ex post facto* Nazi criminal law,
the monstrous punishments instituted by the Nazi regime, such
as castration (not merely sterilization). While the employment
of Nazi law against Nazi criminals would be a peculiarly appropriate instance of poetic justice, the United Nations ought
not, even remotely, to sponsor the monstrosities "legalized" by
the Germans. On the other hand, to employ German law with
objectionable elements removed, would leave many gaps and
loopholes and create numerous complex problems; and a re-
drafting of German ordinary and military codes of criminal
law and procedure would take much time and could hardly be
done by a shattered State. If, finally, the German courts should
go back to German law as it existed prior to 1933, the question
would arise whether the numerous young offenders could lawfully or fairly be punishable, inasmuch as the application of
criminal law rests on the necessary (albeit largely fictional)
assumption that the accused knows the law and what it prohibits. Since many of the German defendants would have been
mere children in 1933, they cannot reasonably be charged with
such knowledge even by a stretch of the customary fiction.

Finally, it should not be at all surprising, if, as a last act of
fascistic irony and defiance, the Nazi legal experts should enact

a law granting a general amnesty for all German war criminals, as Hitler has done on prior occasions in deliberately white-washing his Nazi Party colleagues on the strange ground that they had been irresistibly pushed into crimes by "their over-passionately fighting for the National-Socialist idea." [19]

Since it is generally claimed by representatives of the United Nations and students of Nazi-Fascist militaristic mentality that it is out of the question to permit Germany and Japan to govern themselves for a long time after the close of hostilities, it is difficult to understand the point of view of those who, despite the evidence of Leipzig and of later events, still insist that Germany and Japan should be permitted to try their own war criminals, under their own laws. As one of the tests of the sincerity of protestations of reform and repentance on the part of the government which will succeed the Nazis, the granting of permission to German courts to try a limited number of test cases may perhaps be justified, provided the United Nations reserve the right to retry the accused if the entire performance again discloses the Leipzig mentality. As a general policy based on some ultra-naive conception of "justice and fair play for the poor, innocent German people," it can be but a liberal gesture of a type that so often in the past not only has been wasted on the Germans but has added fuel to the self-conceit and arrogance of their politicians and militarists.

It must inevitably be concluded, then, that at least for several years after the defeat of Germany and Japan, United Nations' tribunals, and not those of the Axis governments or even of their immediate successors, should manage the processes of justice in the case of war criminals. [20] Their stewardship will be subjected to the judgment of history, as were the doings of the Leipzig court.

So much for trials in the local courts of the individual countries. What about prosecutions in *multi-national* tribunals?

(4) While the Moscow agreement for trial in domestic courts will take care of the vast majority of offenders charged with acts contrary to the laws or customs of legitimate warfare or violative of the principles of criminal law generally adhered to by civilized peoples, there are certain malefactors and offenses peculiarly appropriate to the jurisdiction of a multi-national or an international tribunal. The Moscow pronouncement evi-

dently recognized this; for it went on to point out that its declaration respecting trial of offenders in domestic courts "is without prejudice to the case of German criminals whose offenses
have no particular geographical localization and who will be
punished by joint decision of the governments of the Allies."
This statement is ambiguous in respect to both the types of
offenses and the nature of the joint action contemplated. However, until more specific information is available, we may, on
the basis of experience at the close of the first world war and
the needs of the present situation, reasonably assume that the
crimes envisaged in this provision for joint action are the following more serious and widespread atrocities: [21]

(a) Offenses committed by Heads of States (Hitler, Mussolini, Hirohito or Tojo, etc.) and prominent officials, including
leading members of the military and political general staffs
(SS., *Gestapo,* Fascist militia, etc.);

(b) Offenses which have been committed in several countries or against the nationals of two or more countries in combination (such as the torture and murder of American, Belgian,
British, French and Polish prisoners of war in some single Axis
camp); thereby giving simultaneous jurisdiction to two or more
members of the United Nations and creating the possibility of
jurisdictional conflicts;

(c) Offenses over which no single United Nations' country
has jurisdiction (*e.g.*, those against Jews and others rendered
"stateless" by the German government, or against other persons,
who, for the jurisdictional requirements of some particular nation's courts, cannot prove their nationality);

(d) Offenses which some injured nation, for reasons of policy, expediency, impracticability, expense or danger, prefers
not to try in its own courts.

These crimes, it will be observed, include, essentially, the
four classes assigned to the "High Tribunal" in the proposals of
the Inter-Allied Commission of the First World War. It would
seem especially appropriate that proceedings against such major malefactors should be conducted "by joint decision of the
government of the Allies," and it is a matter of necessity that
they be so conducted in the case of category (c) above.[22]

As was indicated at the outset, united action in these cases
could be either by a joint ("mixed") *military* tribunal – a pro-

posal made by the American members of the Commission at
the close of World War I [23] and embodied in the Versailles
Peace Treaty [24] — or by a true and new *International Criminal
Court*.

Even the American members of the Commission on Responsibilities appointed at the close of World War I (Lansing and
Scott), who had strenuously opposed the trial of German war
criminals in an international "High Tribunal" on the grounds
that, it was unprecedented and that there exists no code of international penal law, consented to prosecution in an equally
unprecedented and newly to be established inter-Allied *military* tribunal. A precedent therefore now exists for trial of enemy war offenders by a joint United Nations military tribunal,
not only while hostilities are still in progress or during a period
of armistice, but even after peace has been formally re-estab-
lished. This precedent was not destroyed by the fact that such
a joint military court was not actually used; since the Allied and
Associated Governments had reserved the right to resort to
such procedure.

There are, however, several weaknesses in a plan to employ
a military court consisting of a simple, loose cooperative association of the military tribunals of the sovereignties involved,
weaknesses which the American representatives on the Commission at Versailles seem not to have considered very thoroughly. First, as to rules governing trials, they believed that the
members of the joint military tribunal could merely "bring with
them" the procedure to be applied by the Allied military tribunal, namely, "the procedure of the national commissions or
courts." [25] But since the procedures differ, which national procedure could the new multi-national military tribunal have
applied? The American representatives seem either to have
assumed that "the procedure of the national commissions or
courts" is uniform, or to have overlooked the confusion that
would result from any last minute attempt to amalgamate or
adjust the varying procedures of the different national military
tribunals without careful previous preparation.

Secondly, as to the substantive law under which war criminals should be tried by the joint military tribunal, there was
also basic ambiguity in the suggestion of the American representatives on the Commission. They rejected the proposal of

the other representatives for an International Criminal Court, on the ground that there existed no international statute or convention making violations of the laws and customs of warfare *international crimes*, defining such offenses more specifically than the definitions to be found in the prohibitions of the unwritten or written law of nations, affixing a specific punishment to each crime, and giving jurisdiction to a world court. Yet they took it for granted that for purposes of prosecution in *military* tribunals (and therefore in the proposed joint military tribunal) either the international laws and customs of war applied directly to individuals and therefore need not have been previously implemented by domestic legislation, or such conversion of international into national law had already been uniformly affected in the legislation of all the Allied nations.[26] This, however, is not at all clear. General Marcel deBaer of the Belgian *Cour Militaire*, who has given much study to the problem, points out that

"Lansing and Scott assumed the military courts abroad conformed to the model of United States Military Courts and Commissions, and that they applied the 'laws of war.' This is . . . a mistake: in most countries the military courts have their own statutory law, and they are neither allowed to apply 'martial law'[27] (which simply does not exist) nor 'the law of war.' One can visualize the muddle that would have been created if ever it had been attempted to put Art. 229 of the Versailles Treaty into practice, each judge trying to apply a different law."[28]

The muddle to which Judge deBaer refers would certainly exist if a mixture of military and non-military law of the various States comprising the United Nations were to be applied in any one case. To make the joint military tribunal feasible, both the substantive and procedural law of the State prosecuting the particular case would have to be applied. This means that in certain cases the United Nations' joint military tribunal would follow English or American military law and procedure; in others, Belgian, Polish, Russian, etc. This would render the proceedings clumsy, the precedents unclear, the punishments unequal; and it would moreover entail the appointment of judges acquainted with most of the military law systems of the world, or special judges for each group of cases.

Another difficulty is that a military tribunal might be, or might regard itself as, incompetent to try non-military offenders whose offenses were more in the nature of ordinary crimes than violations of the laws and customs of warfare, especially during a postwar period. Although, by the German and Japanese conception and practice of "total war" almost every criminal act committed by some of their politicians, bankers and industrialists can at least indirectly (as part of a general conspiracy) be deemed an offense against the laws and customs of legitimate warfare, it would seem preferable to entrust to a non-military court jurisdiction over offenders who are charged with ordinary crimes defined in civilized penal codes, especially if many of the trials have to be postponed to a time after the formal conclusion of peace.

Despite the weaknesses noted, there would be a genuine value in the employment of a United Nations Joint Military Tribunal. The procedure might be more expeditious than in a non-military court. Before the forum of public opinion and history the most important offenders would be convicted by the *joint action* of the United Nations. The symbolic significance of a proceeding entitled *The United Nations* ex rel. *The Kingdom of Belgium* v. *Adolf Hitler,* or *The United Nations* ex rel. *The United States of America* v. *Hideki Tojo,* would not be lost on the world. The choice of the moving State in any particular case would rest upon agreement among the member States of the United Nations, depending upon such factors as which State's nationals suffered the greatest injury from the act, which State's law and procedure were the easiest to apply to the particular facts involved, and the like. However, a joint military tribunal would not be a true international court because only the United Nations would be members and because, technically speaking, not directly the law of nations but the *domestic military law of the injured State* would be enforced by it.[29]

(5) Under the second type of joint action a true *International Criminal Court* would be established, in the sense that it would be set up by practically all States in the world, would be the agent of civilized humanity in general, and would, essentially, be vindicating the *law of nations.* Just as the ordinary criminal law grew up under the conception that he who injures another does harm not only to the victim himself but to the society of

which he is a member, so the proposed world criminal tribunal would proceed on the valid assumption that he who does an act contrary to the law of nations offends not only against the individual State whose subject is injured thereby, but also against the rights, security and public order of the entire world community.

Not only does a combination of States have the right to act jointly in the vindication of the law of nations, but it has the duty to do so. Only the fact that most States, individually, are helpless to resort to force when a powerful State defiantly flaunts the law of nations prevents the systematic resort to force in the service of world jurisdiction. Pre-arrangements in the nature of written World Constitutions, or World States, or Leagues of Nations, or Kellogg Pacts are not indispensable legal prerequisites to the exercise of jurisdiction on behalf of the civilized world by a large majority of nations which act because they are convinced the facts show beyond doubt the deliberate and unjustified violation of international duties by a State in the grip of a criminalistic government. In fact, unless the United Nations solemnly fulfill their obligation to prosecute war criminals and punish those found guilty, they themselves will be remiss in their duty to the point of lawlessness. For lawlessness on the international plane consists not only in the failure of a defiant member of the Family of Nations to observe its international duties and commitments, but equally if not more so, in the failure of the rest of the members of the international community to act jointly, if necessary, to vindicate the law. Long ago Elihu Root acutely observed that

"International laws violated with impunity must soon cease to exist, and every state has a direct interest in preventing those violations which, if permitted to continue, would destroy the law. Wherever in the world, the laws which should protect the independence of nations, the inviolability of their territory, the lives and property of their citizens, are violated, all other nations have a right to protest against the breaking down of the law. Such a protest would not be an interference in the quarrels of others. It would be an assertion of the protesting nation's own right against the injury done to it by the destruction of the law upon which it relies for its peace and security. What would follow such a protest must in each case depend upon the protesting nation's own judgment as to policy, upon the feelings of its people and the wisdom of its governing body." [30]

The stage has been reached in the world community where mere protests have again and again been defied by lawless and powerful States, where single States or ordinary combinations of States are not strong enough to compel law observance, where the feelings of the peoples and — it is to be hoped — the wisdom of their governing bodies, will demand the implementation of protests with more effective action. It is because the writer believes conditions to be peculiarly propitious for the establishment of a world tribunal to serve as the agent of the Family of Nations in the trial of persons whose acts are contrary to the laws of warfare or the prohibitions common to the criminal laws of civilized States, that he devotes the entire next chapter to a detailed analysis of the problems involved in the creation and operation of such a tribunal.

CHAPTER VI

AN INTERNATIONAL CRIMINAL COURT

⚖

An unusual opportunity presents itself, in connection with the trial of important war criminals, for the vindication of law and justice on an international plane. Either before the close of hostilities or immediately after the Armistice granted Germany, the United Nations might set up a new International Criminal Court to try those classes of offenses in which not only they but all members of the Family of Nations have a common interest. Such a court could be established by convention entered into by the United Nations (and neutrals if possible) or, perhaps, by executive agreement under the war powers of the President of the United States and of the chief executives of the other interested nations.[1] The jurisdiction of this tribunal would at first naturally be limited to the trial of war crimes, although it might be hoped that in a more interrelated and rational post-war world it could be given jurisdiction also over certain peacetime offenses of a peculiarly international interest.[2]

The concept of an international criminal tribunal is not without precedent.[3] Three of the more significant milestones on the road to the creation of a tribunal with extra-national criminal jurisdiction deserve special mention:

(1) When the Advisory Committee of distinguished jurists who drafted the statute of the Permanent Court of International Justice (the "World Court") first began its labors, a proposal for an international criminal court was made by Baron Descamps of Belgium, President of the Committee. However, this project miscarried.[4] It was too vague regarding the crimes comprehended, leaving it to the proposed court itself to "define the character of the offense, . . . fix the penalty and . . . decide the means by which the terms of the sentence are to be enforced."[5] Elihu Root, a member of the Committee, argued that "unless there is a law to be broken there can be no penalty

for breach of it."[6] In this connection, it was doubted that individuals, not only sovereign States, could commit infractions of international law. Baron Descamps' proposal was finally shelved after a committee of the First Assembly of the League of Nations had reported that "there is not yet any penal law recognized by all nations."[7]

(2) A move toward establishing international criminal justice had been made earlier, as we have seen, in connection with the report of the Commission of Fifteen set up by the Preliminary Peace Conference at the close of World War I, to inquire into and report upon violations of international law chargeable to Germany and her Allies.[8] The proposal of the majority of the Commission was to establish a "High Tribunal," to consist of three appointees from each of the five chief Allied governments and one from each of the lesser powers. The High Tribunal was to try the four classes of cases previously noted.[9] It was to apply "the principles of the law of nations as they result from the usages established among civilized peoples, from the laws of humanity and from the dictates of public conscience."[10] The court was empowered to determine its own procedure. Upon a finding of guilty, it could sentence the convict to such punishment as any courts of the nations represented on the tribunal or of the accused's own country might impose for the offense in question. Selection of cases for trial, and direction of prosecutions, were to be left to a Prosecuting Commission, whose five members were to be appointed by the chief powers and their assistants by the others.

But as we have seen, the creation of such an international tribunal was opposed by the American and Japanese delegations, and the proposal was not incorporated into the treaties of peace with the Central Powers.

(3) Yet another attempt to establish an international criminal court was initiated by the French, following the assassination of Alexander I of Yugoslavia at Marseilles in 1934. A League of Nations committee drafted a convention for the prevention and punishment of "terrorism" and another establishing an international tribunal. Under the first, each High Contracting Party agreed to punish specified acts of terrorism directed against another Party; to make such acts extraditable crimes; and to collaborate in relevant police matters.[11] Under the sec-

ond convention, each Party was permitted to commit violators of its laws against terrorism for trial by the international tribunal instead of in its domestic courts.[12] Neither of these agreements was ratified;[13] but they, too, are significant milestones on the hard road toward a temple of international criminal justice.

These abortive projects[14] should be no discouragement to those who see in an international criminal court a particularly timely, useful and symbolic instrumentality for effective promotion of international law and order.

Let us, then, consider the basic issues involved in the employment of a multi-national tribunal for the trial of war criminals.

In the first place, *what law would the proposed International Criminal Court apply?* Since no world code of penal law is in existence, would not the tribunal be acting contrary to the well-known maxim of civilized justice, "there can be no crime and no punishment without pre-existing law" (*nullum crimen et nulla poena sine lege*)?

These crucial questions were the rocks on which split both the Hague Committee of jurists and the Inter-Allied Commission engaged in planning a program for the prosecution of war criminals at the close of the first world war. Considering the first question — what law might be legitimately applied by the proposed International Criminal Court? — there are several possibilities:

(1) The first that suggests itself is the *statutory criminal law of the prosecuting State, i.e.,* of that nation whose subjects were most seriously injured by the acts of illegality committed by the accused and which nation therefore initiated the prosecution. However, there appear to be several objections to an international court's use of such municipal law in dealing with the trial of war criminals: (a) In many instances of equally flagrant violations of the laws of several States, it would be difficult to decide which State should take precedence. (b) Such a policy would entail expert knowledge of the law of each injured State and therefore the employment of many different judges acquainted with the technical details of each of the numerous legal systems involved; and the other members of the court would naturally tend to give undue weight to the views of the specialists. (c) Enforcement of national law by the international tribunal might involve lack of uniformity in certain legal

defenses, in bases of guilt, and in punishments for the same crimes, thereby giving occasion for resentment. (d) Problems arising from the territorial theory of jurisdiction might, in the case of the existing law of some particular State, greatly limit the scope of the trials, excluding, for example, crimes committed inside German prison camps against British or American nationals. (e) Finally and most seriously, employment of national law by the multi-national tribunal would not develop a general *international criminal law* to serve as a precedent and deterrent for the future.

Despite these difficulties, resort to the domestic legal system of the particular State whose laws had been violated would have one great advantage: it could not possibly be regarded as involving enforcement of laws which did not pre-exist their violation (*ex post facto* legislation); and no valid argument could therefore be raised on the ground that the work of the international tribunal violated the familiar maxim of civilized criminal justice alluded to: "There is no crime and no punishment without pre-existing law."

(2) As another possibility, the International Criminal Court might apply the law of the *enemy defendant's State*. That this is undesirable was shown in discussing German law.[15]

(3) The proposed international tribunal might also apply *international written* ("positive") law in the form of the Hague and Geneva conventions. Standing alone, however, the international agreements governing rules of land warfare and the treatment of prisoners of war and the sick and wounded might not be deemed to furnish a sufficient basis for the administration of criminal justice. It is claimed by most international lawyers with some justification that the relevant international conventions are obligatory only upon States and not their individual nationals. Moreover, such agreements between nations do not embrace many of the offenses which must be deemed within the scope of war crimes as conceived at the present.[16] International conventions do, however, form a body of law which, used in connection with other law, helps to measure responsibility by furnishing a standard for determining which acts of warfare are lawful and which are not. For example, a soldier normally enjoys the defense of "justification" when he kills an enemy in wartime, provided the warfare was *lawful;*

and the German court in the Leipzig trials concerning homicides by submarine commanders legitimately looked to the prohibitions of *international conventions* governing warfare to determine whether or not the particular act of warfare for which a justification was claimed was prohibited and therefore *unlawful.*

(4) The proposed International Criminal Court might apply a new *international penal code* embodied in a convention to be entered into as soon as possible by the countries of the United Nations and such others as may wish to adhere to the agreement. Thereby multi-national written (positive) law would prohibit certain acts, designate them crimes, and affix a specific punishment to each. However, such an international penal code, although desirable, does not yet exist. To frame it in all its technical details and have it agreed to and ratified as an international convention would take a long time. Besides, even after its adoption and promulgation it could, normally, apply only to offenses committed after its enactment. As victors, the United Nations could of course enforce such a code upon enemy nationals, either in the armistice terms or in the peace treaty, even in respect to the crimes committed before the adoption and promulgation of the code. But it would be insisted by purists that such a statute, incorporated in the armistices or peace treaties to come, would run counter to the doctrine already stressed ("No crime and no punishment without pre-existing law"), a principle deemed to be a "minimum standard of Western civilization." [17]

(5) Finally, the new International Criminal Court could, prior to the framing and adoption of a special detailed code, legitimately apply the *common (customary) law of nations.* This last approach to the problem of prosecuting Axis war criminals is important and promising enough to deserve extended consideration.

(a) In the first place, application of the common law of nations to individuals by a multi-national court was strenuously opposed, not only by the German delegation to the Peace Conference at Versailles [18] but by the American representatives on the Commission on Responsibilities, on the ground that there exists no international criminal law. In strongly objecting to the trial of the former Kaiser and other leading malefactors by a

"High Tribunal" to be established anew by the Allies, the Americans argued that a judicial court administers only *existing* law; and that since no international penal code had pre-existed the alleged crimes, the German war criminals could not be tried in the proposed inter-Allied non-military court. Since the American experts admitted that a joint Allied *military* tribunal could legitimately try war offenders even after the legal conclusion of the war, it is difficult to comprehend the force of their purely technical objection to the trial of war criminals in a non-military international criminal tribunal. The *acts* for which the offenders would have been tried would, in the vast majority of instances, have been the very same whether regarded as violations of the joint domestic military laws of the Allies and tried by a newly established joint military commission, or deemed violations of international law directly (*i.e.*, without implementation by municipal law) and tried by a newly established non-military international court. As a matter of fact, the accused would have enjoyed more protections and privileges in the proposed criminal court than in the proposed joint military commission. Military courts are ordinarily more strict and summary in their proceedings than civil courts. Nevertheless, the Americans insisted that,

"an act could not be a crime in the legal sense of the word, unless it were made so by law, and that the commission of an act declared to be a crime by law could not be punished unless the law prescribed the penalty to be inflicted. They were perhaps more conscious than their colleagues of the difficulties involved, inasmuch as this question was one that had arisen in the American Union composed of States, and where it had been held in the leading case of *United States v. Hudson* (7 Cranch, 32), decided by the Supreme Court of the United States in 1812, that 'the legislative authority of the Union must first make an act a crime, affix a punishment to it, and declare the court that shall have jurisdiction of the offense.'"[19]

The American commissioners argued that "what is true of the American States must be true of this looser union we call the Society of Nations."[20] But this is clearly a *non sequitur*. In the *Hudson* case a tribunal of a certain federation of states was interpreting a special written constitution in which powers are distributed between the United States of America and the individual states.[21] The case *might* have been decided the other way.[22] It is in fact highly questionable whether the *Hudson* case — confined to a local 18th century constitutional arrangement within a single nation — is at all relevant to the issue whether an International Criminal Court, to be established in our day by the vast majority of States, could or could not legitimately apply the common law of nations to individuals without some world "legislative authority" having first enacted a statute, made its violations crimes, and affixed punishments to each crime.

A major fallacy of the American representatives on the Commission of Responsibilities, as of the German delegates to the Versailles peace conference, was to take it for granted that the characteristics of a fully developed system of law are indispensable to all "justice according to law." Lansing and Scott wanted a world legislature and world criminal *legislation* to exist before establishment of a world criminal court. But a court can also enforce the common or unwritten law; and the situation with reference to the laws and customs of war as a branch of the law of nations is more analogous to that of the early English *judge-made* common law than to that of a sophisticated system of legislature-made law, of which a detailed penal code is typical. During the early stages of any system of law the courts must, in a certain sense and to some extent, "legislate." Whenever a common-law court for the first time held that some act not previously declared by a legislature to be prohibited was a punishable offense for which the accused was now liable, or whenever, for the first time, it more specifically than theretofore defined the constituents of a crime and applied that definition in a new case, it made law to some extent, despite the fiction that it only "found" or "declared" pre-existent law. Yet, fundamentally, it did no violence to the technique of law-enforcement or the requirements of man-made justice. True, the legal "command" (in the Austinian sense) which the actor was held to have violated did not come directly and specifically from the sovereign or a legislature; but since the prohibition of the act in question represented the consensus of opinion of the people as reflected in customary usage, it had enough of the imperative element to warn its prospective violators, to impel common law judges to declare it to be part of the law of the land, and to hold its violators punishable. As Sir James Stephen points out, "it is not till a very late stage in its history that law is regarded as a series of commands issued by the sovereign power of the state. Indeed, even in our own time and country that conception of it is gaining ground very slowly. An earlier, and to some extent a still prevailing, view of it is that it is more like an art or science, the principles of which are at first enunciated vaguely, and are gradually reduced to precision by their application to particular circumstances. Somehow, no one can say precisely how . . . certain principles came to be accepted as the law of the land." [23]

That branch of the law of nations which deals with prohibited acts of warfare is as yet as undeveloped as was the early English common law. No world legislature exists. No international penal code has been enacted. No special court has as yet been set up to enforce the obligations. Yet all the belligerents are bound by the law of nations to observe certain rules of warfare commonly agreed upon. As members of the World Community, they are mutually obligated to vindicate the law by punishing their own nationals who have committed acts prohibited by it; [24] and they have the duty as well as the right to prosecute and punish *enemy* nationals, as well, for such offenses. [25] In enforcing its own international obligation to punish violators of the law of nations each State is, in effect, acting not only on its own behalf but as agent of the Family of Nations each of whose members is both bound by, and interested in vindicating, international law. And in acting jointly, the vast majority of civilized States establishing an international tribunal for the punishment of war criminals will need no preexistent World State or World Legislature to justify their jurisdiction. The fact that they agree to pool their rights and duties to punish violators of the law of nations *is* in itself an exercise of world sovereignty on behalf of world law.

Because German doctrine on the common law is so little known and may become very important at the close of the present war, it may be well to mention the views of two German authorities. Thus, Schätzel, who has thoroughly investigated the technical problem we are discussing from the point of view of German doctrine and precedent, says:

"Anyone who acted . . . as a criminal judge in the occupied territory and there administered justice, not according to . . . expediency but . . . to legal principles," [knew that if he wished to apply] "the principle *nullum crimen sine lege, nulla poena sine lege,* which is the cornerstone of the entire criminal law, in the occupied territory," [he found] "that the existing provisions of *national* law are often inadequate. There are cases where the prestige of the occupying power simply demands that certain acts be punished. And they can be punished on the basis of the *customs of war, which supplement the rule of national law.* . . .

". . . The Laws and Customs of Warfare are law not because they are reproduced in the Field Manual but because they are international law.

"The Imperial Decree [of 1899] speaks of punishment, 'in accordance with the laws, the customs of war and special decrees of competent military authorities' (Art. 2). This shows clearly that the customs of war are recognized as a source of law. They are binding on individuals by virtue of the Imperial Decree which orders the authorities administering justice to follow these rules.

"The customs of war are substantive penal law as good as the State's penal legislation." [26]

Another distinguished German scholar, Verdross, after a painstaking analysis of German law and practice, also sustains the view that when a State wishes to punish a violator of the laws and customs of permissible warfare, the fact that it has not previously enacted a penal code setting forth detailed definitions and prescribing various punishments is irrelevant, since it can legitimately resort to the customs of war as part of the common law of nations.[27]

So much for the first objection to trials in an international court under the common law of nations.

(b) In the second place, it was argued at Versailles and is still generally contended by international lawyers that the law of nations (including the rules and customs of legitimate warfare) addresses its prohibitions only to States, *not to individuals;* that, therefore, it cannot be applied directly to persons who do acts contrary to such law. Lawful prosecution for the acts in question, it is argued, requires prior "implementation" of the law of nations by, or its "transformation" into, national

legislation of the prosecuting State.[28] But while this is generally
true, it is not always or necessarily so. The claim overlooks the
fact that the question of the *means* employed by a State in carrying out its international duty to punish violations of the laws
and customs of warfare is not one of international law but
rather of municipal or domestic law — the constitution of the
particular State. A State may enforce its international obligations in respect to war criminals either by first interposing its
own statutes or military rules the violation of which is an injury
to its sovereignty, or *by direct application of the law of nations
to individual malefactors.* If, for example, it deems its formal,
written undertakings (such as the Hague and Geneva conventions) [29] to bind only the High Contracting Parties and not their
individual nationals, a State if it wishes, can resort to the *common law.* This includes the common (unwritten) law of nations
and, as part of such body of general law, the rules and customs
of legitimate warfare.[30]

That the generalization regarding the absolute non-liability
of individuals under the law of nations [31] is not altogether sound
is shown by the classic case of piracy. Violation of the rule that
prohibits piracy — regardless of whether or not it has also been
constituted a crime by the statutory law of the State which happens to have seized the pirate — is clearly a violation of a norm
of the *law of nations.* The punishment is directed not against
the State of which the pirate is a national (or its "citizens col-
lectively"), but rather against the accused as an *individual.* In
the absence of a world authority or "sovereign" and an international criminal tribunal, the prosecution must perforce be
conducted in the courts of the State which has seized the pirate;
but the violation of the law involved is one which concerns the
entire Community of Nations, and the prosecuting State is acting, in effect, as agent of all civilized States in vindicating the
law common to them all.

There are other instances which illustrate the fact that despite the general rule that only States are obligated under the
law of nations, significant exceptions exist [32] to demonstrate that
the rule is open to such modifications as are dictated by necessity, reason, and the general welfare of all nations. Indeed, there
are instances in which both English and American courts have,
on the basis of the common law, convicted persons even for non-

piratical acts deemed contrary to the law of nations, *without prior statutory stigmatization of such acts as domestic crimes.* Thus, an English court in 1796 sustained a conviction for "knowingly, wilfully, deceitfully and maliciously" supplying French prisoners of war with unwholesome food, "to the great discredit of . . . the King," despite an argument that the act in question had not been done "in breach of any contract with the public or of any moral or civil duty." [33] English courts have also held that "malicious and scurrilous reflections upon those who are possessed of rank and influence in foreign states" may be prosecuted as criminal libels. [34]

So also those American States which administer the common law of crimes punish violations of the law of nations by individuals, without prior legislative prohibition of them as crimes. Thus in Pennsylvania a defendant was convicted and sentenced to imprisonment and fine for insulting and threatening bodily harm to the Secretary of the French Legation. [35] The indictment set forth that the victim was then "under the protection of the law of nations and this Commonwealth." The court rejected the defendant's contention that "the reparation sought, and the remedy offered, are confined to the *municipal law of Pennsylvania,* where the offense was committed; and [that] in all cases of menaces, the law of Pennsylvania yields no further relief than the imposition of a legal restraint on the execution of those menaces." The prosecution argued "the necessity of sustaining the law of nations, of protecting and securing the persons and privileges of ambassadors; the connection between the law of nations and the municipal law, and the effect which this decision must have upon the honor of Pennsylvania, and the safety of her citizens abroad. . . . Upon the same principle that the infringement of a statute is an indictable offense, though the mode of punishment is not pointed out in the act itself, an offense against the laws of nations, while they compose a part of the law of the land, must necessarily be indictable." The court expressed the opinion that the case "must be determined on the principles of the law of nations, which form a part of the municipal law of Pennsylvania; and, if the offenses charged in the indictment have been committed, there can be no doubt that those laws have been violated." In imposing sentence of a large fine, two years' imprisonment and the furnishing of heavy "security to keep the peace, and be of good behavior to all public Ministers, Secretaries to Embassies, and Consuls . . . for seven years," the court said: *"The first crime in the indictment is an infraction of the law of nations.* This law, in its full extent, is part of the law of this State, and is to be collected from the practice of different nations and authority of writers. The person of a public minister is sacred and inviolable. Whoever offers any violence to him, *not only affronts the Sovereign he represents, but also hurts the common safety and well-being of nations*: — *he is guilty of a crime against the whole world."*

Under the American *Federal* system there can, since the *Hudson* case, be no crime without prior statutory enactment by Congress.[36] That body is specifically empowered (not ordered) by the Constitution (Article I, Section 8, Clause 10) "to define and punish . . . offenses against the Law of Nations." Nevertheless, the Supreme Court of the United States, in the "Saboteurs' Case,"[37] had recently held, in effect, that individual offenders against the laws and customs of warfare can be punished under the law of warfare branch of the common law of nations, without prior intervention of specific domestic legislation:

"It is no objection that Congress in providing for the trial of such offenses has not itself undertaken to codify that branch of international law or to mark its precise boundaries, or to enumerate or define by statute all the acts which that law condemns. . . . By the reference in the 15th Article of War to 'offenders or offenses that . . . by the law of war may be triable by such military commissions,' Congress has incorporated by reference, as within the jurisdiction of military commissions, all offenses which are defined as such by the law of war . . . and which may constitutionally be included within that jurisdiction. Congress had the choice of crystallizing in permanent form and in minute detail every offense against the law of war, or of adopting the system of common law applied by military tribunals so far as it should be recognized and deemed applicable by the courts. It chose the latter course." [38]

Thus the *Saboteurs' Case* decision "is impressive judicial testimony to the effect not only that" the "law of nations may, and oftentimes does, address its injunctions to *individuals* by attaching an *internationally* illegal quality to particular acts," but that "the law of war as a part of the law of nations is a part of the local law," and "also that its applicability by the courts in reference to penal matters need not await precise legislative appraisal or definition." [39]

It may of course be argued that by the very enactment of the Articles of War Congress has in fact "converted" offenses against the law of nations (which can be committed only by States) into offenses under Federal law (which can be committed by individuals). But even if this be accepted as a theory, it makes little difference practically. For the code of Articles of War is not in any real sense, *i.e.*, in any sense that makes much of a difference to the *accused*, a penal code. The 15th Article of War, to which reference is made in the above quotation from the opinion in the *Quirin* case, gives him no prior notice of the exact constituents of the acts prohibited or of the punishments they entail; it does not specifically define the crimes that can be committed by individuals under it. On the contrary, it merely refers back to the "offenses that . . . by the law of war may be triable by . . . military commissions," which means to the vast reservoir of the *law of nations* and not to municipal penal law. It is not some detailed Federal penal statute that can be consulted to determine the definitions and constituents of the offenses, the matters that constitute justifications or excuses, the punishments, but rather the general common "law of war." Even the Army's Basic Field Manual, *Military Government* (FM 27-5), which may be regarded as an implementation of the law of nations by domestic regulations having the force of law, goes no farther to define the offenses than to give jurisdiction to military commissions over "offenses against the laws of war" (Sec. V, Par. 25 b); and no farther to define the punishments than to aver that "a military commission may impose any lawful and appropriate sentence, including death or life imprisonment" (Sec. V, Par. 28 a (1)). Fundamentally, therefore, and in any meaningful sense, it cannot be said that the laws and customs of warfare, as part of the law of nations, are not applicable directly to individuals in the absence of their prior statutory conversion into crimes against the United States.

The German Supreme Court, also, was impelled, during the Leipzig trials, to acknowledge the direct obligatoriness of the

law of nations upon individuals. In the trial involving the torpedoing of the British hospital ship *Llandovery Castle* and the
machine-gunning of survivors in lifeboats, the German court
said:

"The firing on the boats was an offense against the *law of nations.*
. . . *Any violation of the law of nations in warfare is* . . . *a punishable offense,* so far as in general, a penalty is attached to the deed.
. . . The fact that his deed is a violation of *international law* must
be well-known to the doer. . . . The rule of *international law* which
is here involved is simple and is universally known. . . . The court
must in this instance affirm Patzig's guilt of killing contrary to
international law." [40]

And in the trial of General Karl Stenger on the charge of slaying
of wounded French soldiers who had surrendered, the Leipzig
court also applied international law in order to judge the responsibility of a defendant who claimed his killings were justifiable as acts of war:

"The lawfulness or unlawfulness of an act of war is determined
by the rules of international law. The killing of enemies in war is in
accordance with the will of the State which wages the war and
whose laws are decisive for the question of legality or illegality *only
to the extent that it is done under the conditions and within the
limits which international law establishes.*" [41]

It should be pointed out that at the time the accused committed
the offense, the Weimar Constitution with its embodiment of
the law of nations as part of the law of the Republic, was not
yet in force.

The authorities cited and others [42] amply support the conclusion that the relevant principles of the law of warfare, a
branch of the law of nations, may and do obligate *individuals;*
and that there is nothing in the law of nations itself that necessarily prohibits the direct application of its prohibitions to individuals if a State chooses to do so. The duty of a State as a
member of the Family of Nations to prohibit and punish violations of the obligations of international law is a matter of the
law of nations; but whether it requires prior "implementation"
or "conversion" of acts constituting such violations of the law
of nations into prohibitions of municipal criminal or military
law, or punishes them directly without such intercession of do-

mestic legislation, is a matter of each State's own constitution — an arrangement of municipal law. No State whose national is being proceeded against in a foreign nation's military or criminal courts has any right to claim that before he can be prosecuted for acts prohibited by the laws and customs of warfare those prohibitions must first have been "transformed" into the prosecuting State's statutory criminal law. All it can claim is the same treatment of its nationals as is afforded the prosecuting State's own subjects.

Since, therefore, individual States can prosecute and punish offenders against the laws and customs of warfare without intervention of domestic statutory law, there would seem to be no legitimate obstacle presented by the law of nations to this being done by an international tribunal established by the great majority of States and operating, in effect, as the agent of all members of the Family of Nations.[43]

(c) Nor would there be anything inherently unfair to the accused in such a procedure. The position of flagrant violators of the laws and customs of permissible warfare is ordinarily more favorable than that of violators of the early English common law. The first person to be convicted under any provision of that law could not, in strict fairness, have been charged with knowledge of its existence or its exact constituents. To be sure, the court looked to customary usage; but before the violator of a particular custom was hailed into court and prosecuted for an alleged crime, he had had no notice that the custom in question would be declared to be *law*. Modern violators of the laws and customs of legitimate warfare, on the other hand, know full well that the killing of surrendered soldiers, the torture of prisoners of war, the slaying of non-offending civilians, the kidnaping of women for soldiers' brothels, and similar atrocities are prohibited by the laws and customs of legitimate warfare and by the criminal law of civilized States. If tried in an international tribunal, they could not legitimately complain that no pre-existing law had bound them to observe the rules and customs of warfare or of ordinary criminal law.

It has, however, been recently insisted that

"International law knows of no crimes. It forbids certain acts. But it provides no punishment for them. It follows that no international court can punish any accused person in accordance with the rules of international law, except by a flagrant violation of the rule of 'nulla poena sine lege.' . . . To depart from the rule of nulla poena sine lege would mean to let international law sink to the depth of Nazi jurisprudence, amongst whose minor 'discoveries' is the abandonment of a rule which the rest of the civilized world quite rightly continues to hold in esteem."[44]

It is submitted that such a view reflects a slavishly superficial conception of the doctrine, "no crime and no punishment without pre-existing law." While, formally, the trial by an International Criminal Court of offenders against the laws and customs of warfare by direct application of the law of nations might be deemed to violate the principle in question, *substantively* it would do no such thing. The formula, *nullum crimen et nulla poena sine lege,* summarizes a protest against penal legislation with retroactive effect.[45] It is deemed unfair to punish a person for an act, which, at the time he committed it, was not an offense; because the offender had no advance notice that the act was a crime and that a penalty attached to it;[46] to punish a person under a law passed after he has already committed an act would be changing the legal consequences of what was an innocent act when it was done. But the principle of non-retroactivity deals with protection of *substantial* rights. It is not merely a fetish to be blindly worshipped regardless of whether or not its non-observance in form but observance in substance works any injury to the accused. No substantial right would in fact be denied a person accused of war crimes for acts well known by all concerned — whether members of the State's government or other persons — to be prohibited by both the law of warfare and the fundamental principles of civilized criminal law. Since the various States either have implemented those systems of law by domestic legislation[47] or have long been prosecuting offenders directly under the common law without such implementation, an international tribunal would be doing no practical violence whatsoever to the doctrine that prohibits retroactivity in applying *directly* the general law which is the *common basis of the law of all civilized States.*

Of course the accused could not in such an international court claim as a defense that under the law of *his* State the acts he had done were lawful, any more than he could in a State court.[48] The provisions of a highly atypical system of law, which run counter to the general principles of the law of nations and the principles of civilized criminal justice, cannot prevail against the law accepted by the great majority of the Family of Nations. Otherwise, the most lawless State could demand immunity for its own nationals for the most heinous offenses while not granting reciprocal immunity to the nationals of other States.

The foregoing analysis indicates that the proposed International Criminal Court could legitimately resort to the common law of nations as a principal source, without doing violence to the historic maxim of civilized criminal justice, *"nullum crimen sine lege."*

But there is another element to the maxim: not only *nullum crimen,* but also *nulla poena, sine lege.* It has been objected by international lawyers and publicists that the law of nations cannot be applied directly to individuals because it provides no "sanctions," no punishments, for violations of the laws and customs of legitimate warfare. Its sanctions, like its prohibitions, are supposedly directed only against *States.* Historically, and in any practical sense, this traditional view, also, is open to serious question. Thus Grotius, the father of modern international law, clearly implies that the law of nations provides for the death penalty in case of its violation by individuals:

"There is no danger from prisoners and those who have surrendered or desire to do so; therefore in order to warrant their execution it is necessary that a crime shall have been previously committed; such a crime, moreover, as a just judge would hold punishable by death." [49]

Any lesser punishment is merely a matter of grace to the offender; and a State is free under international law to impose the penalties it deems appropriate to the particular offense. Holland, a distinguished modern authority, after an exhaustive study of the most reliable sources of customary international law, concludes that

"Individuals offending against the laws of war are liable to such punishment as is prescribed by the military code of the belligerent into whose hands they may fall, or, in default of such code, then to such punishment as may be ordered, in accordance with the laws and usages of war, by a military court." [50]

Following the practice of nations, the proposed International Criminal Court could therefore either impose death penalties for all offenses, in accordance with customary international law, or be guided by punishments prescribed for similar offenses in the statutes of the defendant's or the victim's country, or enforce a schedule of penalties set out in the instrument establishing the court or even in rules of the court's own making. Non-military war crimes — those violative of prohibitions usually found in civilized systems of criminal law — may be punished as customarily provided therein or as provided for in the penal code of the accusing State.

It will be seen, from the foregoing analysis, that proceedings before an International Criminal Court will *in essence* not violate any of the protections enjoyed by an offender under the principle, "no crime or punishment without pre-existing law." Certainly, to claim that such proceedings would be on a level with Nazi *ex post facto* legislation and court proceedings is to do gross violence to the facts. [51]

If, therefore, the United Nations, acting on behalf of all civilized States, were to organize an International Criminal Court for the trial of war offenders, that tribunal could begin to function immediately, even without implementation by an international penal code defining specific crimes and affixing specific penalties. It could legitimately apply to individuals the laws and customs of warfare and the general principles of criminal law recognized by civilized nations.

The rejection by the Paris Peace Conference of the suggestion for trial of war criminals by an inter-Allied "High Tribunal" prevented the establishment of a specific precedent. But precedents must have a beginning some time; and there is ample basis in justice and common sense for the United Nations to take the step at the close of the present world war which was prevented by the objections of the American and Japanese representatives at the close of the last.

(d) However, to say that the proposed International Criminal Court can legitimately begin to function by applying the common law and need not depend upon the enactment of an international penal code is not enough. Some guidance in respect to the various *sources* of the law it should apply would have to be given the court in its organic act, as was done in the case of the Permanent Court of International Justice at the Hague.

The majority of the Commission on Responsibilities appointed at the close of the last world war had proposed that the High Tribunal should apply "the principles of the law of nations as they result from the usages established among civilized peoples, from the laws of humanity and from the dictates of public conscience." [52] This formula was criticized by the American representatives as altogether too vague. [53] What then would be the various sources of law to which an International Criminal Court could turn?

The following formula, adopted as Article 38 [54] of the Statute of the Permanent Court of International Justice might, with slight modification, be employed at once as the source of the law for the proposed tribunal:

1. International Conventions, whether general or particular, establishing rules expressly recognized by the contesting States;

2. International custom, as evidence of a general practice accepted as law;

3. The general principles of law recognized by civilized nations;

4. . . . Judicial decisions and the teaching of the most highly qualified publicists of the various nations, as subsidiary means for the determination of rules of law. . . . [55]

In drafting a statute for an International Criminal Court, Items 1, 2 and 4 may remain as they are. The first is necessary as one means of determining which acts sought to be justified by the accused as lawful acts of warfare are in fact prohibited and therefore illegal. Although the second item in the above enumeration will likewise afford a means of measuring the legality of acts sought to be justified, its main service will be, as we have indicated, as a reservoir of common law prohibitions directly applicable to individual offenders. Apart from this, even in the interpretation of the relevant conventions the proposed International Criminal Court, as would be true of any other tribunal, would occasionally have to resort to common law (or customs as evidence of general practices accepted as law) to fill in gaps and clear away ambiguities.[56]

Item 4 illustrates the fact that tribunals sometimes have to resort to the views of outstanding scholars in the field of law. Thus American criminal law has been influenced not a little by the treatises of Bishop and Wharton.

This leaves for discussion Item 3 in the above formulation. It should not be forgotten that the "general principles of law recognized by civilized nations" include, also, those of *criminal* law. This fact would provide a particularly rich source of law for the proposed International Criminal Court, in addition to the laws and customs of legitimate warfare. A statement by Professor deLapradelle, representing France on the Advisory Committee which drafted the Statute of the Permanent Court of International Justice, gives a clue to the justification for an international tribunal's employment of the general principles of law recognized by civilized nations and to the limits of the doctrine.

While admitting that "the principles which formed the bases of national law, were also sources of international law," Lapradelle insisted that "the only generally recognized principles which exist, are those which have obtained unanimous *or quasi-unanimous* support."[57] This does not mean, as Holland implied, that "the law of nations is but private law 'writ large.'"[58] It means that where a legal principle is so generally accepted by various nations as to be a *common denominator* of practically all civilized systems, it is justifiably applicable also by an international tribunal.

Lapradelle properly spoke of "quasi-unanimous support." If absolute unanimity were required, the peculiarities of some highly atypical system of law would forever block the recognition and enforcement of a principle by an international tribunal, although the rest of the world recognized it. Such an argument from necessity must have been in the minds of the draftsmen of the Statute of the Permanent Court when they limited the applicability of the source of international law in question to the "general principles of law recognized by *civilized* nations."[59] It has been said that "the word 'civilized' can do no more than exclude primitive systems of law."[60] This may have been what the drafting Committee had in mind; but the principle behind the exclusion of "primitive" systems of law would apply with equal force to what might be denominated *pathologic* systems. While a sovereign State is free to adopt any legislation it sees fit — however much it turns back the clock of civilization — the Family of Nations is not obligated, either in law or in morals, to be bound by such aberrations. Public policy on the international plane must necessarily limit the kind of provisions of a foreign State which either a domestic court or one established by the Family of Nations is bound to respect; otherwise, the most regressive nation would always have it in its power to render the rest of the world legally sterile.[61] There is ample justification for the International Criminal Court's exclusion of the pathologic legislation of Nazi Germany in the process of determining the principles of civilized justice.[62]

A detailed, systematic study in comparative criminal law, to determine exactly which of the provisions may truly be regarded as reflecting "general principles of law recognized by civilized nations," would be very helpful to the International Criminal Court. However, such an elaborate analysis is not indispensable to the early functioning of that tribunal. As litigation proceeds, the Court can determine relevant commonly accepted principles in dealing with the questions raised in the earlier cases; and its decisions on those questions will then become basic precedents for subsequent ones. It will be helpful, however, to illustrate the type of principles comprehended, by mentioning some of the provisions of penal codes which reflect those principles.

First, as to the *substantive law, which defines crimes,* it is generally found that there are public wrongs (crimes) and private wrongs (torts); that legal systems do not customarily take cognizance of offenses against the moral order, unless these have also been prohibited by law (statutory or common); that certain acts are generally recognized as serious crimes (denominated "felonies" or by some equivalent term, and including murder, manslaughter, rape, robbery, aggravated assault and battery, arson, burglary, and thefts of property of considerable value), and others as minor offenses (denominated "misdemeanors" or by some equivalent term).

Secondly, in civilized systems, proof is generally required not only of certain legally prohibited *behavior* (the "act element") but also of a *bad state of mind* ("criminal intent," "*mens rea*," "malice aforethought," etc.).

Thirdly, as to *defenses,* in civilized systems of penal law it is generally true that proof of (a) certain excuses or justifications, as well as (b) certain mitigating circumstances, is permitted the accused. Excuses and justifications usually include such factors as infancy, insanity, self-defense, compulsion, killing in the execution by an official of a lawful order of a court, killing by a soldier of an enemy in battle, in *lawful* warfare.[63] Mitigating circumstances customarily embrace voluntary killing in "heat of blood" upon legally adequate provocation, and involuntary killing through negligence usually amounting to a greater degree than that required in civil litigation.[64] On the other hand, while reasonable mistake or ignorance of operative fact usually constitutes a good defense in indicating the absence of a guilty mind, ignorance of law is customarily no excuse in the penal systems of civilized nations.

Fourthly, as to *punishment,* it is generally true in civilized penal law that murder is punishable by death or by life-long incarceration in a prison; the other crimes, by terms of years; that there are subsidiary penalties, such as fines and loss of certain civil rights; that the prior criminal record of the accused and other circumstances of aggravation (and mitigation) of punishment may usually be taken into account by the court, after conviction, in imposing sentence.[65]

Fifthly, as to basic *protections,* it is generally true in civilized systems of law that *ex post facto legislation* in a fundamental sense — the punishment of persons for acts which were not prohibited before they were committed — is avoided. It is also generally true that punishment more than once for the same offense is prohibited; although this, or at least the universality of the test of "double jeopardy" employed, is less certain.[66]

Sixthly, as to *procedural matters,* the International Criminal Court could legitimately frame its own rules; but it would probably and ought properly to take into account certain basic considerations of fair play generally observed. For example, although various legal systems differ, practically all include the right of the accused to receive a sufficiently adequate statement of the complaint against him to enable him to know what crime he is charged with, to prepare his defense, and to record his trial against a possible later attempt to hold him a second time for the same crime; the right of the accused to be heard, and to have witnesses, in his own defense; his right to cross-examine the witnesses for the prosecution; to have evidence presented before an impartial [67] trier of facts, be it judge or jury; to employ counsel. These are merely illustrations; but they demonstrate that despite the fact that there are certain differences between Anglo-American and Continental procedures, [68] certain elements in the administration of civilized criminal justice are nowadays so customarily accepted as to be legitimately drawn upon by an International Criminal Court as evidence of "the general principles of law recognized by civilized nations."

It will be seen from this brief sketch that the formula in question can readily be vitalized by an enumeration of elements of sufficiently common acceptance to justify their enforcement by the proposed court.

It is reasonable to conclude, then, that when it comes to the law to be administered by an International Criminal Court, prior world "legislation" setting up a detailed international penal code is not a *sine qua non* to the Court's beginning to function; nor would trials, in its absence, be fundamentally unfair or illegal. Such a code, though furnishing details, would in essence be but declaratory of the existing law of and common to nations, a part of which prohibits certain illegitimate acts of warfare and permits of their punishment when the malefactors fall into the hands of the injured nation, and another part of which, derivable from "the general principles of law recognized by civilized nations," permits of the punishment by an international tribunal of infractions of those principles of criminal law, the violation of which is deemed to endanger the world community or public order on the international plane. As citizens of a State and members of an army or navy, the defendants are presumed to have had notice of such provisions of civilized law. [69] And their governments have on several occasions been solemnly warned by official spokesmen of the United Nations that their subjects will be held to strict legal accountability for their atrocities.

By whom and how would the proposed International Criminal Court be organized and staffed?

It was claimed by the German delegates to the peace conference at the close of the last war (and has been argued since by some American publicists and lawyers) that such a court would not be a truly international tribunal, nor even a just court, unless and until Germany (and, now, Japan and the Axis satellite nations) participated in its establishment and in supplying of the personnel of the court. While, in the abstract, there is merit in this contention, it is necessary to be realistic in these matters. Even the Permanent Court of International Justice at the Hague was not established by all the nations; the United States, for example, not participating. Yet it was and is a true international court and its decisions have won respect. If and when the successor governments to the Axis misrulers have demonstrated to the world their sincere desire and capacity to administer justice according to civilized standards regardless of race, creed or nationality, they too will be welcome to adhere to the International Criminal Court. In the meantime, it cannot be reasonably expected that the nations which have suffered most by Axis aggression and illegality should postpone their seeking of justice through an international tribunal until some distant time when it is feasible and convenient for Germany, Japan and the others to join. So to put off the project would mean — as turned out to be the case after the last world war — that the evidence would become "cold," many of the accused and witnesses would disappear or die, and Justice would once more be outwitted. It is not amiss in this connection to recall the Allies' reply in 1919 to the Germans' appeal to suddenly hallowed principles of legality and justice as barring the trial of the former Kaiser and other violators of the laws and customs of warfare:

"As regards the German contention that a trial of the accused by tribunals appointed by the Allied and Associated Powers would be a one-sided and inequitable proceeding, the Allied and Associated Powers consider that it is impossible to entrust the trial of those directly responsible for offenses against humanity and international right to their accomplices in their crimes. Almost the whole world has banded itself together in order to bring to naught the German plan of conquest and dominion. The tribunals they will establish will therefore represent the deliberate judgment of the greater part of the civilized world. The Allied and Associated Powers are prepared to stand by the verdict of history as to the impartiality and justice with which the accused will be tried." [70]

How clairvoyant this statement was, and how thoroughly sound was the argument of the Allies, have been proved beyond doubt by the Leipzig trials and the entire attitude and proceedings of the Germans in respect to their war criminals. To ensure greater fairness, however, there is no good reason why some of the distinguished jurists who have been hounded out of Nazi Germany or the other Fascist States should not be eligible for judgeships on the International Criminal Court even before their countries are admitted to the family circle of nations participating in that tribunal. [71]

It will doubtless be insisted by Germany and her satellites that they too should have the right to file complaints in the International Criminal Court against soldiers and officials of the United Nations' countries, and that without such a right the proceedings will necessarily be unjust. Judging by the behavior of the Germans during the two world wars, and considering the skill with which they forge documents and manipulate propaganda, it is a foregone conclusion that if the Nazis were permitted to file complaints before the international tribunal, they would present the world with a farrago of falsified "proof" deliberately designed to tar United Nations' generals, admirals and officials with the same stick of infamy which they themselves have so ruthlessly wielded. Even their immediate successors in government cannot be trusted to be too prejudiced in favor of the truth in the light of their *"Deutschland über Alles"* obsession, if one may judge by the attitude of the officials of the Weimar Republic toward the attempt to punish German war criminals. Yet there will be American apologists for the Axis powers who will raise their voices in high moral indignation at "one-sided justice," whilst discreetly failing to mention the kind of Germanic justice the victims of Nazi tyranny "enjoyed" at the hands of their oppressors. That there have been some violations of the laws and customs of warfare and of criminal law on the part of American and English soldiers cannot be denied; this is to be expected of any army. Such violations have, however, been promptly handled by the military tribunals of the armies involved. Not even the Nazis dare resort to the colossal lie that English and American war crimes were officially inspired and directed or that they ran into huge numbers, as is most assuredly true of Axis war crimes.

Despite the dangers and difficulties involved, however, successor governments in former Axis nations should be permitted to file charges of United Nations' war crimes that are within the jurisdiction of the International Criminal Court, in cases where preliminary examination of the proferred evidence discloses "probable cause" to believe that an offense against the laws and customs of warfare or a crime according to the tenets of civilized criminal law has in fact been committed. Keen and fearless judges can usually detect manufactured complaints and forged proof; while legitimate charges against United Nations' offenders ought, in fairness, to be subjected to a judicial airing.

There would be nothing fundamentally unfair in prosecuting enemy war criminals in a newly established international tribunal instead of in some State court or military commission. If the Germans were to try an American soldier for violating a German statute implementing the laws and customs of warfare, in a newly established type of military tribunal, the accused would not be heard to complain that he had had no prior notice that a new type of court had been set up. Provided the international tribunal affords as adequate a trial as the accused would have had in the court of any injured belligerent, he has no valid ground for complaint. As a matter of fact, he would be likely to enjoy more protections in a world tribunal than he would ordinarily obtain in a military tribunal of either his own country or that of the enemy.

Limitations of space prohibit a detailed description of the organization, personnel and procedure of the proposed International Criminal Court. The United Nations Commission, established in London in the summer of 1943 for the gathering of evidence of crimes, particularly "organized atrocities," and the planning of trial and punishment, is at present considering several plans of international criminal tribunals together with other types of trial organs. It is not yet known (Autumn, 1944) whether or not the United Nations will finally decide to set up an International Criminal Court, but adequate drafts of con-

ventions for such a tribunal are at present under consideration.[72]

The great majority of the accused will be tried in the domestic courts and under the local law of the various States on whose
territories or against whose nationals or laws their offenses were
committed. Yet the number of leading Axis military, political
and business figures chargeable with the most heinous war
crimes, as well as as the defendants involved in crimes against
"stateless" victims, not to stress the other two classes of crimes
previously mentioned as especially suitable to trial under the
joint auspices of the United Nations, will be very large. The
time, expense and personnel necessary to try all war criminals
would be fantastic. Consequently, as is true of the overbur-
dened and understaffed large city prosecutor in the United
States, the prosecuting agency will have to limit itself to certain classes of cases. The United Nations may decide, for example, to exempt from prosecution all accused below a certain
military or political rank, save in exceptional cases. But even
with such limitations, and taking into account the internicine
slaughter that will occur when the Nazi and Junker thieves and
murderers fall out and begin to take vengeance on each other,
the docket of cases to be tried by an International Criminal
Court will be extensive.

This means that the Court will have to be large, and a considerable number of judges will have to be appointed. The
central headquarters of the Court could be at The Hague, in
London or in Geneva, but a circuit of branches or divisions will
have to be set up in various parts of Europe and Asia, including Axis lands.

Appointments of the original panel of judges might be left,
simply, to the chief executives of the various countries comprising the United Nations and of such neutrals as wish to participate in the establishment of the tribunal. So far as the
United States is concerned, this could probably be done under
the war powers of the President, especially if the court's operations were confined to the war period only. However, because
the court will probably have to continue to function long after
the armistice, and because it is to be hoped that its conduct of
war criminals' trials will win for it a more permanent status and

jurisdiction over international offenses of peacetime,[73] the advice and consent of the Senate ought wisely to be sought in appointment of American judges.[74] The executives should not be limited to their own nationals in appointing their State's quota of judges; each might be given the privilege of selecting an agreed number of his own nationals and one or two foreigners. Elections to fill vacancies or to enlarge the court, if need requires, should be by majority of the court from among candidates specially nominated for such purpose by the chief executives of the member-States of the court, each State being permitted an equal number of nominees, including, if it wishes, non-nationals. Judges should be selected from among candidates who are acknowledged authorities on criminal or international law and are or have been members of courts of criminal jurisdiction or possess qualifications required for appointment to high judicial office in their own country.[75]

The prosecuting staff, as well as a public defenders' staff for indigent accused, might be appointed from panels or nominees submitted by the chief executives of the countries establishing the Court;[76] bailiffs, sheriffs, clerks and interpreters could be appointed by the Court on its own motion. United Nations officers experienced in military government ought to be a good source of such personnel.

The procedure in the International Criminal Court should consist of a simplified combination of the best features of the Anglo-American and Continental systems, guaranteeing the fundamental rights and defenses[77] enumerated above. That it is possible to amalgamate such systems satisfactorily is shown both by the procedure in the Mixed Courts of Egypt[78] and by the draft convention for an International Criminal Court prepared by the London Commission of the League of Nations Union.

Rules of evidence should be simple. Since the trials are to be before panels of judges trained in the evaluation of proof, rather than before lay juries, exclusionary rules should be few.[79] It would seem legitimate for the court to adopt a general principle to the effect that membership in certain organizations notorious for their policy and program of cruelty, such as the Gestapo and employees of concentration and extermination camps, should create a presumption of guilt and throw the burden of proof of innocence upon the accused.

Appeals on points of law and on the ground that the verdict is manifestly against the weight of the evidence should be permitted — but only sparingly and in legally important cases — to an Appellate Division of the Court.

Now that a United Nations Commission exists for the gathering of evidence of atrocities and the solution of related problems, it ought to be easier to arrive at a reasonable agreement among Powers interested in the vindication, on a world plane, of an important branch of the law common to civilized nations. It is especially appropriate that the war crimes committed by major military and political malefactors and involving general plans for and execution of wholesale atrocities, as well as the cases involving crimes against the numerous innocent persons rendered "stateless," right-less and property-less by Nazi-Fascist arrogance, should be tried in a tribunal that represents the conscience and justice of all civilized peoples in common. For practical as well as technical reasons, jurisdiction to punish States for violations of treaties (which, in the jurisprudence of the future, may be denominated international crimes), as well as to try individuals for peacetime offenses of a peculiarly international interest, ought to be postponed. Nevertheless, the time is ripe for symbolizing a new era of neighborly cooperation of civilized peoples in vindication of law and justice on behalf of mankind in general. First things come first, and acts by high-placed individuals which are violative of the laws and customs of legitimate war or of the general principles of civilized criminal law are sufficient for the pioneer business of an International Criminal Court.

One of the arguments advanced by the American participants on the Commission on Responsibilities at the close of World War I against the establishment of an international criminal tribunal was that it was unprecedented.[80] But all courts were at one time unprecedented. The problems presented by our epoch are unprecedented. The atrocities committed by Axis powers led by Germany, even by comparison with their behavior in World War I, are unprecedented. Can history show a better age than our own for mankind to initiate a series of much needed precedents? Few symbols of this new era which heralds the neighborly cooperation of civilized peoples in the vindication of the laws of civilized humanity would be more impressive than an International Criminal Court, in which the plaintiff would be the World Community. And the early announcement of its establishment by the United Nations [81] might exert some sobering and deterrent effect on Axis-Fascist militarists and a restraining effect on their surviving victims.

International concensus on the need of cooperation in the world community is much more likely to survive if it begins in a limited area and originates in the "grass roots" of the sense of justice of the common man. The International Criminal Court would be a more vivid symbol of the reign of justice on an international plane than even the Permanent Court at the Hague has been. The common man is hardly interested in, nor can he even understand, the latter's technical decisions. He *could* understand that justice had been done if, with the "People of the World Community" as the plaintiff, Hitler, Tojo, Mussolini, Himmler, Goering, Goebbels and the rest of the master criminals were to be subjected to trial in a world tribunal, were given a fair procedure and an opportunity to defend, and, upon legal proof of guilt, were properly punished in vindication of law and justice.

CHAPTER VII

LIABILITY OF HEADS OF STATE

⚖

THE defendants in trials before the proposed International Criminal Court will be the chiefs of government and other ringleaders in the planning and execution of atrocities. However, some international lawyers insist that Heads of State are not triable in courts other than those of their own country, if at all.

This problem caused considerable difficulty at the close of the last World War. The American members of the Commission on Responsibilities strongly insisted that the former Kaiser was not amenable to a foreign jurisdiction.[1] They did not deny responsibility of the Heads of States for acts committed "in violation of law, including, in so far as their country is concerned, the laws and customs of war." However, they insisted that while, "from the moral point of view the head of state, be he termed emperor, king or chief executive, is responsible to mankind, . . . from the legal point of view they expressed themselves as unable to see how any member of the Commission could claim that the head of a state exercising sovereign rights is responsible to any but those who have confided those rights to him by consent express or implied."[2] Chiefs of State "are not and . . . should not be made responsible to any other sovereignty."

In the case of militaristic tyrannies the likelihood of lawless Heads of State being punished by their own people is so remote as in effect to exempt such prime malefactors from all punishment no matter how flagrant and extensive are their crimes. But the Americans strongly held to their point of view; and they were supported by the Japanese representatives on the Commission who, with an acumen which time has shown not to have been uncalculated, bolstered the Americans' position with the observation that it was "important to consider the consequences which would be created in the history of international law by the prosecution for breaches of the laws and customs of war of enemy heads of States before a tribunal constituted by the opposite party."[3]

But the argument of the American representatives is in error. In the first place, even granting the immunity of a sovereign under international law except in relation to his own people and law, the rule does not apply to *ex*-sovereigns, because the reasons for the rule have ceased.[4] At the time the Allies wanted to subject Wilhelm II to trial, he had renounced the throne and had fled to Holland where he was an *ex*-Kaiser. It is possible if not probable that by the time this is published, Hitler will be an *ex*-Führer of the German Reich, and, far from his status as a former wielder of high official authority excusing him, President Roosevelt warned on July 28, 1943, after Mussolini had "resigned," that "no criminal will be allowed to escape by the expedient of resignation."

Secondly, *Schooner Exchange* v. *McFaddon*,[5] the decision cited by the American members of the Commission on Responsibilities at the close of World War I in support of their claim that a sovereign is always immune from the jurisdiction of foreign courts, is a very old case; and there is nothing immutable about ideas of sovereignty. They have undergone several changes in the course of time.[6] Furthermore, the *Schooner Exchange* case pertains to property rights [7] and not to the question of the triability of a Chief of State for violation of international and criminal law common to all sovereignties. Most important of all, the *Schooner Exchange* case (as Chief Justice Marshall was careful to indicate) deals with the *normal, peacetime relations of friendly sovereigns*. The immunity granted a sovereign by other sovereignties has nothing to do with any immunity a Chief of State may enjoy inside his own country and under his own laws. It is based rather on international comity and courtesy; and this in turn depends upon the sovereign in question conducting himself in conformity with international law as a respectable and trustworthy member of the Family of Nations. By invading neighboring countries in flagrant violation of treaty obligations and for purposes of aggression, conquest and the mass-extermination of human beings, a sovereign strips himself of any mantle of immunity he may have claimed by virtue of international comity. He outlaws himself. The im-

prisonment of Napoleon at St. Helena was partly founded on
the legitimate argument that a gross breach of faith by an absolute sovereign renders *him* (not merely his State) personally responsible for an offense against the law of nations.
By his breach of the convention "which had established him in
the Island of Elba, Bonaparte destroyed the only legal title on
which his existence depended," leading the Powers at the Congress of Vienna (March 13, 1815) to "consequently declare that
Napoleon Bonaparte has placed himself without the pale of
civil and social relations and that as an enemy and a disturber
of the tranquillity of the world he has rendered himself liable
to public vengeance." [8]

Clearly, the sovereign immunity involved in the *Schooner
Exchange* case can in no way be said to apply to the situation
of a Head of State of the Hitler stripe, the leader of a ruthless
band of gangsters, who, in time of an unjust and unlawful war
brought on by himself, institutes, approves, rewards, fails to
prevent, and even boasts about wholesale violations of the
laws and customs of war and of civilized criminal law.[9] Unless
such a qualification of the doctrine of sovereign immunity existed, the most brutal and aggressive sovereign would always
be protected. If he won the war, he would surely not only
escape punishment himself but deal harshly with the losers.
If he lost it, he would always be sure to save his own skin; he
could claim immunity from foreign trial and his servile people
would hesitate to try him in a domestic court.

There can be little doubt that a Head of State is subject to
capture and treatment as a prisoner of war, the same as lesser
men.[10] Since prisoners of war are subject to trial for violations of
the laws and customs of war, as well as for ordinary crimes,
sovereigns may be so treated. They cannot have the advantages [11] of a prisoner of war's status without its obligations.

There is therefore little foundation for the dogmatic assertion that under international law a person is always necessarily
exempt from foreign trial and punishment for the most flagrant
crimes simply because he is Head of State.

It is, moreover, the height of absurdity as well as injustice to
punish underlings who were forcibly compelled to carry out the
illegal orders of a sovereign and his military and political
cliques, while sparing the leader who, under no compulsion to

violate the law, deliberately and cold-bloodedly planned and ordered wholesale atrocities. One is reminded of Burke's eloquent speech at the trial of Warren Hastings:

"We have not brought before you an obscure offender, who, when his insignificance and weakness are weighed against the power of the prosecution gives even to public justice something of the appearance of oppression; no, my Lords, we have brought before you the first man of India in rank, authority, and station. We have brought before you the Chief of the tribe, the head of the whole body of eastern offenders; a captain-general of iniquity, under whom all the fraud, all the peculation, all the tyranny in India are embodied, disciplined, arrayed and paid. This is the person, my Lords, that we bring before you. We have brought before you such a person, that, if you strike at him with the firm and decided arm of justice, you will not have need of a great many more examples. You strike at the whole corps if you strike at the head." [12]

As was pointed out by the French during the last war, the Kaiser (like Hitler) was in a fundamental sense of the term responsible for atrocities committed by the generals and others under him:

"It was necessary to go beyond the individual, the actual author of the act complained of; it was necessary to search for the chiefs; from chief to chief we must go to the top. In the German army there is one supreme chief, the Emperor.[13] Let us know, for example, whether the act of General Stenger, who was accused of having issued a proclamation ordering his troops to give no quarter, was ever disavowed. We do not know whether it was so or not; but it is certain that this proclamation reached the ears of the Kaiser and it is he who is responsible." [14]

And again:

"It is evident that the Kaiser knew it and perhaps one may even say, ordered it. Of course he did not give directly all the barbarous orders issued by his generals, but the latter knew that their acts had his approval; they were only the executors, high or low, of measures decreed by their master who felicitated, decorated, or promoted those who distinguished themselves by their ferocity." [15]

With how much more assurance can all this be said of Hitler! In his writings and harangues he has again and again boastingly declared himself the author and inspirer of the enormities perpetrated against the Czechs, Jews, Poles, and other helpless minorities within his grasp,[16] and of the destruction of international law:

"Brutality is respected. . . . The most horrible warfare is the kindest. I shall spread terror by the surprise employment of all my measures. The important thing is the sudden shock of an overwhelming fear of death. . . . These so-called atrocities spare me a hundred thousand individual actions against disobedience and discontent." [17]

"Any leniency or humane attitude towards war prisoners is severely deprecated. The German soldier must always let war prisoners understand his superiority. . . . Every delay in resorting to arms against war prisoners is pregnant with danger. The Commander-in-Chief hopes that this order will be fully observed." [18]

"The leadership must explain to our troops the meaning of the present struggle. The supplying of food to local inhabitants and prisoners of war is unnecessary humanitarianism. . . ." [19]

"I shall shrink from nothing. No so-called international law, no agreements will prevent me from making use of any advantage that offers. . . . I make no distinction between friends and enemies. . . . There will be no such thing as neutrality." [20]

These statements of policy and practice, as well as many others that might be quoted from Hitler's sadistic harangues, demonstrate the premeditated nature of this Head of State's crimes. To say that such a man is exempt from punishment while the common soldier puppet who obeyed his orders must be punished is to fly in the face of reason, justice and elementary decency; and no interpretation of law that arrived at such a conclusion could or ought to withstand the wrath and the sense of fair play of the civilized peoples of the world.

If Chiefs of State are not above the law, for what offenses should Hitler and the others be prosecuted?

The Allies at the close of the first World War made the serious mistake of not charging the ex-Kaiser with being a principal or accessary to the common crimes of murder,[21] robbery, kidnaping, and the like, in addition to various well-known offenses against the law of nations, in ordering, countenancing and rewarding flagrant and wholesale atrocities against prisoners of war [22] and civilians. Had they formally accused him of ordinary familiar crimes, Holland's legal position would have been far less sure than it was when it claimed that the crime called for in the extradition demand — "a supreme offense against international morality and the sanctity of treaties" — was not included in the list of crimes embodied in the extradition treaties it had with the Allied nations. Even if one were to grant that under existing international law there is no provision for punishing the act of starting an unjust, aggressive war in violation of solemn treaty obligations,[23] there can be not the remotest doubt whatsoever that Hitler is chargeable with the commission of countless ordinary crimes against civilians, as well as a great many violations of the laws and customs of warfare.

It has been shown that international law does not necessarily prohibit the trial and punishment of a Head of State for war crimes. But if doubt still remains respecting the purely technical legal basis of prosecution, it may be insisted that the punishment of Hitler and other responsible Nazi-Fascist leaders is justifiable as a morally legitimate exercise of a *political* policy on the part of the civilized nations of the world, a policy of expediency enforceable by the will of the victorious United Nations. In such an approach to the problem, it matters little whether or not technical international law recognizes the responsibility of Heads of State; it is simply a question of expediency, a prerogative to be exercised by the victorious belligerent or not, as he may judge fit; [24] "a high exercise of executive and conquering force submitting itself to the judgment of history." [25] For such a course, the Allied public arraignment of "William II of Hohenzollern, formerly German Emperor," in Article 227 of the Treaty of Versailles, is in itself an adequate precedent. Only because the government of the Netherlands refused to surrender him for trial did the Allied action fail to result in the trial and punishment of the "All Highest"; and not because there would have been anything "illegal" in punishing him. The United Nations have a right, founded on precedent and morality, to do as they please (within the limits of reason and civilized justice) with Hitler and the other misguided Chiefs of State. They can, in the treaty of peace, in the armistice, or in the bill of particulars laying down the terms of their announced policy of "unconditional surrender," arraign such Heads of State for a "supreme offense against international morality and the sanctity of treaties," as Wilhelm II was arraigned in the Treaty of Versailles. Or, without arraignment or without trial, the United Nations can simply declare the implicated Chiefs of State guilty of the violations of the laws and customs of warfare and the principles of civilized penal codes to which, in their oral and written utterances, they have confessed or which they are commonly known to have committed. Moreover, they can punish them as they see fit — by shooting, electrocuting, or, in most appropriate "poetic justice," by use of the very gas autos and death chambers which diabolical Nazi ingenuity employed in the cold-blooded murder of hundreds of thousands of *innocent* men, women and children. Or, the malefactors. If a precedent be needed, the imprisonment in United Nations can decide to imprison or banish the chief Axis exile of Napoleon Bonaparte after Waterloo amply supports the punishment of Hitler and the other Chiefs of State by the joint action of the United Nations without benefit of trial.[26]

The plan of the Allies at the close of World War I with reference to the former Kaiser was, then, basically sound and proper. They could have charged him with instigating the wholesale violations of the laws and customs of warfare and of civilized criminal law, and subjected him to trial like everyone else for such offenses; he, like his fellow-nationals, was not above the law. On the other hand, they could simply have disregarded the legalistic approach altogether and declared that they were exercising the right of the victor to dispose as he sees fit of an enemy not deserving of the graces of chivalry or the quality of mercy.[27] But instead of resorting to either extreme, the Allies blended the two. They wished to give the former Kaiser, whom, as victors, they could have stood up against a wall and shot without any hearing at all, "the guarantees essential to the right of defense"; and they therefore set up a special tribunal and provided that in its decision it was to be "guided by the highest motives of international policy," in order to vindicate "the solemn obligation of international undertakings and the validity of international morality." As they pointed out, in reply to German objections,

"the public arraignment under Article 227 framed against the German ex-Emperor has not a juridical character as regards its substance but only in its form. The ex-Emperor is arraigned as a matter of high international policy as the minimum of what is demanded for a supreme offence against international morality, the sanctity of treaties and the essential rules of justice. The Allied and Associated Powers have desired that judicial forms, a judicial procedure and a regularly constituted tribunal should be set up in order to assure to the accused full rights and liberties in regard to his defence, and in order that the judgment should be of a most solemn judicial character." [28]

President Roosevelt long ago stripped the mask off the Nazi claim of legality of their wholesale violations of the law of nations and ordinary criminal law, when in September, 1941, he said bluntly that the attack of the German submarines on the American destroyer *"Geer"* was "piracy legally and morally" and that the aggressors were "international outlaws." He again characterized them correctly from both a legal and a moral point of view when, in October, 1941, he called the Nazi leaders a "band of gangsters and outlaws." [29] As such, they deserve little right to any orderly judicial determination of their guilt for specific crimes. As was said in another connection by the United States Government, a State which "confesses itself unable or unwilling to conform to those international obligations which must exist between established Governments of friendly States, would thereby confess that it is not entitled to be regarded or recognized as a sovereign and independent power." [30]

However, even pirates,[31] who may be punished by any State capturing them (regardless of whether or not the piracy was committed in its territorial waters, or against its nationals, or it injured its special interests) must, according to modern international law, be given the benefit of a trial, if it be feasible.[32] To set an example of fair and just proceedings, the United Nations had therefore better subject Hitler and the other implicated Heads of State to trial by an international criminal tribunal as was proposed by the Allied and Associated Powers at the close of World War I. Thus, what may originate as a "political act" will at all events be blended with and transformed into a legal act of justice, after the manner of the origin of much law; and will become a solid legal precedent for future action against lawless Heads of State who think they can ride roughshod over the rights of other peoples with impunity. In fact the most effective way of stressing the normal immunity of sovereigns from foreign jurisdiction is to emphasize its basis in their conducting themselves lawfully; and that can best be done by a demonstration to offending sovereigns and to their peoples that those Heads of State who flagrantly violate international law thereby strip themselves of such immunity.[33] In the meantime, only a stiff-necked legal conceptualist could complain that, because something which could have been done without affording the accused any of the familiar protections of a trial at all, has been done by a court under orderly procedure and with the accused given an opportunity to be heard through himself, his witnesses, and counsel, the procedure has not been "strictly in accord with international law."

There remains the question of high policy: Would it be wise to subject Hitler, Tojo (and perhaps Victor Emmanuel[34] and Hirohito) and the other Chiefs of State to trial and punishment? Even to ask such a question would arouse the moral indignation if not the anger of many. Yet matters of "high policy" are often settled by statesmen and their legal advisers with but little regard to the true state of public opinion. It will not be amiss to remind the reader of the official attitude of the American representatives on the Commission on Responsibilities at the close of the last war. One of these gentlemen waxed almost lyrical in his satisfaction at the frustrating of the plans of the Allies to prosecute and punish the former Kaiser.

"I am bold enough to say that the American Commission rendered a service to the world at large in standing as a rock against the trial of the kaiser for a legal offense, and that Holland has made the world its debtor by refusing to surrender the kaiser for the commission of an offense admittedly political. . . . That little country had too much honor to think of it — more honor than the Allied and Associated Powers which dared to suggest it. However, the Allied Powers were without shame. . . . Our allies were disappointed at the time that the kaiser was not tried and that an international tribunal was not created for the trial and punishment of persons accused of breaches of 'the laws and customs of war or the laws of humanity': The time will come when they will be glad that they did not succeed. Perhaps it has come already. *'La nuit porte conseil.'* " [35]

This is the sort of preoccupation with legal concepts at the expense of elementary justice that must be frankly and firmly put in its proper place in coping with the master criminals of the present war. For, it is indeed true that *la nuit porte conseil* — the black night of Nazi-Fascist tyranny!

Objection is already being made that by punishing the German, Japanese and other Axis Heads of State and military leaders, the United Nations would only "martyrize" them and thereby give the Axis peoples an excuse for starting World War III. This theme, too, was harped upon at the close of the last war. James Brown Scott emphasized the point:

"One shudders to think what might have happened if the British and French commissioners had had their way, for they were the two who really seemed set upon getting the Kaiser. Heroes are sometimes made out of very cheap stuff, and it apparently takes but little persecution to make a hero of a monarch. As James Russell Lowell puts it in 'The Biglow Papers,' the best way to make a goose a swan is to cut its head off." [36]

But does anyone really still believe that if the Kaiser had been "martyrized" the German violations of treaties and their brutalities in the second world war would or could have been more flagrant and widespread than they have actually turned out to be? The question answers itself. The argument against martyrization involves the fallacious assumption that by letting the Axis leaders go scot-free, we would be sure that their peoples would never wage another aggressive war, or if they did, that they would adhere to legal limitations on methods of warfare. But the causes of war and the causes of a policy of lawlessness are multiple. There is no guarantee whatsoever that the whitewashing of the crimes of Hitler and the rest through the grant of immunity will so satisfy their peoples as to render them loath to start another war or induce them to be more law-abiding in its conduct. In fact, history following the debacle of justice at the close of the last war points to just the opposite conclusion. It is high time that the civilized world stopped appeasing the aggressor nations out of fear of offending them. Neither domestic nor international security can be obtained by surrender to the blackmail tactics of criminals, whether they be petty gangsters or those who plan to enslave the whole world.

Far from a policy of impunity for war crimes having acted as a deterrent, it seems reasonable to assume that the opposite policy — of enforcing justice through law — a program suggested by the majority of the members of the Commission at Versailles — might actually have had some deterrent effect. Punishment of high-placed malefactors is more likely to influence humanity in general desirably than is undeserved impunity. As was said by the then Attorney-General of England, Lord Birkenhead, with reference to the former Kaiser,

"If this man escapes, common people will say everywhere that he has escaped because he is an Emperor. In my judgment they will be right. They will say that august influence has been exerted to save him. It is not desirable that such things should be said, especially in these days. It is necessary for all time to teach the lesson that failure is not the only risk which a man possessing at the moment in any country despotic powers, and taking the awful decision between Peace and War, has to fear. If ever again that decision should be suspended in nicely balanced equipoise, at the disposition of an individual, let the ruler who decides upon war know that he is gambling, amongst other hazards, with his own personal safety." [37]

However, the trial of Hitler and the other major war criminals can take place only if the United Nations succeed in getting hold of them. Perhaps Hitler and his immediate entourage will prefer to precipitate a Wagnerian *"Götterdämmerung"* finish, thereby continuing the myth of their heroism.[38] But every effort should be made, as the United Nations armies close in on the heart of Europe, to seize the planners and instigators of the most widespread regime of misery that any tyrant ever imposed on his victims. They may, however, escape to one of the few remaining neutral States. The rich loot which they will carry with them or have deposited in foreign vaults, as well as fear of the vengeance of a *Reich* that in future years may again wax strong — not to stress the morbid sentimentality of many ordinary citizens and statesmen when "ex-royalty" is involved — these considerations may well defeat Justice in the end. Unless the United Nations can induce the States to which the Axis leaders may flee, to surrender them for trial, the entire plan of prosecution will dissolve into thin air.

Chapter X is devoted to this crucial problem — how to get hold of the Axis war criminals for the purposes of trial and punishment. However, before considering the issues involved in the caption and extradition of persons accused of war crimes, it is necessary to examine two other technical problems, the proper solution of which is indispensable to a realistic program: The defenses of "acts of States" and "superior orders."

CHAPTER VIII

ACTS OF STATE

⚖

THERE are two technical defenses to a charge of violation of the laws and customs of warfare which may entirely bedevil the administration of justice in the case of war criminals. The first, related to a question already discussed — whether the law of nations is ever obligatory upon individuals — is that for any acts of a soldier which his State either ordered or affirmed and made its own, he cannot lawfully be punished; liability, if any, is limited to the State of which he is a subject. The second is that if the prohibited act had been ordered by a military superior, the doer of the deed cannot lawfully be punished; only the giver of the illegal order, not the subordinate, is liable, and even the former escapes liability if, in turn, he was merely carrying out an order of *his* superior.

The problem presented by the doctrine of "acts of State" is considered in this chapter; the problem of superior orders will be taken up in the following chapter.

The reason given for the doctrine that international law prohibits punishment of individual violators of the laws of warfare if their acts were ordered by the accused's State is that, legally, the acts in question are not at all those of the individuals who commit them, but rather those of their nation, *i.e.*, "acts of State."[1] International law, it is claimed, forbids a State to make a foreign subject individually responsible for an act committed as an act of his State, even if that act is a flagrant war crime and as such clearly contrary to international law itself. Responsibility for such a violation rests not on the individual, who acted as a mere instrument or "organ" of his State, but upon the "collectivity of individuals" which comprises that State. Unless this were so, it is argued, no violation of international law by *States* would ever be possible; for collective responsibility (*i.e.*, that of the State) "as a rule" excludes individual responsibility.[2] An injured State cannot evade this principle of general international law by declaring the act of a foreign State a crime under its own national law and prosecuting the individual perpetrator of the act if he falls into its hands. "For, prosecution of an individual for an act that has been performed as an act of a foreign State is directed against the foreign State itself," and therefore runs counter to the "generally accepted principle that no State has jurisdiction over the acts of another State" *without the latter's consent,* a principle allegedly not suspended by the outbreak of war between the States involved.[3]

So runs the argument; but examination of the act-of-State theory demonstrates its artificiality, legalistic nihilism and inapplicability when dealing with the effective enforcement of the laws and customs of warfare.

In the first place, the very fact of a State's membership in the Family of Nations and its adherence to international law immediately limits its theoretically absolute sovereignty and its consequent immunity from judgment by other States acting as representatives of the Family of Nations in the vindication of the law of warfare. When a State subjects violators of the laws and customs of legitimate warfare to trial — be they its own or enemy nationals — it is in effect not that State alone which is sitting in judgment on another State; it is the prosecuting State as representative of the Community of Nations which, in the final analysis, is enforcing not only its domestic penal law but the law of nations as well.[4] The non-existence of an *international* criminal court makes trial in State tribunals the only practical means of enforcing this branch of the law of nations against individual violators. Without any possibility of its enforcement it is no law; and to limit enforcement to acts done on the initiative of the perpetrator or his commander and grant immunity for all acts done in the name of a State, however lawless, is to permit the most lawbreaking States to emasculate this entire portion of the law of nations.

It is true, that punishment of war prisoners who have violated the laws and customs of warfare is not the only remedy open to an injured State. It may take various steps to influence the offending nation itself. But as both the last war and the present one have amply demonstrated, such remedies are of little avail, in dealing with States which defy international law. Postwar indemnification is at best a very inadequate requital for wholesale murder. Reliance upon "punishment" of States for unlawful acts by means of reprisals alone leads inevitably to competition in brutality, in which the most ruthless States have all the advantage. The military leaders of an injured belligerent may be too humane to imbrue their hands in blood through indiscriminate reprisals against innocent enemy nationals in their power as hostages or otherwise; not all military commanders are Germans or Japanese. It would indeed be a strange interpretation of international law that not only would encourage violations of the law instead of deterring them, but would bring about the deliberate lowering of all States to the inhumane level of the most brutal and lawless State!

Nor is there any sound basis to suppose that provision for various types of action against the guilty State logically or justly excludes the right to proceed against individual violators of the law who have acted at the command, or with the approval of, their Government.[5] The remedies against a State must of necessity be limited to monetary compensation in the nature of indemnities or fines; only natural persons can be subjected to imprisonment or the death penalty.

Secondly, no State can claim its acts to be in fact completely, at all times and under all conditions, immune from the jurisdiction of other States, however much it may theorize about it. A recent commentator[6] who insists upon the applicability of the act-of-State doctrine to the war crimes problem himself applies the familiar distinction between a "just war" and an unjust one; yet whenever a State enters upon what it conceives to be a just war (e.g., one in self-defense) it has in fact previously subjected to its own jurisdiction the acts of the State against which it wars. For no neutral tribunal, acting on the basis of a fair hearing in which all relevant evidence was presented on both sides, has in such cases previously adjudged whether the contemplated war will be just or unjust.[7]

Thirdly, it is questionable whether the doctrine of "act of State" is at all applicable to the problem of liability of individuals for violations of the laws and customs of legitimate warfare.[8] It is not surprising that the act-of-State problem is almost invariably discussed by authorities on international law in connection with civil suits and within the framework of normal, *peacetime* intercourse of the Family of Nations, and not in connection with war crimes.[9] The very fact of the existence of customary usages and conventional agreements regarding warfare, and the recognition that among the remedies open to an injured State is the punishment of individuals who act contrary to such rules, strongly suggests that the act-of-State principle does not apply to such cases. For to interpose such a principle means, in effect, to deprive the injured State of its most powerful deterrent to atrocities committed during a war, and to encourage violations of international law and criminal law by defiant and ruthless States.

This brings us to the most serious result of the blind adherence to the act-of-State dogma when applied to the problem of war crimes: it would prevent the United Nations from doing anything "lawfully" — at least during the progress of the war — about punishing individual perpetrators of the most revolting atrocities in the history of mankind.[10] For practically all Nazi-Japanese violations of the laws and customs of legitimate warfare during the present conflict have in fact been ordered by the German and Japanese governments, or could easily be ratified by them and rendered "acts of State." True, for an ordinary nation to resort to the act-of-State doctrine in the case of the flagrant war crimes of its agents would mean the placing of that nation in the embarrassing position of publicly admitting that its government had encouraged wholesale lawlessness and crime in the name of the State. But brazen governments of the Nazi-Japanese politico-military stripe would not hesitate over a little matter of embarrassment when their entire program has in fact been deliberately planned to violate international law as a matter of national policy; especially when they could thereby prevent the punishment of their field marshals, generals, admirals and lesser officers.[11]

Thus the act-of-State dogma applied generally could easily render the entire body of the laws and customs of warfare a dead letter; any government could easily arrange to have all of its subjects' violations of the law of nations in warfare declared "acts of State." The result would be that most lawless, aggressive States could never lose: If they won the war, their militarists who had ordered and executed even the most flagrant atrocities would of course not be punished. To add insult to injury, only alleged *enemy* violators would be. If they lost the war, they would claim immunity on the ground that *under their own law* (*e.g.*, Hitler's decrees "legalizing" all sorts of atrocities) their criminal deeds were "acts of State." Consequently, just the opposite effect would be brought about from that intended by the prohibitions of the law: instead of deterrence from crime, there would be inducement to crime because of pre-guaranteed impunity. But in order to protect themselves, naturally law-abiding peoples would also have to encourage lawlessness in the name of their States. Thus would all nations be pulled down to the lowest level of international morality.

There is no rule of jurisprudence or abstract justice which requires blind support of an alleged principle of law that not only involves a *reductio ad absurdum* but is highly dangerous to peace-loving and law-abiding members of the Family of Nations. On the contrary, the most realistic and just view of law is that it is the systematic application of the "rule of reason" to litigation. The rule of reason impels the conclusion that "it is difficult to regard" the view under criticism as "expressing a sound legal principle." [12] Whatever the ordinary rule as to acts of State may be, reason and justice combine to dictate its modification when dealing with the problem of war crimes.

It is the concept of "the State" as an almost mystical entity that has prevented the realistic analysis of the power, authority, responsibility and punishability involved in the flagrant violations of plain mandates of the law of nations. By hiding behind the facade of the State, a government made up of scoundrels and murderers intent upon trampling upon all the laws of God and man to achieve their tyrannous purposes can evade personal responsibility through a dilution of individual guilt into the watery concept of "acts of State." It has been acutely pointed out that "if international law took the position, as it has tended to do, that, while a state may commit a tort or a breach of contract, it cannot commit a crime, it would be abandoning a large sphere of international relations to lawlessness, unless it at the same time recognized that a government which in the name of the state resorts to violence in disregard of the state's obligations to the community of nations as a whole is itself criminally responsible to that community." [13] Whether the de-

sired result be obtained through such a rational dissection of
the reality of a changing government of human beings [14] from
the abstraction of a more fixed but impersonal entity known as
the "State," or it be obtained by recognizing the direct and immediate criminal responsibility of the continuing State as well
as its temporary governmental agents for flagrant violations of
the law of nations, does not matter as much as does the practical task of preventing guilty individuals from escaping responsibility and punishment through flight into the mystical State.
Not only does such a mechanism of escape protect scoundrels
and encourage their successors in government to be equally
scoundrelly, but it unjustly spreads the punishment (through
monetary reparations, etc.) upon the masses who have been
the tools (more or less unwilling) of their lawless governments.
The doctrine of immunity of criminals on the ground that they
acted as agents of their State ought therefore to be emasculated
from the body of jurisprudence.

It is true that either the armistice or the treaty of peace or
both can remove the act-of-State obstacle to the trial and punishment of war criminals, by forcibly imposing the "consent"
of the Axis powers to the trial of their war criminals without
regard to whether or not the accused has violated the law at the
command of the offending State. The treaties of peace with the
Central Powers at the close of the first world war made no distinction between those who had committed war crimes on their
own initiative and those who had done so upon the orders of
their government acting for the State. They speak merely of
"the right of the Allied and Associated Powers to bring before
military tribunals persons accused of having committed acts in
violation of the laws and customs of war." [15] But the nations of
the world which twice in a generation have suffered from German military lawlessness should not be placed in the false position of doing something which, without such imposed consent,
is deemed to be necessarily contrary to principles of international law.

Besides, many Axis war criminals are being captured and
will continue to be captured before the conclusion of an armistice with Germany and Japan; and reason and justice require
that the unrealistic argument that would exempt even the most
flagrant violators of the laws and customs of legitimate war-

fare from punishment should not stand in the way of their immediate trial.

The theory that individuals cannot lawfully be prosecuted and punished for crimes which their own government designates acts of State is therefore subject to the reasonable and necessary qualification that individuals carrying out the orders of their government for clear violations of the laws and customs of warfare or of the principles of civilized criminal law generally observed by the members of the Family of Nations are triable and punishable by an injured State or the Community of States acting in the interest of the vindication of international law.

If joint action by the great majority of civilized States comprising the United Nations is contemplated in certain cases of a general interest, by means of an International Criminal Court, the convention or executive agreement setting up such a tribunal should eliminate the act-of-State defense where the accused knew or under the circumstances ought to have known that the act involved was illegal.[16]

CHAPTER IX

ORDERS OF A MILITARY SUPERIOR

⚖

IN addition to the act-of-State dogma discussed in the pre-ceding chapter, one of the most complex technical problems which will arise in the trial of Axis war criminals is presented by the defense that in doing the prohibited act the accused was merely acting in obedinece to the orders of his military supe-rior. A few authorities hold that a soldier or sailor who violates the laws and customs of warfare is not immune from trial and punishment merely because his acts have been ordered by a superior; and most of them apparently make no distinction be-tween the government (or the State it represents) and an offi-cer as the "superior."[1] However, copying the principle incor-porated in the British *Manual of Military Law*,[2] Paragraph 347 of the American *Rules of Land Warfare*, after listing typical "offenses by armed forces," specifically provides that a soldier has a valid defense if his act was ordered by his government or by a commander:

". . . Individuals of the armed forces will not be punished for these offenses in case they are committed *under the orders or sanc-tion of their government or commanders.* The commanders ordering the commission of such acts, or under whose authority they are committed by their troops, may be punished by the belligerent into whose hands they may fall."[3] [Nothing is said as to the liability of States or their governments.]

A little reflection will show that this provision, if followed literally, would give almost the entire band of Axis war crimi-nals a valid defense. For the most widespread and brutal atroc-ities grew out of the plans and orders of the governments tem-porarily in power in Axis lands; and as for the orders of "com-manders," the most heinous of these came, ultimately, from the respective commanders-in-chief who are also, in most instances, Heads of State.

Here, as in the case of other technical obstacles to an efficient as well as just coping with the war criminals' problem, critical examination of the underlying principles may lead to legitimate ways of overcoming the obstacles.

Paragraph 347 of the American *Rules*, quoted above, provides that while individual members of the armed forces will not be punished for violations of the laws of warfare in case these were committed "under orders or sanction of their government or commanders," the "commanders ordering the commission of such acts . . . by their troops, may be punished by the belligerent into whose hands they fall." This provision contains a triple ambiguity: it is not clear from the language whether it was intended to distinguish acts of members of a government from acts of State (discussed in the previous chapter); it is not clear whether commanders, as opposed to ordinary soldiers, may be punished for acts of State; and, finally, it is not clear where the line should be drawn in interpreting "commander."

The first and second ambiguities may be disposed of by assuming that they are due to inept draftsmanship and that it was intended to exempt commanders as well as lower officers and soldiers when acting under orders of their government or the State. The third ambiguity may lead to the absurd result of climbing higher and higher in the hierarchical ladder until the commander-in-chief or "Head of State" is reached. Since, in turn, a Head of State is held by many authorities not to be amenable to the jurisdiction of foreign tribunals,[4] we should have the Alice-in-Wonderland consequence of everybody escaping punishment for atrocities — including, in the case of the Germans, Hitler! One sensible way of interpreting "commander" would of course be to hold liable any officer who had complete discretion in respect to the issuance of or obedience to the order in question.

But what of officers and enlisted men below the rank of commander, wherever that line may be drawn?

The provision in the American *Rules* quoted above seemingly protects them against punishment (be they American or enemy nationals) not only in the case of orders of their government (and perhaps acts of State) but also if, in doing the prohibited act, they obeyed the order of a military [5] superior, *even though they knew their acts to be contrary to the laws and customs of legitimate warfare.*

This result is obviously undesirable; nor has such a rule always existed either in American or European law or military practice. As a matter of fact, the provision in question did not enter into the American *Rules* until 1914, through the British Manual of Military Law.[6] Neither the original Lieber Code [7] of the Civil War, on which codifications of rules of warfare are based, nor the 1898 revision of the Lieber Code, even mentioned "superior orders"; and, presumably, the military courts-martial and commissions had previously followed the rule laid down in American judicial decisions. By these, a soldier is *not* under all circumstances protected in obeying his superior's order; he is criminally as well as civilly liable if the order he obeyed is illegal.[8]

Considering the serious possibility that under Sec. 347 and its English progenitor practically all ordinary violators of the laws and customs of warfare to the injury of American and English nationals or interests would have a valid defense, we may well inquire whether the rule should not be changed.

Admittedly, the ordinary soldier is in an unenviable position in time of warfare. He has a dual obligation: to the ordinary criminal law which prohibits certain acts on pain of punishment, as well as to the military law which compels him to obey the orders of his superior. Receiving a command from his officer to carry out an act contrary to the laws and customs of legitimate warfare, he may or may not know the act to be unlawful under the circumstances. Even if he does know it to be illegal, it seems hard to hold him responsible when all his military training has stressed the duty of instant and unquestioning obedience; and this is still more true if he does not know the order to be unlawful.

It is not generally realized that in respect to the duty of obedience, there are gradations that make the task of the soldier especially difficult. At least three situations are possible: (a) The order appears to be regular and lawful on its face; (b) the order is "so manifestly beyond the legal power or discretion of the commander as to admit of no rational doubt of

[its] unlawfulness"; [9] (c) there is room for reasonable doubt as to whether or not the order on its face is lawful. In case (a), a soldier's prime duty of obedience is such that he is not required to go behind an order regular and lawful on its face to inquire whether it is so in fact; he should assume it to be lawful and authorized, and "in obeying it he can scarcely fail to be held justified by a military court." [10] In case (b) — where the order admits of no rational doubt of it *un*lawfulness — the soldier need not obey it, and a court-martial will usually deal lightly with him if he refused obedience. [11] Thus while Article 64 of the American *Articles of War* provides that a soldier or officer who wilfully disobeys a "command of his superior officer shall suffer death or such other punishment as a court-martial may direct," it is confined, specifically, to disobedience of "any *lawful* command." This qualification has existed in the Articles of War since the beginning of an organized American army; and it embodies a principle which, seemingly, is recognized by the military law of civilized nations generally. [12]

Under the heading of "orders so manifestly beyond the legal power or discretion of the commander as to admit of no rational doubt of their unlawfulness," a leading authority on military law includes, among others, "a command to violate a specific law of the land or an established custom or written law of the military service, or an arbitrary command imposing an obligation not justified by law or usage." [13] Yet in time of hostilities, a soldier — certainly a German or Japanese officer or soldier — may hesitate to disobey even the most glaringly unlawful and criminalistic order. Suppose, for example, his captain orders him to commit wholesale homicide by machine-gunning unoffending enemy civilian old men, women and children or unarmed and surrendered troops, as many a German and Japanese soldier has been ordered to do. This is so patently unlawful that either he actually knows it to be so or, as a reasonable man, he ought to be held to know such acts to be prohibited not only by international law but by the criminal law of all civilized peoples. [14] He is then, however, between the Charybdis of defying an order patently and shockingly unlawful and being disciplined (perhaps shot on the spot) [15] and the Scylla of obeying it and being later charged with murder. The situation is illustrated by a case in which, during the last war, a German officer, when reproached for having committed atrocities in a Belgian village, replied: "Yes, I know it was contrary to the law of nations, for I am a doctor of law. I did not wish to do it, but I did it in obedience to the formal order of the Governor General of Brussels." [16]

In the various gradations of situation (c) — where the subordinate has some suspicion that the order may be unlawful but is in doubt whether or not it is so — there may be even greater difficulty in arriving at a just solution of the soldier's dilemma. He is expected to obey such an order without cavil. Yet the very fact that he questions its legality indicates his awareness that in obeying it he may be committing an offense against the laws of warfare or an ordinary crime. On the other hand, he may in some cases gladly acquiesce in the order which he knows *may* be unlawful. Why should he then be protected by the duty of obedience when his own criminal intent and vicious motive have participated with those of his superior?

In order to arrive at a reasonable and just accommodation of the conflicting interests involved in the various situations mentioned, it will be necessary to analyze some of the leading decisions in the field. In considering the following precedents, it is well to bear in mind two distinctions which may well have animated the judges in arriving at their decisions, even though they did not always make reference to them: the difference in consequences between a civil suit and a criminal prosecution; the difference between a soldier's situation in time of peace as opposed to his status in time of war.

The earliest American pronouncement upon the defense of superior orders was made by Chief Justice Marshall speaking for the Supreme Court in 1804, in the important case of *Little* v. *Barreme*.[17] An act of Congress prohibited American ships from trading with France or her dependencies, authorized the President to issue instructions to commanders of American public armed ships to stop and examine American vessels on the high seas suspected of such prohibited commerce, and permitted their capture and forfeiture if they were found to be sailing *to* a French port. Officers of an American armed ship stopped a suspect vessel which was *en route* to the United States and took her into Boston. When the ship turned out to be not American but Danish a court ordered her restored. The owners then sued the officers for damages. The defense was that the President's instructions, issued to them through the Secretary of the Navy in compliance with the act of Congress, specifically included the order to see that vessels actually American "but covered by Danish or other foreign papers, and bound *to or from* French ports, did not escape." Chief Justice Marshall concluded, after much doubt, that "the instructions cannot change the nature of the transaction, or legalize an act, which, without those instructions, would have been a plain trespass."

Here, then, is a case wherein the defendants, far from having actual knowledge that what they were doing was illegal, had excellent grounds to believe that they were following the letter of the law. Yet because the order under which they acted was subsequently declared by a court to be unlawful, they were held personally liable in damages for acts done in obeying it. One can only speculate what the decision would have been if the act of Congress had permitted the use of all necessary force against resisters to seizure of a vessel and the defendants had killed the resisting master and been prosecuted for murder. The great majority of adjudications in civil suits are in accord with *Little* v. *Barreme*.[18]

The next important decision on our question, that of *Ensign Maxwell,* grew out of the Napoleonic wars. Though not an American decision, it may be considered here as part of the historical development of the superior orders doctrine. Some French prisoners in a Scotch jail had neglected to extinguish a light in their cell window when so ordered by a guard, and the latter, under the direct orders of Ensign Maxwell, fired at the light, killing one of the prisoners. We are not told what happened in the case of the guard, but Maxwell was tried and convicted of murder, before the High Court of Justiciary of Scotland. His plea that he was merely executing orders of higher officers was rejected by the court, which charged the jury as follows:

"If an officer were to command a soldier to go out to the street, and to kill you or me, he would not be bound to obey. It must be a legal order given with reference to the circumstances in which he is placed; and thus every officer has a discretion to disobey orders against the known laws of the land." [19]

Here we have a situation in which the accused mistakenly believed that obedience to the order of a superior is always a valid defense and that a superior could lawfully order enforcement of discipline through shooting. His belief in the legality of his action in executing the order of his superior is less clear than the belief of the officers in *Little* v. *Barreme*.[20] The situation was such that he could perhaps have taken the time and trouble to verify the lawfulness of the order, something not often possible in active military operations. The Scottish court, as did the United States Supreme Court, evidently looked only at the question whether, in subsequently examining the action of a defendant, it turns out that the order he obeyed was in fact unlawful; and both held that if it does, the defendant cannot claim a justification for his act.

Consider, next, the leading American case of *United States* v. *Jones*, a prosecution for piracy. During the War of 1812, some of the crew of an American "privateer" ship stopped and searched a neutral (Portuguese) vessel on the high seas, assaulted the captain and crew, and stole valuables. At their trial, Circuit Justice Washington, charging the jury, said with reference to the defense of Jones and others that they had only obeyed their Captain's orders:

"This doctrine, equally alarming and unfounded, . . . is repugnant to reason, and to the positive law of the land. No military or civil officer can command an inferior to violate the laws of his country; nor will such command excuse, much less justify the act. Can it be for a moment pretended, that the general of an army, or the commander of a ship of war, can order one of his men to commit murder or felony? Certainly not. In relation to the navy, let it be remarked that the 14th section of the law for the better government of that part of the public force, which enjoins on inferior officers or privates the duty of obedience to their superior, cautiously speaks of *lawful* orders of that superior. Disobedience of an unlawful order, must not of course be punishable; and a court martial would, in such a case, be bound to acquit the person tried upon a charge of disobedience. We do not mean to go further than to say, that the participation of the inferior officer, in an act which he *knows, or ought to know to be illegal,* will not be excused by the order of his superior." [21]

It will be noticed that this decision sets up as a standard of criminal responsibility either (a) the possession of *actual knowledge* of the illegality of the act ordered, or (b), in the case of actual *ignorance* or doubt, proof that under the circumstances the soldier *ought* to have known the order to have commanded an illegal act. The second half of the test of responsibility here enunciated would seem to set up an objective standard, the knowledge expected of a reasonable man under the circumstances. As in the case of criminal negligence, the accused, although he claims to have been actually ignorant that the deed he was ordered to do was illegal, is seemingly *chargeable at his peril with knowledge of the unlawfulness of the ordered act, if the average soldier would then and there have known it to be unlawful.* Under such a rule, if the legality of the order is open to reasonable doubt, then the soldier should be acquitted, because he ought not then to be expected to have known it to be in fact illegal.

In 1851, *Mitchell* v. *Harmony,* another important case involving the defense of superior orders, reached the Supreme Court. During the Mexican War an American Army officer in Mexico unlawfully seized the goods of a trader in occupied territory. When later sued for the price of these goods, his claim that he acted under orders of his superior was rejected. Chief Justice Taney wrote: "Upon principle, independent of the weight of judicial decision, it can never be maintained that a military officer can justify himself for doing an *unlawful* act by producing the order of his superior. The order may palliate, but it cannot justify." [22] In this civil case, then, we are confronted by a stricter rule than that seemingly enunciated in the Jones (criminal) case; because according to the principle of *Mitchell* v. *Harmony,* if the order turns out to be in fact *unlawful,* the defendant is liable even though he may have had reasonable grounds to believe it to have been lawful when he acted. The court is dogmatic in limiting exemption only to a case where the order was in fact lawful.

The reference to the palliative effect of the order is a significant dictum. It authoritatively calls attention to a means of mitigating harsh results in individual cases while retaining a strict legal standard of liability.[23]

In several preceding lower Federal court decisions the doctrine of obedience to superior orders as an unqualified defense had also been rejected.[24] These cases occurred in peacetime. It may well be that the rigid rule they enunciate should operate only in peacetime. In time of war a soldier ought to receive greater protection for obeying an order that turns out to be unlawful; for at that time, especially during a period of active hostilities, the discipline of a soldier should be more severe because failure to obey an order on the ground of doubt as to its legality could have very serious consequences for an entire company or regiment.[25]

The principle which denies justification of the act if the order turns out to have been in fact unlawful seems excessively harsh. Military men argue that for a soldier to be placed in the position of first definitely determining whether or not the order he received is in fact unlawful would often amount to insubordination and would subvert military discipline.[26] Some later decisions of varying reliability reflect a similar point of view. In *In re Fair*, the accused, a corporal, together with another soldier was called upon by the sergeant of the guard to pursue two prisoners who had assaulted their guard and attempted to escape. The order was: "If you sight them, and are positive it is the right party, halt them; and, if they do not halt, halt them a second time; and if they do not halt, then fire upon them, and fire to hit them." Fair and his companion, showing some caution, did substantially as ordered; and one of the fugitives was killed. They were acquitted by a court-martial of the charge of manslaughter and were later prosecuted in a civil court for murder. The main question was whether a civil court could thus take jurisdiction; and on a hearing on *habeas corpus*, the judge, following a test laid down in the civil case of *McCall* v. *McDowell*,[27] said that "the illegality of the order, if illegal it was, was not so much so as to be *apparent and palpable to the commonest understanding*. If, then, the petitioners acted under such order in good faith, without any criminal intent, but with honest purpose to perform a supposed duty, they are not liable to prosecution under the criminal laws of the state."[28] However, the matter of superior orders was a collateral question in this decision; and, whatever may be the actual practice in American military tribunals, it is doubtful whether *In re Fair* has overthrown the prior decisions holding the defense invalid if the order turns out in fact to have been unlawful. It is, however, possible to regard the test of "palpable illegality" as essentially the same as the one suggested in the *Jones* case, — "an act which he knows, or *ought to know* to be illegal" — inasmuch as a patently illegal order is one which the ordinary soldier should have known to be unlawful.

To summarize the status of American judicial authority, the earliest, most authoritative decisions held the accused to strict criminal liability if the order he obeyed turned out to be in fact unlawful even though there was reasonable doubt of its illegality when the accused acted. The question whether or not the order was so patently or palpably unlawful that he should have known it to be so was ignored.[29] In some later decisions there is a tendency to take the military point of view and to qualify the absolute rule. This is accomplished either by reference to conditions under which the soldier "ought to have known" the order to have been unlawful (which evidently acquits the ignorant defendant if a reasonable man under the circumstances would also not have known of its illegality), or by the grant of immunity if the order was not "palpably illegal." The American law has not yet completely crystallized.

The English law is best reflected in the leading case of *Regina* v. *Smith,* which embodies a principle much like the American "palpable illegality" cases. During the Boer War a patrol of British soldiers, sent out on a dangerous mission, indulged in an argument with a recalcitrant native who hesitated about finding a bridle for them. Under orders of his superior, Smith, one of the soldiers, killed the native on the spot. Under the Indemnity and Special Tribunals Act set up after the close of the war[30] for the trial of war crimes, a special court tried him for murder. In acquitting the accused, the court stated the superior orders rule in terms which in emphasis are more advantageous to the soldier than the rule usually embodied in the older American decisions, but which nevertheless lay him open to conviction in extreme instances:

"I think it is a safe rule to lay down that if a soldier honestly believes he is doing his duty in obeying commands of his superior, and if the orders are *not so manifestly illegal* that he must or *ought to have known* that they were unlawful, the private soldier would be protected by the orders of his superior officer."[31]

This rule is reminiscent of that in the American *Jones* case above, but the general emphasis is more in favor of the defendant. Honest belief that he is doing his duty[32] protects him in executing most orders, excepting only the manifestly illegal. If an order is not clearly and unmistakably unlawful, he has a valid defense even though he actually had some doubt about its legality and it later turns out to have been in fact unlawful.

In 1914, not long after the *Smith* case doctrine was enunciated, the British *Manual of Military Law* for the first time embodied a rule on superior orders; and, as already pointed out, this provision, enforced to the letter, would result in the acquittal of a majority of Axis offenders, unless the term "commanders" be very liberally construed to include all discretion-exercising personnel:[33] "Members of armed forces who commit such violations of the recognized rules of warfare as are ordered by their government or by their commander are not war criminals and cannot therefore be punished by the enemy. He may punish the officials or commanders responsible for such order if they fall in his hands, but otherwise he may only resort to the other means of obtaining redress."[34] And it was this dogmatic rule of *absolute non-liability* which was then for the first time embodied in almost identic terms in the *Rules of Land Warfare* of the United States Army, in 1914.

There would thus appear to be lack of harmony between the official *Rules* and the pre-existent judicial decisions. That the English and American rules are inadequate to coping with many classes of war criminals is evident. Before suggesting a revision, it will be instructive to examine the doctrines of another member of the United Nations, The Union of Socialist Soviet Republics, and of the leading Axis State, Germany.

The Russian view regarding superior orders was expressed in the argument of the prosecutor during the Kharkov trials in December, 1943. Echoing the Leipzig court in the *Llandov-*

ery Castle case, N. K. Dunayev, Public Prosecutor and Colonel of Military Justice, pointed out that the German tribunal had laid down the principle that "though the acts of the accused were consequences of direct or indirect orders given by their superiors, that did not release them from responsibility, since there was no doubt whatsoever that the defendants were perfectly aware of the criminal and dishonest intentions of their commanders." He then emphasized the fact that "numerous orders of the Hitler government and Hitler military authorities call for the commission of acts which are clearly and unequivocally the greatest crimes and flagrant violations of international law. A member of the German army who sets fire to peaceful cities and villages, kills the civilian population and forces women, children and old men into burning houses knows perfectly well that such acts constitute a violation of international law and of the laws prevailing in all civilized countries." Further, "since Hitlerite Germany's warfare has the character of large-scale, organized military brigandage, criminal responsibility must be borne both by the instigators and perpetrators of the crimes, for otherwise the majority of the monstrous crimes perpetrated by Fascist criminals would remain unpunished, inasmuch as the perpetrators would be allowed to cover themselves by the defense of superior orders."[35] The court seems to have agreed with this reasoning. However, the prosecutor noted the further fact that the crimes were committed not only "by order of the Hitler government and the German High Command," but also "on the initiative of the defendants, who issued orders to their subordinates for the extermination of Soviet citizens," something which the "defendants fully confessed . . . during the trial." Consequently, the decision excluding the defense of superior orders may be partially based on the fact that, independent of their orders, the defendants *on their own motion* ordered or committed the offenses for which they were tried in Kharkov. Apart from this, the Russian point of view condemned the German defendants out of the mouth of German law itself.

The German law on superior orders was expressed in one of the Leipzig trials (*Llandovery Castle* case). Submarine officers Dithmar and Boldt, on trial for the machine-gunning to death

of helpless life-boat survivors of a torpedoed Canadian hospital
ship, raised the defense of superior orders. In rejecting it, the
German Supreme Court said:

"It is true that according to the Military Penal Code, if the execution of an order in the ordinary course of duty involves such a violation of law as is punishable, the superior officer issuing such an
order is alone responsible.[36] However, the subordinate obeying such
an order is liable to punishment *if it was known to him* that the
order of the superior involved the infringement of *civil or military
law*. This applies to the case of the accused. Military subordinates
are under no obligation to question the order of their superior officers, and they can count upon its legality. But no such confidence
can be held to exist if such an order is *universally known to everybody, including also the accused, to be without any doubt whatever
against the law.* . . . They should, therefore, have refused to obey.
As they did not do so, they must be punished."[37]

Elsewhere the Court said:

"In examining the question of the existence of this knowledge, the
ambiguity of many rules of international law, as well as the actual
circumstances of the case, must be borne in mind, because in war
time decisions of great importance have frequently to be made on
very insufficient material. This consideration, however, cannot be
applied to the case at present before the court. *The rule of international law, which is here involved, is simple and is universally
known. No possible doubt can exist with regard to the question
of its applicability.* The court must in this instance affirm Patzig's
guilt of killing contrary to international law."[38]

Evidently the German rule does not protect the soldier if he
actually knows the order to be illegal; and an inference of such
knowledge is used against him when the order is one which "is
universally known to everybody . . . to be without any doubt
whatever against the law." It would appear on the basis of this
decision that even a German tribunal could not legitimately
permit an accused German war criminal to argue in defense
that he did not know it was against international law or the
municipal law of civilized States to torture, gas, electrocute, or
machine-gun innocent civilians whose only offense was that

they did not belong to the Aryan "master-race"; or to employ children as a shield in the invasion of Norway and other lands overrun by the Nazi hordes, in order to prevent native soldiers from defending themselves against the invader; or to kidnap the enemy's women into white slavery in German and Japanese soldiers' brothels; or to do any of the other acts in flagrant violation of both the well-known laws of warfare and the criminal law of every civilized land, with which the Nazi hordes are chargeable.[39]

But that German courts would take such a stand is by no means a certainty, when one examines German law on this subject more deeply.

The Leipzig court's decision in the *Llandovery Castle* case is in general conformity with the German Military Penal Law, but it does not specify the exact states of mind that must be proved for conviction. To find a soldier guilty in these cases, a German court must evidently find proof of two constituents: (a) that the superior's order was in fact aimed at the commission of a crime; (b) that the subordinate actually *knew* that such was the *superior's intention* in giving the illegal order.[40] This knowledge is, according to the *Llandovery Castle* decision, evidently imputable only in the very rare case where "the rule of international law . . . involved is simple and is universally known."

The inadequacy of German law on this question, even in the extreme case of the atrocities mentioned above, is shown by examining the Leipzig Court's decision in the *Dover Castle* hospital-ship torpedoing case, in the light of the principles of the German Military Penal Law. The Court in that case acquitted the defendant on a finding that he knew that the German Admiralty had issued memoranda charging the misuse by the British of hospital ships for military purposes, and that he was therefore of the opinion that the "measures taken by the German Admiralty against enemy hospital ships were not contrary to international law but were legitimate reprisals." In other words, the accused did *not know* that in ordering the torpedoing of British hospital ships it was the Admiralty's intention to commit a crime. The Court pointed out that the defendant's "conduct clearly shows that this was his conviction. . . . The accused accordingly sank the 'Dover Castle' in obedience to a service order of his highest superior, an order which he considered binding. He cannot, therefore, be punished for his conduct." [41]

However, under the principles of German military law mentioned above, the defendant would have been acquitted even if (a) he had actually had some *doubt* about the legality of the German Admiralty's order instead of believing it definitely to be legal; or even if, (b) though he had absolute certainty of its *illegality,* the prosecution could not prove (1) that the high officers of the Admiralty actually *intended* a breach of international law resulting in the crime of murder and (2) that the accused had definite *knowledge of such intention* on the part of his superiors.

This shows how extraordinarily difficult it is to convict a subordinate under German law when he sets up the defense of obedience to superior orders, especially since the question of the illegality of the order usually depends upon interpretation of international law, a matter in which the German militarists are notoriously biased. Evidently, therefore, the German rule is little better than one which completely exempts from responsibility *all* subordinates acting upon *any* orders of military superiors.

The foregoing review suggest several alternative treatments of the defense of superior orders, ranging all the way from absolute justification regardless of full knowledge of the illegality of the act to absolute responsibility if the act is in fact illegal even though the accused had no reasonable grounds to believe it to be illegal. Which position is most likely to do substantial justice?

In regard to this problem, as well as the others involved in the trial and punishment of war criminals, blind legalism, or even the need of inculcating the military habit of instant and unquestioning obedience, should not be permitted to expunge common sense. That both the United States and Great Britain were willing to throw overboard the defense of superior orders altogether in the case of submarine warfare, is shown by their signing and ratifying the Washington treaty of February 6, 1922, Article 3 of which expressly provides that in connection

with submarine attacks on merchant vessels, it shall be imma-
terial whether or not the attacker "is under orders of a governmental superior," the offender being "deemed to have violated
the laws of war and . . . [to] be liable to trial and punishment
as if for an act of piracy . . . before the civil or military authorities of any Power within the jurisdiction of which he may
be found." [42] This treaty was ratified not only by the United
States and Great Britain, but also by Italy and Japan; [43] and it
was only France's failure to ratify (for a reason other than
elimination of the defense of superior orders) that prevented
it from coming into force and demonstrating realistically that
certain conceptions have got to be modified if the law of warfare is to have any teeth in it.

Since the application of the principle of absolute non-liability
found in the English and American *Rules* would render impossible many convictions of Axis war criminals, and since
there are differences among the various member States of the
United Nations in respect to the regulations and decisions
governing the subject of superior orders, a new and realistic
rule is necessary both for prosecutions in domestic courts (especially English and American) and those in the proposed
International Criminal Court. Such a rule need not be as
sweeping in its protection of the subordinate as is that embodied in the English and American *Rules*, nor need it depart
altogether from the German rule. At the same time it need not
be the complete opposite of the English and American *Rules*
exemplified in the early American decisions — that is, a refusal
to accept the plea of obedience to superior orders under any
circumstances. [44] What is needed is a rule which will serve as
a deterrent upon extremes of brutality and at the same time
take account of the soldier's peculiar position, as "between the
devil and the deep blue sea." It is submitted that the following
principle most closely supplies these desiderata, provided it is
implemented with a sound sentencing policy:

*An unlawful act of a soldier or officer in obedience to an
order of his government or his military superior is not justifiable
if when he committed it he actually knew, or, considering the
circumstances, he had reasonable grounds for knowing, that
the act ordered is unlawful under (a) the laws and customs
of warfare, or (b) the principles of criminal law generally pre-*

vailing in civilized nations, or (c) the law of his own country. In applying this rule, whenever the three legal systems clash, the last shall be subordinate.

This rule avoids the extremes of the early American decisions, on the one hand, and the English and German decisions and English and American military manuals, on the other. The provision of "reasonable grounds" for knowledge of unlawfulness under the particular circumstances provides a necessary elastic standard for intermediary situations. This category would include not only situations in which the act ordered is so "patently" or "manifestly" or "universally known to be" unlawful that the defendant ought to have known it to be so, but also less extreme situations.

Since, however, it will be impracticable to prosecute the many hundreds of thousands of Axis subjects who have done unlawful acts, trials will probably be limited to the most extreme instances of patently unlawful acts generally known to be such. In most cases these will probably be the acts of highly-placed policy framers and others in the upper brackets of command or authority who have issued unlawful orders, rather than the ordinary soldiers and non-commissioned officers who have executed them. These issuers of unlawful orders can, in practice, often be proved to have been actually aware of the illegality of their orders.

In the *Jones* case it was said that obedience to an illegal order "may palliate but it cannot justify." This dictum wisely suggests that it is through the careful individualization of the *punishment*, rather than the attempt to make the substantive rule of low take cognizance of nice gradations in the moral responsibility of different offenders, that the special difficulties and hazards to which any particular defendant was subjected when he committed the offense may best be taken into account. Methods and degrees of punishment can be very flexible. The court ought to consider, by way of mitigation or aggravation of punishment, the following factors among others: The age and intelligence of the accused; his military rank; the amount of discretion he enjoyed; the nature and extent of the injury caused by his obeying an illegal order; the kind of unlawful act that was involved (whether it was one generally known to be illegal or one as to the illegality of which there was obscurity); the amount of instruction he had received in respect to the laws and customs of warfare and the kind of manual of rules with which he had been supplied; the circumstances under which he obeyed the illegal order (if it occurred during a time of great danger, or hasty retreat, or of occupation of enemy lands behind the lines, when the danger was less and there was more opportunity to check upon the order); whether the order required instant obedience,[45] or involved an act that could be done later or postponed for a considerable period; and other like considerations. This would mean that many ordinary soldiers would receive but a nominal punishment, while officers chargeable with more knowledge of law and greater discretion would be punished more severely.

The complete and absolute protection of those below the status of "commander," in Section 347 of the American *Rules,* was probably adopted because the framers had primarily in mind our own soldiers, and the aim was to relieve them entirely of liability *in war time* in order to encourage greater discipline and obedience. However, the principle in the rules applies also to any *enemy* soldiers it may be desirable to prosecute; and in that respect the Anglo-American standard may prove to be troublesome. The matter comes down to a question of policy — whether it is more desirable, all around, to retain the principle now in the military manuals or modify it along the lines suggested. So far as concerns proceedings in American military commissions, the President as Commander-in-Chief can clarify the matter by a revision of the *American Rules of Land Warfare* through the War Department. In the convention or executive agreement for establishing an International Criminal Court to try certain serious classes of war criminals, a rule of the kind proposed, if implemented by a sound sentencing policy, ought to furnish a satisfactory solution of the superior orders problem.[46]

There remains the technical question, *Which law shall be applied in order to determine the illegality of the order?* Normally, in law and in justice, it would have to be that of the accused, since he could not justly be expected to know the law of the enemy nation that prosecutes him; and the proposed rule has accordingly been stated in such terms. However, if the rule be limited to illegality of the act under the law of the accused,

the most lawless nations could easily whitewash their militarists
for the most flagrant violations of the laws of warfare by simply
enacting that such deeds are legitimate under their own municipal law.[47] In fact much of Nazi decree-law clearly illustrates
this danger. Some of it is so contrary to the most elementary
principles of generally recognized fair play that, in the interests
of German defendants themselves as well as of the administration of civilized justice, it may legitimately be ignored as patho-
logical.[48] As was pointed out in an earlier chapter, while a
sovereign State is free to adopt any legislation is sees fit — however much it may, in doing so, turn back the clock of civilization — the Family of Nations is not obligated, either in law or
in morals, to be bound by such aberrations. Otherwise the most
backward nation would always have it in its power to stultify
the progress of justice. An indispensable provision has therefore
been included in the second sentence of the suggested rule governing superior orders. There is nothing fundamentally unfair
in providing that wherever the law of the defendant's own
country clashes with well-known tenets of the law of nations,
the latter shall take precedence; for the laws and customs of
warfare (as well as the ordinary principles of normal civilized
criminal law) are generally known and they ought to be applicable in Germany, Italy, Japan, Rumania and other Axis
lands, as well as in the countries of the United Nations. There
can be no injustice in employing such laws and principles in
the case of enemy war criminals as well as those of the United
Nations, since they ought to be at the foundation of Axis domestic military and criminal law as well as that of the United
Nations. Where Nazi-Fascist domestic law clashes with the
well known provisions of the law of nations respecting the rules
and customs of legitimate warfare or with almost universally
accepted principles of criminal law, it will, under the proposed
rule, have to give way to such generally accepted norms and
principles.[49]

CHAPTER X

THE CAPTION OF ACCUSED

⚖

A s the victorious United Nations' armies draw the military noose tighter and tighter around Europe and the Pacific islands, there will doubtless be outbursts of popular fury against the local Axis personnel, resulting in the summary liquidation of many of the petty tyrants. Even inside Germany proper, there may still be sufficient opposition spirit left in enough survivors of Nazi oppression for an expeditious and bloody settling of accounts, especially against officers of the hated S.S. and *Gestapo*. Certainly, the falling out of the Junker military clique with the Nazi gang, climaxed by the genuine or staged attack on Hitler in July, 1944, has already resulted in much bloodletting. There may also be periods of revolutionary activity inside Axis lands, with justice meted out by businesslike, fast-moving revolutionary tribunals.

However, the time will come when the United Nations' armies will be in full control of affairs within Europe, and when fairer methods of trial of war criminals will be in order. The problem of getting hold of those accused of war crimes, as a preliminary step to their orderly prosecution, can best be considered by dividing them into four classes: (a) those among prisoners of war interned in the prison camps of the United States, England, Soviet Russia and other United Nations countries, who are ligitimately chargeable with war crimes committed before their capture or surrender; (b) those Axis subjects who, when the United Nations' armies march into Germany, Japan and other lands released from the Nazi-Fascist tyranny, will be seized or surrendered there; (c) those who will be found in the territories of the various States overrun by Nazi-Fascist hordes; and (d) those who will have fled to seek "asylum" in the territories of the few remaining neutrals.

At the present writing, these are Argentina,[1] Portugal, Spain, Sweden, Switzerland, Turkey and Vatican City.

(a) Although prisoners of war must be treated with the consideration provided for in the Hague and Geneva conventions as well as the common law of war, those who have previously committed offenses against international law provisions governing warfare, or crimes prohibited by the tenets of civilized penal law generally, are legally amenable to trial and punishment. It will be recalled, for example, that Sec. 347 c of the American *Rules of Land Warfare* provides, among the remedies open to an injured belligerent State, for the "punishment of captured individual offenders." This group includes a considerable number of German officers already in the hands of members of the United Nations, especially Russia.

(b) The offenders who will be seized by the United Nations' forces on non-German soil will, in accordance with the Moscow Statement of November 1, 1943, be turned over for trial to the authorities of the countries whose nationals have suffered from their atrocities. There should be little difficulty in the members of the United Nations exchanging the accused among each other. This process need not and should not entail the technicalities of extradition law, but would be based, simply, upon agreements entered into among the interested member-States of the United Nations.

(c) So, also, the offenders who will be captured by United Nations' troops on German territory or taken into custody as part of the terms of unconditional surrender will be turned over to the appropriate national tribunals or detained for trial by the joint action of the United Nations, as the cases may require.[2] Many instances of revolting mass atrocities have already been investigated and listed, with appropriate proof, by governmental commissions (especially that of Soviet Russia[3] and the recent American and British investigators of Japanese atrocities against prisoners of war) and by the joint United Nations' Commission for the Investigation of War Crimes, aided by various underground organizations. More accused and their crimes will be listed as time goes on. Toward the end of the last war (November, 1918), the Allies agreed, in Article 6 of the Armistice Agreement to abstain until the Peace Treaty came into force (January, 1920) from prosecuting war criminals found in occupied Germany, *i.e.*, in the only part of Germany in which they could have seized them! It is to be hoped that this misplaced chivalry to "fellow-soldiers" will not be repeated at the close of the present conflict. Assuredly, the perpetrators of wholesale atrocities against helpless civilians and prisoners of war are entitled to none of the sportsmanlike graces of the profession of arms. The Allies at the close of World War I also made little attempt to obtain information from the German Government regarding the residence of persons accused; they never published the details of the list of war criminals. As one authority summarizes the Allied attitude,

"it can be inferred that after the last war the Allies made no efforts to lay hands on the war criminals, so that the defects of the machinery may be less to blame than the defective way in which that machinery was used.

"The reason for this absence of retribution was that after the last war the world was permeated with the idea that it was unnecessary to punish the guilty because there would be no more wars, the institution of the League of Nations having marked the beginning of a new era of peace and good will; it was optimistically believed that a lasting peace would be secured by the appeasement of Germany and that it was unwise to create bitterness."[4]

A major problem of the modern war and peace will be the detection of those Nazis, members of the *Gestapo,* the *S.S.* and other guilty persons who may resort to the protective coloration of submergence, under false identities and disguises, into the great mass of the German people. The Nazis will doubtless destroy records, identity cards, military and police reports and even as many eyewitnesses as they can, in order to sow chaos and confusion and make the task of criminal investigation and assemblage of judicial proof as difficult as possible. To counteract this, appeals should now be made to German anti-Nazi and foreign slave-labor underground elements, to obtain and store away documentary proof of atrocities; warnings should be issued that the destruction of official military, police and other records and other proof of atrocities will be severely punished; and rewards should be offered for information leading to the arrest of perpetrators of war crimes. Large numbers of German-speaking criminal investigation officers should accompany

United Nations armies in the occupation of Germany. A similar plan ought to be followed in other Axis lands.

(d) There remains the fourth group of war criminals — those major offenders who will have fled by plane, submarine or other means to some neutral country, who will there be granted asylum, and who will do everything in their power to resist extradition to the United Nations. Hitler, Mussolini, Tojo, Goering, Goebbels, Himmler, Frank and many other Nazi and Fascist chieftains in brigandage have doubtless deposited vast sums of looted money in neutral countries. With these spoils they can employ expensive counsel and attempt bribery of officials. The example of the untroubled and prosperous long life of ex-Kaiser Wilhelm II in his castle at Doorn should arouse the strongest desire among the peoples of civilized nations to see to it that such a crowning of iniquity with impunity be not repeated.

To that end, President Roosevelt, on July 30, 1943, addressed a note of warning to neutral countries as follows:

". . . There are now rumors that Mussolini and members of his Fascist gang may attempt to take refuge in neutral territory. One day Hitler and his gang and Tojo and his gang will be trying to escape from their countries. I find it difficult to believe that any neutral country would give asylum to or extend protection to any of them.

"I can only say that the Government of the United States would regard the action by a neutral government in affording asylum to Axis leaders or their tools as inconsistent with the principles for which the United Nations are fighting and that the United States Government hopes that no neutral government will permit its territory to be used as a place of refuge or otherwise assist such persons in any effort to escape their just deserts." [5]

This warning was supported by the diplomatic representations of Great Britain and a note to like effect by the Soviet Union to Turkey and Sweden.

The Nazis foamed at the mouth at this step. They were suddenly seized with a tender regard for the sovereign prerogatives of neutrals; they shed copious crocodile tears over the outrageous infringement by the United Nations of the sacred humanitarian principle of sanctuary:

"This declaration is characteristic of the pitch of arrogance, impudence, and contempt for law which the Allied Governments have reached. It is one of the most elementary human rights to grant refuge to the persecuted. The political right of refuge plays a special part in international law: In times of war and political unrest it is one of the unassailable privileges of neutral states. . . . Switzerland, for example, considers the right of refuge the most ancient foundation of Swiss neutrality. Any insult to, or infringement of, this right would act like a landslide, sweeping away five hundred years of Swiss tradition." [6]

The incredible hypocrisy of this girding on of the sword of Justice by the Nazis is evident not only when their numerous violations of the most elementary tenets of civilized law are recalled, but from their insolent statement, only a year earlier, when this same Switzerland for whose status as an asylum State they now professed to have such a sympathetic regard, had opened its doors to Jewish refugees from the Nazi terror in France:

"The latest Jewish invasion from France has increased the number of Jewish emigrés in Switzerland to almost 15,000. . . . The advance guard of the war criminals (!) who have pushed one country after another into the world-wide conflagration has knocked at the door of Switzerland and the Swiss have readily admitted it. The slogans with which they welcome the sons of Ahasuerus are 'Traditional Right of Asylum' and 'Pity the Innocent Victims.'" [7]

Extradition between nations is governed by a network of bilateral and multilateral treaties and conventions. Many of these exist between the various States comprising the United Nations and the neutral countries to which war criminals might escape. These conventions, as well as domestic statutes on the subject, customarily contain clauses exempting from extradition, in the discretion of the asylum State, persons charged with "political crimes" or offenses connected with such crimes. At the close of the first world war the Dutch Government argued, with some legal justification, that the crime for which the Allies demanded that the former Kaiser be "handed over" for trial under Article 227 of the Treaty of Versailles — "a supreme offense against international morality and the sanctity of treaties"

— was a political crime and not one for which they were justified under their own law in granting extradition.[8] Of course,
Holland could simply have expelled the former Kaiser to any
country that would receive him, expulsion being merely an administrative measure applicable by any government to any
alien whom it deems undesirable as a resident.[9] But expulsion
of even a former ruler of a chronically warlike neighboring land
could not be expected of little Holland. While the Allies could
have demanded the extradition of the ex-Kaiser as accessory to
one or more specific crimes included in all extradition treaties,
such as murder, they doubted the soundness of this approach.
At all events, they seemed disinclined to press the matter.[10]

A position similar to that taken by Holland may be assumed
by one or more of the few remaining neutrals at the close of the
present war, inasmuch as there is no generally accepted definition of a political offense. Thus, for example, the Argentine
Government replied to President Roosevelt's statement of July
30, 1943, that it appreciated the "just objectives" of the various
warning notes, "inasmuch as they contemplate the punishment
of common crimes which may have been committed during the
course of war;" it recalled that Argentina has consistently held
that asylum "can be granted only for political motives or
crimes;" but it also adverted to the too easily overlooked fact
that the determination of what is or is not a "political" offense
lies within the power of the asylum State, pointing out that
whenever in doubt as to whether asylum should be granted any
war criminal it will "exercise the faculties that belong to it to
decide in each particular case."[11] What this could mean in the
case of such Fascist-minded governments as those at present in
power in Argentina and Spain can readily be imagined. The
Embassies of these two countries in Washington announced, on
September 5, 1944, that their countries would not become post-
war havens of refuge for Nazi leaders; but only time will tell
whether the leaders of those countries, who have long kept
silent about German atrocities, have really undergone a change
of heart.

On the other hand, a government is very jealous of its sovereign prerogatives, especially if it enjoys a long-standing tradition as a haven of refuge for political offenders. It was perhaps
asking too much to demand that neutral States put themselves

on record long ahead of time with reference to a matter which, until some specific war criminal actually seeks its shelter, must remain a hypothetical case.

It should be emphasized that the determination of whether or not any particular crime falls within a State's obligations under an extradition treaty with another State is a matter within the decision of the officials and courts of the asylum State.[12] As to ordinary crimes, little difficulty can be anticipated. Examination of some of the extradition treaties existing between member States of the United Nations and neutral States, shows that they include long lists of specific crimes which would cover many of the acts of atrocity committed by Axis military and political offenders, such as murder (including attempts and conspiracies), manslaughter, rape, robbery and arson; on the other hand, certain widespread war crimes, notably kidnaping and false imprisonment, are either not included in some of the relevant conventions or hedged about with qualifications.[13]

However, there may be pitfalls of legal interpretation even in the case of the ordinary crimes; for it might be argued that the acts in question were done in pursuance of a political "motive" and are thereby political crimes.[14] It is difficult to conceive of any modern court sincerely concluding that the wholesale butchery and torture of non-offending civilians attributable to Hitler, Tojo, Himmler and the other Nazi-Fascist leaders are "political crimes."[15] Political crimes are those committed by one group of citizens within a country against another group, with a political motive, such as a change in government. A basic reason why asylum nations reserve the right to refuse extradition of political prisoners is the fact that the victorious political clique will probably not grant the refugees impartial justice in their own courts; another is that the offenses in question may not be deemed crimes in the asylum State. While the "blood purge" mass murders by Hitler of his Nazi partner, Roehm, and the rest of the opposition clique within the National Socialist Party, or, more recently, of opposition generals, might by liberal construction be deemed political crimes, this assuredly cannot be said of the wholesale murders, kidnapings, tortures and lootings carried on in countries overrun by Nazi-Fascist hordes.

The defects in existing extradition treaties might be remedied either by the United Nations' countries negotiating new conventions with the few remaining neutral States, or by a limited special agreement with them to cover only war crimes without affecting existing extradition treaties. The latter course seems more likely to succeed, and could be more quickly followed, than the former. In this connection, the Commission on War Criminals of the London International Assembly, League of Nations Union, has made the following sensible suggestion:

"A separate and temporary agreement [should be made by the United Nations] with the neutral countries, concerning only war criminals. Without modifying anything in the existing extradition treaties, those countries should, *during a limited period*, after the war, be asked to undertake to deliver to the United Nations all persons accused of such war crimes. The list of those crimes should of course be drafted, and a new word, such as 'delivery,' should be used in this respect to avoid confusion with ordinary extradition. In the agreement it should be specified (1) that delivery is a purely administrative measure, connected with the safety of the State, which applies not only to crimes which have been committed in the territory of the requiring State, but also to crimes committed abroad against nationals of that State, or property belonging to that State or to its nationals; (2) that the traditional custom of refusing extradition when the crime was of a political nature does not apply to delivery; (3) that delivery will take place even if exemption from punishment has been acquired by lapse of time; (4) that the circumstance that the crime for which delivery is demanded is punishable by death shall not be a reason for refusing it; (5) that the circumstance that the accused alleges to have committed the crime by order of his superior will not be a reason for refusing delivery." [16]

It may well be that neutrals would be far more willing to enter into such an agreement or to construe "political crimes" more reasonably if the demanded persons were to be tried by an International Criminal Court than if prosecution were planned in some national tribunal; since the former would represent the weight of public opinion of the civilized world and might, on the whole, be deemed more likely to provide a fair trial than a domestic tribunal operating amidst embittered survivors of

Nazi-Fascist atrocities. In this connection, if the request for extradition or "delivery" comes from the United Nations as a whole, rather than from any particular injured nation, it will carry much more weight with neutrals and give them a greater sense of security against future German-Japanese attempts at reprisal.

One of the important tasks of the official United Nations Commission now sitting in London is the preparation of the proposed agreements with neutral states for delivery of war criminals, if exploration of the possibility of new extradition conventions shows that to be too remote. Another task is the preparation of lists of accused war criminals whose extradition and delivery would seem to be reasonably expectable because of the great extent and heinous nature of their criminalistic activities and the solidity of the proof against them of violations of the law of nations or the principles of criminal law common to civilized peoples.

In all these attempts to lay hold of the malefactors who will have fled to neutral countries, public opinion in asylum States will have weight with their governments and courts. In some of the neutral States, however, the press and other organs for the development of an informed popular opinion are not free. But even in these, the force of freely expressed world opinion may well be felt and may repulse attempts to manipulate political intrigue or legal interpretation in the case of malefactors whose atrocities are as notorious as those committed by the Nazi and Japanese leaders. Whatever the state of public opinion may be when the crucial period arrives, it now seems, in some of the neutral States, to be emphatically opposed to granting asylum to Nazi-Fascist war criminals. Thus, Swedish papers state bluntly that "it would be repulsive to imagine Quisling and his supporters enjoying Swedish hospitality:"[17]

"If pyromaniacs, murderers, and thieves succeed in coming to power in a country, they cannot escape punishment by crossing the frontier into another country when their time is up. Their crimes do not become political just because they claim they have committed them for political reasons.

"Asylum cannot be granted to persons who, while they are in power, have mocked at all the rights of asylum."[18]

So also the Swiss press, despite the particularly strong reputation of Switzerland as a haven of refuge for political offenders, draws a clear line of distinction:

"The right of granting sanctuary is our own affair. We decide who is worthy and who is not. However, we have refused sanctuary to many worthy people during the war, and even before that. Let us hope that no one in Switzerland will be in favor of sanctuary being granted to those who have to answer for war crimes. They had courage enough to commit the crimes: we hope they will also have the courage to answer for themselves. They should not bring any neutral country, which they have often mocked, into difficulties by seeking protection here." [19]

And again:

"Among the Swiss, who have a sound instinct for questions such as the right of asylum and its administration, we have noticed for some time that something was in the air. Hardly had Mussolini fallen when we began to hear in mocking tones the remark that the fallen dictator would be sure to take a villa somewhere in Switzerland and take advantage of our tradition of asylum.[20] We have no support for this theory. But we know that there are by-ways in diplomacy, and that certain high financial circles have interests and thoughts different from those of the people. The people want to keep the tradition of asylum unsullied. It is not for criminals, it is not for those who, during the last decade, have planned the present war, who have worked from the outside against our land, filled it with espionage organizations, bribed spies and agents, and themselves provided a refuge for traitors. Switzerland must never become a city of refuge for such as these, who have scorned democracy, overrun the small states of Europe, terrorized their populations and designated as a crime punishable by mass executions the struggle for national freedom and independence. The Federation will do well to abide by the wholesome sentiments of the people. This feeling of the people cannot be wrong." [21]

The peoples of these small countries, in the very shadow of the Nazi colossus, have thus bravely spoken out in favor of a realistic and just interpretation of their sovereign rights in the matters of asylum and extradition. Moreover, they have recently also bravely acted. Commemorating the 633d anniversary of the Federation, the Federal Council of Switzerland recently announced a revision of its age-long policy in respect to asylum. The new set of instructions and rules communicated on July 14, 1944 by the Federal Ministry of Justice and Police to the Swiss frontier authorities contains this significant paragraph:

"The authorities are empowered to forbid a special category of refugees all access to Swiss soil; namely, foreigners who, because of reprovable deeds, appear to have made themselves unworthy of being given asylum, or else, by their own activities, have impaired or endangered Swiss interests." [22]

This means, in effect, that the "traditional right of asylum," so characteristically associated with the Alpine federation, is no longer to be deemed a "natural right," to be claimed by any refugee regardless of his past, and subject only to judicial examination into the issues involved when an extradition demand is later made. It is rather a right to be regulated, in the first place, by border authorities empowered to bar entry to those appearing *prima facie* unworthy on moral and legal grounds.

On September 5, 1944, the Swedish Ministry of Social Affairs announced that Sweden, too, will treat the problem of refugee Axis war criminals with realism and justice. It promised that Sweden will return to their own countries fugitives of both the Quisling and war criminal classes who may have slipped into its borders:

"During this war . . . there have been committed terrible deeds of such a nature that hardly anybody previously would have thought them possible in a world calling itself civilized. Such deeds have been committed above all in the occupied countries. It is probable that many people, knowing that they are responsible for actions that have shocked the minds and sense of justice of ordinary people and that they cannot be justified by the requirements of war, will try to escape to neutral countries, including Sweden, to elude punishment. Our policy so far has been to keep our frontiers open for refugees, but it should not be concluded that Sweden will be open, or is prepared to grant asylum, to those who by their actions have defied the conscience of the civilized world or betrayed their own countries. It can be taken for granted that Sweden will close its frontiers in the face of a large or a small invasion of such 'political' refugees and, should anyone slip through, he will be returned to his own country." [23]

Thus have public opinion and public will, sustained by the relentless victorious march of the United Nations armies in August and September, 1944, been translated into sternly effective action in at least two neutral countries. But in the case of neutrals whose peoples are not permitted free expression of opinion (e.g., Spain and Argentina) even the impending victory of the United Nations may not be sufficiently effective, and it may be necessary to implement the warnings of the United Nations with practical economic and political measures. Food and oil may yet turn out to be the most effective handmaidens of Justice! [24]

CHAPTER XI

PUNISHMENT AND CORRECTION

W HAT *shall be done with those found guilty of war crimes?*

There are many who would have the United Nations, either individually or jointly, dispose of all Axis war criminals by the expeditious method of shooting or hanging. But a little reflection shows that this too simple solution might be contrary to the best interests of the people who have been victimized by Nazi-Fascist cruelties. To kill off much of the manpower of the Axis States would be to destroy the labor needed to rebuild the thousands of roads, canals, power plants, factories and homes laid waste by Germany's and Japan's mad bid for world domination. Apart from this, the question will surely be raised whether extermination or even temporary disablement of the guilty is in harmony with the best modern thought in criminology and penology.

Numerous volumes have been written purporting to tell us whether the Germans are bad people or good people, curable or incurable, reformable or irreformable, inveterate devotees of brute force in human relations or only *gemüthliche* believers in self-discipline; capable or incapable of governing themselves and keeping the peace under a democratic form of government. As to the Japanese, present opinion seems to be widespread, since the news of the atrocities committed against the heroes of Bataan and Corregidor, that they are hopeless savages for whom the only "cure" is wholesale extermination. Most of the evidence thus far supplied by the statements and behavior of the Germans and Japanese themselves is not very encouraging with respect to the more hopeful and humane possibilities of reform and rehabilitation of convicted war criminals. On the basis of the attitude and behavior of the Germans and Japanese, the United Nations could well justify a Draconian policy of painful punishment. Axis leaders remain ruthless, cruel, murderous despite numerous warnings and appeals, and this even in the face of (partially because of) clearly impending doom. Axis prisoners of war — especially the Germans — give little evidence of sincere remorse or even regret. On the contrary, they remain typically defiant and arrogant; and some of the Nazi war prisoners inside American prison camps even have the temerity and insolence to carry on their methods of terrorism against the small minority of their fellows who show signs of disillusionment with Hitler and his "New Order."

Moreover, the large numbers of war criminals involved[1] — even if the United Nations should perforce adopt a policy of prosecuting only ring leaders and higher personnel — will make routine mass-methods of penology almost imperative.

On the other hand, the trend in modern peno-correctional policy in respect to ordinary, domestic criminals is one of "individualization"; of careful study of the assets and liabilities of each particular offender; of fitting a special program to each, which is designed to make the most of his assets, develop new ones, counteract his liabilities and, through intelligent and kindly guidance, gradually restore the offender to a law-abiding and useful station in society.

Can and ought such a policy to be followed in the case of the Axis war criminals?

This is a most difficult question if one insists upon consistency. Yet consistency is not always a sign of good sense. Because of the difference in the psychologic and moral nature of the two types of criminalism and the differing urgencies and proportions of the ordinary local criminal problem and the international war-criminal problem, a valid distinction can be made between the treatment of peacetime offenders under a State's modern domestic polity and the treatment of Axis war criminals, especially those to be coped with by joint action of the United Nations. In the case of ordinary, local offenders, who commit a proportionately small number of crimes during the course of a year and whose victims are rarely subjected to the horrible brutalities chargeable to the Nazis, Japanese and their Balkan satellites, society can afford to experiment with humane and essentially rehabilitative measures; and the public, even the victims and their families, can, as a rule, be made to agree to so patient and generous a disposal of the problem of wrong-doing in their midst. When it comes to war atrocities, however, there are vital differences both in the quantity and quality of the crimes committed; hence there will be differences, also, in the receptivity of the public, particularly the victims and their relatives, to any United Nations' plan of reformation and reha-bilitation as opposed to disablement and extermination of the Nazi and Japanese war criminals.

However, not all convicted war criminals can be executed. There are too many of them. Only the Germans have been will-ing and eager to demonstrate to the world how huge masses of persons can be scientifically *"spurlos vernichtet."* Even in cop-ing with the most heinous guilty criminals, the civilized peo-ples comprising the United Nations will surely hesitate to employ the large-scale extermination methods used by the Ger-mans to do away with innocent people. As to ordinary impris-onment, that may be wasteful in certain cases. It is possible that even among the ardent Nazi warriors there may be some who are capable of re-education and rehabilitation, once the wall of defiance and fanaticism has been pierced. Yet until the better resources of modern criminology and penology (psychiatric and psychologic examinations and therapy, social case work, education, vocational guidance, the teaching of trades and skills, supervisory probation and parole) are applied, there is little way of knowing which types of Axis war criminals are "curable," what mental mechanisms have been developed by the Nazi and Japanese techniques of "education for death," and how those mechanisms might be counteracted, reconditioned or destroyed. The possibility of obtaining such significant knowledge is so important for the future security of the world that it should be taken into account in planning a program of punishment and correction for war criminals.

On the other hand, we must not make the too common mis-take of thinking only or largely of the effect of United Nations' penal policy on the Germans and Japanese and ignoring the fact that the opinions and feelings, indeed the very moral and mental health, of their surviving victims also deserve to be taken into account. Millions of innocent men, women and chil-dren will feel cheated and shocked if, to the awful injuries they have suffered, are added what to them will appear to be the crowning insult of affording their torturers the privileges and immunities of reform and rehabilitation. All too human emotions are brewing in the breasts of the survivors of Fascist brutality. Unless some socially controlled catharsis is permitted, unless these emotions are given play in approval of the program of retribution, explosions will follow despite the fact that "justice according to law" has been done. To the victims of the Nazis and Japanese, the looters, rapers, torturers and butchers will be deemed to have won out though convicted, if they are permitted to escape with their lives; all the more so, if they not only "cheat the gallows," but are comfortably housed in modern correctional institutions, mental hospitals and other establishments.

Considering these various currents of opinion that must influence decision, it may be predicted that capital punishment or long-term imprisonment at hard labor—especially in rebuilding shattered Europe—will be the lot of most convicted Axis war criminals.

However, in the case of those imprisoned, an observation and quarantine period might well be provided for, to serve the dual purpose of a "cooling off" stage for all concerned—victims as well as prisoners—and of scientific study with a view to ascertaining which individuals give promise of sufficient response to constructive educational and rehabilitative efforts. Extramural supervision for such offenders is not only dictated by humanitarian reasons, but will be far less expensive than continuous incarceration.

Younger offenders might be distinguished as a class for whom imprisonment ought to include a regime of strict discipline for a stated period, to be followed by careful selection of individual prisoners for re-education and rehabilitation, with gradual return of responsive offenders to normal life in their own countries. In such cases there is not only a greater possibility of moral fumigation and mental rehabilitation because of the youth factor, but a great ethical justification for furnishing such an opportunity; since we are dealing with a generation of still youngish and therefore more pliant fanatics who had been deliberately manufactured by their cynical overlords into ruthless destroyers and killers. Perhaps the process of education for death is in individual instances reversible.

So far as concerns those convicted in the local military and civil tribunals of the States whose subjects have been victimized and laws violated by war criminals, the outcome for the accused — whether execution or imprisonment with or without rehabilitative opportunities — will depend upon the accident of local laws, the nature of the crimes, and the state of public opinion. However, the principal miscreants — the Chiefs of State, the responsible members of the general staffs, the high officials of the *Gestapo* and other political terrorist organizations, as well as certain categories of offenders noted elsewhere,[2] are, it is to be hoped, to be tried under the joint auspices of the United Nations (and participating neutrals) by means of an International Criminal Court. Such an international organ of justice possesses no penal, correctional and psychiatric establishments and personnel. Therefore, the International Criminal Court will have to have its mandates carried out in local prison systems of the various member States of the United Nations. It might, however, have to construct or rent its own houses of detention for those awaiting trial. The United Nations, on behalf of the international tribunal, will probably also have to set up a Bureau of Punishment and Correction, to make arrangements with various governments for the housing, feeding, and employment of those convicted by international action; to keep track of their progress; to consider applications for commutation and parole, and like problems.

As in the case of offenders convicted in State tribunals, so also with regard to those convicted in the International Criminal Court, the taking of full account of the feelings of mankind would dictate almost universal employment of capital punishment. This would also solve the problem of imprisonment and support of the convicts. However, even among the more serious cases tried by the world tribunal there will be degrees of culpability and of moral guilt; and it might be politically wiser and more deterrent in the long run for the court to bring out such distinctions by imposing, in some cases, not absolute but conditional and suspended sentences of death accompanied by imprisonment at hard labor. Normally, suspended sentences are imposed only in non-capital crimes and are accompanied by probation — the extramural supervision of offenders under conditions of good behavior to be followed by execution of the sentence for violation of the conditions. However, imprisonment of those convicted in the world criminal court, with the death-sentence sword of Damocles hanging over them, may both satisfy the emotional demand for retribution and subject them to a regime of hard labor in partial repayment of the damage they have wrought. While it would be useless to attempt corrective and rehabilitative measures in such cases, psychiatric clinics might well subject them to careful study, in order to increase the store of scientific knowledge of human aberration.

Trained penologic and psychiatric personnel is available in most of the United Nations, particularly the United States.

In all cases the United Nations ought to impose, as one of the conditions of armistice and peace, the obligation of Germany, Japan and their satellites to pay the expense of the trials and punitive and corrective regimes. Whatever one may think of the wisdom and feasibility of reparations for the damage wrought in Europe and Asia by the Fascist hordes, there should be little difference of opinion as to the fairness and necessity of compelling them to bear the expense of that regime of justice under law which they have so ruthlessly destroyed in every land upon which they have trampled. No matter how large may turn out to be the cost of this financing of justice, it will nowhere equal the financial burdens imposed by Germany and Japan upon the helpless peoples whose governments and institutions they have destroyed, nor the billions of dollars' worth of property they have burned or looted.

It is to be hoped the the United Nations Commission on War Criminals in London will before long work out policy agreements among the different governments concerned, covering the classification of offenders for purposes both of trial and punishment; the use of various penal and correctional facilities in the case of those convicted by the International Criminal Court; the employment of different classes of prison labor in the devastated areas; and such other matters as may be necessary for the effective implementation of courts of law with instruments of punishment and correction.

It will doubtless have occurred to the reader that the enforcement of the sentences of international criminal tribunals will have to be spread over a very long period. This is but one problem the solution of which will require the placing of Germany, Japan and other lawless States under indefinite control and tutelage by the law-abiding and peace-loving members of the Family of Nations. No greater historic mistake can be made than to repeat the fatuous policy of the Allied and Associated Powers at the close of World War I. The militaristic disease is so dangerous to the health and life of the peace-loving peoples of our modern shrunken globe that political quarantine of paranoidly ill nations until they give unmistakable signs of recovery has become an indispensable measure of international public hygiene and safety.

CHAPTER XII

SUMMARY AND CONCLUSIONS

⚖

IN domestic polity, the administration of criminal justice is the strongest pillar of government. The doing of justice on an international plane and under international auspices is, nowadays, if anything, even more important. It is indispensable to the survival, in the intercourse of nations, of the very traditions of law and justice. The besmirching of the prestige of international law is not the least of the evils perpetrated by the Axis powers led by Nazi Germany. The fearless and efficient administration of justice in the case of Axis war criminals is today indispensable as a token to the peoples of the world, a sign that crimes committed by one country's subjects against the people of another member of the Family of Nations will be relentlessly punished even though they run into huge numbers, are committed by men in uniform, and are instigated by a *Führer* endowed by himself and his intoxicated followers with the attributes of a demigod.

The debacle of justice at the close of World War I must not be repeated. Two extremes must be avoided: On the one hand, unrestrained, undiscriminating and illegal vengeance; on the other, the bewilderment and betrayal of Justice through blind-alley, legalistic technicalities.

The ordinary remedies available to an injured belligerent in the case of flagrant violations of the laws and customs of war are sanctions to be taken against the guilty *State*: Publication of the facts in order to influence world opinion against the offending belligerent, protest and demand for punishment of enemy individuals who have acted contrary to the requirements of permissive warfare, reprisals. But these are grossly inadequate in the case of belligerents — such as the Axis powers — whose deliberate policy it is to trample upon all law in order to achieve their goal of unholy conquest. Punishment of *individual male-*

factors remains as the only deterrent and retributive remedy; and, while not excluding post-war penalties and indemnities to be imposed upon the Axis States, it is recourse against individual war criminals upon which the United Nations ought largely to rely.

The justice of the judicial proceedings under United Nations auspices can confidently be left to the judgment of history, which has already rendered its verdict as to the "justice" of Nazi and Japanese judicial proceedings.

Because of the widespread murders and lootings of innocent civilians initiated by Germany in supplementing traditional warfare with ordinary crime as a politico-military policy, Germany and her satellites have given a new meaning to the concept of "war criminals"; and this broader definition should be used in proceedings against Axis malefactors. Such a modernized concept of war criminals embraces offenses and crimes cognizable under one or more of the following systems of law: international common (unwritten) law, international conventional (written) law, the criminal law of the vast majority of the civilized nations of the world. It includes among the implicated, not only Heads of States and leading military figures, but also responsible politicians, industrialists, bankers and others who have participated in a lawless nation's criminalistic conspiracies and programs.

Germany and Japan should not be given the privilege of trying their own subjects for war crimes in their own courts, under their own law, and by their own judges. Nothing in the past history of the administration of justice by these powers in the case of war criminals suggests that if they were given this privilege they would discharge their duty faithfully and fairly. On the contrary, the Leipzig performance and the uncivilized legislation and judicial administration in Nazi Germany, as well as the Japanese treatment of non-offending prisoners of war, point strongly to the opposite conclusion.

The claim that trial of Axis war criminals for crimes committed inside Germany and Japan would violate the territorial principle of jurisdiction and therefore be unjust should not be given weight. The territoriality of sovereignty depends on friendly relations between States at peace. Besides, many States have expanded their jurisdictional claims to include crimes against their nationals wherever committed. However, countries which adhere slavishly to the territorial principle can readily and should shortly modify their legislation as necessary for the special problem of war criminals.

Offenders of the Quisling type will most properly be tried and punished by the States to which they have proved traitors. The great majority of enemy war criminals should also be prosecuted and punished by the countries on whose territory or against whose nationals they have committed their atrocities. But a large number — the Heads of State and other military and political leaders, those who planned, executed or consented to widespread atrocities in two or more countries, those who committed crimes against entire classes of persons whom they first had rendered "stateless" and whom they slaughtered *en masse* in pursuance of a calculated policy of destroying allegedly "inferior races" — such super-malefactors ought properly to be tried and punished under the solemn auspices of the entire civilized world. Legitimate charges of war crimes alleged to have been committed by United Nations' offenders ought also to be considered by the court.

This task of administering justice on an international plane ought to be performed by an International Criminal Court, staffed by representatives of the United Nations, neutrals (if they wish to participate) and, if possible, eminent jurists who have been driven from Germany, Italy and other Axis lands because of their anti-Fascist views or ethnic or religious background.

Adequate law for use by an International Criminal Court now exists; and its enforcement by such a tribunal would violate no fundamental tenets of civilized justice. The law for an international tribunal can be drawn from the rich reservoirs of common and conventional law of nations and the principles, doctrines and standards of criminal law that constitute the common denominator of all civilized penal codes. It may be desirable, later, for the nations of the world to enter into a convention setting out the general principles and specific definitions of crimes and punishments to be cognizable in the future by the international tribunal; but the pre-existence of such an international penal code is not a *sine qua non* to the just and efficient functioning of an International Criminal Court in the case of the criminals of the present war.

The punishments to be applied by domestic military and civil courts depend upon local law and practice. Those to be imposed by the international tribunal could be based either upon the punishments permitted by the law of nations in the case of piracy and violations of the laws and customs of warfare or upon those provided for crimes of similar nature and gravity by the law of the accusing State, taking into account, also, where necessary in individual instances, the law of the defendant's State.

The United Nations have already profited from one lesson of the miscarriage of justice after the close of World War I. Then the Allies did not establish the Commission of Fifteen on war criminals until January 25, 1919, long after the armistice; this time, the United Nations have set up a commission for investigating war crimes well before the capitulation of Germany, Japan and their satellites. This Commission is already preparing long lists of major war criminals and assembling the necessary detailed proof of guilt.

Another lesson which the United Nations should take to heart is the failure of the Allies, at the close of the first world war, to occupy all of Germany and seize those persons wanted for trial as war criminals. The cessation of hostilities in the present war should find the United Nations complete masters of Axis territory and in a position to incarcerate for trial as many persons charged with war crimes as still remain and can be ferreted out. There is still another lesson not to be overlooked in connection with the seizure of the accused; namely, the failure in 1918 to make surrender of the war criminals a condition precedent to the granting of an armistice. This has been promised by United Nations' statesmen; and the armistice terms signed by Rumania and Finland tend to fulfill the promise. Unquestionably, one chief provision in the list of terms of unconditional surrender of the remaining Axis States ought to be the handing over of the chief, named malefactors for trial. No excuses for not doing so should be tolerated, except convincing proof of death. Those with whom the United Nations' military and political leaders deal in negotiating for surrender must be held strictly and personally accountable for seeing that none of the principal war criminals escapes to neutral countries, and that all are immediately arrested and kept in custody until they can be taken over by representatives of the United States.

Related to this is still another World War I lesson from which the United Nations should profit; namely, the matter of getting hold of war offenders from other countries. As between member States of the United Nations, an agreement for free exchange of wanted war criminals can at once be negotiated. As to those who may escape to neutral lands, the first step in the right direction has already been taken: solemn warning of neutrals, in accordance with the Moscow Statement's policy of pursuing "to the uttermost ends of the earth" those who have "imbrued their hands with innocent blood," and delivering them up to their accusers for justice. However, the replies received are not too revealing or promising. The United Nations ought therefore as soon as possible to initiate frank discussion with the neutral States, looking to just and sensible agreements in the matter. They must be prepared, further, to impose economic and political pressure for defiant refusal to deliver up notorious war criminals by neutrals acting upon some obviously specious or unreasonable ground, such as the claim that the mass-butchery of hundreds of thousands of civilians, war prisoners and stateless peoples are mere "political offenses." Instead of the crime for which extradition of the former Kaiser was demanded and refused — a "supreme offense against international morality and the sanctity of treaties" — requested master-criminals should be plainly and bluntly charged with being principals, accessories or conspirators in such ordinary crimes as murder, arson, kidnapping, rape, robbery, larceny and others usually listed in extradition treaties.

Heads of State should be included in the roster of those to be tried. It is not legally sound to hold that a Chief of State is necessarily exempt from trial by a foreign jurisdiction in wartime for offenses contrary to the laws and customs of legitimate warfare and to the principles of civilized criminal law. Although there is valid legal basis to justify foreign jurisdiction in such cases, the disposal of Chiefs of State is, in the final analysis, essentially a political problem. By simple agreement between his captors, a sovereign or ex-sovereign can be executed, imprisoned, or banished without any trial at all. However, for the sake of further supporting the structure of international justice and of establishing a precedent of fair dealing with Heads of State, such high-placed malefactors should be subjected to trial before an International Criminal Court and given every facility of defense.

The defense of "acts of State" — appropriate in the peacetime relations of law-abiding States — should not and need not have any standing when dealing with members of governments who have consistently and defiantly, albeit officially, violated both the laws of warfare and the basic principles of civilized penal law. Otherwise, the most flagrant malefactors could always escape punishment by shifting individual responsibility and guilt from themselves as the lawbreaking manipulators of the "State" to the State itself; and the punishment would always have to be limited to a generalized fine or indemnity to be borne alike by the innocent as well as the guilty citizens of the State.

So, also, the defense of obedience to the orders of a military commander ought not to be permitted to defeat justice. As a reasonable and fair policy for modification of Anglo-American rules and as a just principle to be applied by an International Criminal Court, it seems sound to provide that the commission of a war crime in obedience to the order of a State or military superior is no defense if the accused actually knew or had reasonable grounds for knowledge, that the act commanded was illegal. Where there is conflict, in respect to the illegality of the act, between the offender's domestic criminal law and the law of nations or commonly accepted tenets of civilized criminal law, the accused's law should give way. The fact of the order, the circumstances under which the act was committed, the amount of discretion lodged in the subordinate, his education and training, and like relevant matters should be weighed in the balance in assessing the punishment.

The problem of punishment and correction of Axis war criminals is unprecedented and highly complex. Because of the nature and multiplicity of the atrocities committed by them and the deeply indoctrinated bigotry of Axis troops, a philosophy of correction, reform and rehabilitation must yield first place to one of punitive retribution. The deeply injured sensibilities of the survivors of Axis atrocity are more to be taken into account than are the feelings or reformative possibilities of the war criminals; for unless the survivors of Nazi-Fascist tyranny see at least the chief contrivers of bestiality punished, the very foundations of their mental and moral well-being will tend to be undermined. There has been altogether too much cynicism about law and justice; it is high time that the awful power of disciplined punishment for violation of law be made evident throughout the world.

But a program that stresses retribution for wrongdoing does not necessarily rule out the opportunity for individualized corrective and therapeutic measures in especially worthy and promising cases. What each of the various countries will do with its convicted war criminals is its own concern; a United Nations policy might well be more elastic and experimental. In non-capital cases, the jails, penal and correctional establishments and reformatory agencies, including probation and parole as well as hospitals for the criminal insane usually employed by the prosecuting State — if these are still available — should be resorted to also by the international court. It will, however, probably need to have detention and punitive facilities of its own to some extent. A Bureau of Imprisonment and Correction will also have to be set up, to work with the international tribunal in supervising the execution of its sentences. A basic consideration will be the need of hundreds of thousands of able-bodied workers to rebuild what they have destroyed. Work in labor battalions ought for years to come to be the fate of the vast majority of convicted Axis war criminals. However hard such labor may be, it will at least be imposed as a lawful penalty following conviction for crime and not as the result of some program of deliberate enslavement and extermination of supposedly lesser men by a self-styled master race. Moreover, it will be imposed under conditions vastly more humane than those to which innocent men, women and children have been subjected by German and Japanese tyranny. Let those good people who are so concerned about the future welfare of the Germans, and who will decry the employment of Axis convicts to rebuild that which they destroyed as "cruel and unusual punishment," remember such simple facts.

The task confronting the United Nations in all this is tremendous. The making out of long lists of accused and summaries of the proof available against them is but one step on a very tortuous road. It is necessary that the United Nations Commission be fully empowered to work out details of general policy and to implement the entire program with conventions and executive agreements, new tribunals, prosecuting and defending agencies, sheriffs and court officers, penal and correctional authorities and facilities; and to cope with other perplexing problems. Above all, the well-known "law's delays" must find no place in the program. To permit two and a half years to elapse between the accusation and the trial — as was done last time — means the strangulation of justice, through the death, disappearance or intimidation of complainants and witnesses and loss of public interest.

In quality if not in quantity, the task of doing justice in the matter of war criminals is the joint responsibility of the United Nations. The symbolic value of joint action on the part of the vast majority of States to do justice in the case of those who have flagrantly murdered and pillaged and scorned all law can hardly be exaggerated. If, out of the travails of the present global war, there is to emerge even a germ of the "international organization" that so many publicists have called for, then an International Criminal Court for the trial of war criminals can be the nucleus of that germ. The mere fact of the continued participation of the member States of the United Nations and neutrals in the doing of at least one post-war job jointly, efficiently, firmly and fairly will awaken hope that the forward-looking members of the Family of Nations can continuously cooperate in the more pleasant and fruitful activities of peace. The performance of justice, more than any other task that confronts the world today, is one in which the United Nations must present a continuing united front.

NOTES

CHAPTER I

1. *In re Piracy Jure Gentium*, Jud. Com., House of Lords, A.C. (1934), 586, 592, per Viscount Sankey, L.C.

CHAPTER II

1. Commission on the Responsibility of the Authors of the War and on Enforcement of Penalties, 14 *Am. J. Int. L.* (1920), 95 et seq. (Hereinafter cited as *Commission Report.*)

2. *Commission Report*, p. 113.

3. Id., p. 116.

4. *New York Times, Current History*, Vol. XI, Pt. II (March 1920), p. 377.

5. *Commission Report*, pp. 121-2.

6. Id., p. 122. The above expression is part of the preamble to the Hague Conventions of 1899 and 1907, having been cautiously put in so that if some matter were not specifically covered by the Convention in question it would not be construed to mean that it was to be left to the arbitrary will of the military commander.

7. *Commission Report*, pp. 134, 135, 144, 145.

8. Id., pp. 142, 146.

9. Id., p. 145.

10. Id., p. 152.

11. Id. Article 227 provided that a "special tribunal" to try the former Kaiser would be set up, to be composed of five judges, one each to be appointed by the United States, Great Britain, France, Italy and Japan. Since Holland refused to extradite him, the tribunal was never set up.

12. This principle has been recognized by German authorities. See Verdross: *Die Völkerrechtswidrige Kriegshandlung und der Strafanspruch der Staaten* (1920).

13. There are differences in the exact count given by various sources. A German authority claims the original list consisted of 890 cases against 900 Germans and 10 Turks. Berber: *"Das Diktat von Versailles"* (1929), pp. 1216-17. Some authorities give the number of British cases as 100 and Belgian as 265. The figures in the text

are from "Punishing War Criminals," *New York Times, Current History*, Vol. XI, Part II (1920), p. 373.

14. Von Lersner: *"Die Auslieferung der deutschen 'Kriegsverbrecher,'"* in *Zehn Jahre Versailles*, ed. by Schnee and Draeger (1929), Vol. I, pp. 15, 22, 23.

15. Id., p. 26.

16. ". . . I am willing at this fateful hour to stand up for my compatriots. If the allied and associated powers want a victim, let them take me instead of the 900 Germans, who have committed no offense other than that of serving their country during the war. Wilhelm." *New York Times, Current History*, Vol. XI, Part II (1920), p. 375.

17. Von Lersner, op. cit., p. 26.

18. Miscellaneous No. 15, Protocols and Correspondence between the Supreme Council and the Conference of Ambassadors and the German Government and the German Peace Delegation between January 10, 1920 and July 17, 1920, respecting The Execution of the Treaty of Versailles of June 28, 1919, Cmd. 1325, 1921, No. 34, pp. 28–9.

19. Kraus and Rödiger: *"Urkunden zum Friedensvertrage von Versailles,"* in *Kommentar zum Friedensvertrage*, ed. by Schücking (1921), p. 943.

20. Mullins: *The Leipzig Trials* (1921), pp. 29–31.

21. Id., p. 39.

22. Id., pp. 41–2.

23. Judgment in the Case of Emil Müller, 16 *Am. J. Int. L.* (1922), 674, 695.

24. In the other cases submitted by the French Government, Lieutenant Laule was acquitted of the charge of having had a French Captain killed after he had been made a prisoner, the court finding that the soldier who had shot the prisoner of war had acted without orders. But the soldier was never prosecuted. Generals von Schack and Krushka were charged with having caused the death of 3,000 prisoners of war through negligence, the conditions under which the prisoners were housed and fed having been outrageous in the extreme and death having been due largely to typhoid. The court followed the prosecution's request for acquittal. Dr. Michelson was accused of having beaten and mistreated several French prisoners in his hospital and willfully causing the death of several. Despite much convincing evidence, the defendant was acquitted.

25. Speaking of the conviction of Lieuts. Dithmar and Boldt, Claude Mullins says: "When the judges had withdrawn, I saw several members of the public go up to the condemned men and sympathize with them. There was an electric atmosphere both in the Court and amid the crowd outside. The British Mission retired quietly to its private room, and then left the Court by a side door, closely guarded by German police. Thus the possibility of an unpleasant incident was avoided." Op. cit., p. 134. Speaking of the trials instituted on behalf of the French, a reporter in the contemporary issue of the *Journal du Droit International* tells how, "when General Stenger, acquitted, left the Court House by automobile, the crowd acclaimed him with ovations. The four members of the Commission named by the French Government to be present at the trials followed in a second vehicle. They were scorned by those present. They confined themselves to an ironic smile. M. Matter, Commissioner of the French Government, raised himself in his automobile and looked fixedly at those nearest him, whom his calmness and *sangfroid* overawed." Clunet: *"Les Criminels de guerre devant le Reichsgericht, à Leipzig,"* 48 J. du Droit Internat. (1921), p. 440.

26. Mullins, op. cit., pp. 17, 43.

27. The German Government made public Poincaré's note of protest with the comment that "the fact that the note emanates from all the principal Allied Powers is especially surprising, in view of the fact that England has on several occasions recognized the perfect impartiality of the Leipzig Tribunal." 49 J. du Droit Internat. (1922), pp. 855–6. German commentators made much of the fact that, as one of them put it, "foreign witnesses of the highest juristic repute, among them the English Solicitor General Sir Ernest Pollock, the English Attorney General Sir Gordon Hewart . . . have acknowledged the Impartiality of the *Reichsgericht.*" Berber: *Das Diktat von Versailles* (1939), p. 1217.

28. Meurer: *Völkerrecht im Weltkrieg* (1927), Vol. III, pp. 58 et seq.

29. Berber, op. cit.

CHAPTER III

1. On several occasions in the past and present wars, the Germans, hoping to achieve victory through treachery and surprise, have first solemnly entered into international engagements with other States and then suddenly and arbitrarily changed the rules of

the game. This was true, for instance, of Germany's violent protests against the removal of the wives and children of the Boers into concentration camps, which were followed by the German brutalities against civilians in Belgium and France during both the first and the second world wars. It was true of Germany's surprise use of poison gas in the last war and her recent employment of "robot bombs" which cannot be aimed, and wreak death and destruction on non-military as well as military objects. So, also, the diabolical invention of "total war" was sprung upon an amazed but soberly saddened world by the Germans. By this action Germany has forced the United Nations to expand the traditional concept of war criminals to include the cold-blooded mass murders to which has been affixed the infamous trademark, "made in Germany."

2. Many definitions of war crimes have been proposed. The definition in the text *excludes* (1) armed hostilities by individuals not members of the enemy armed forces, (2) espionage and "war treason," (3) marauding acts. These are not the sort of deeds that have shocked the world as atrocities; they present special problems; they are the type of offense that has long been successfully coped with by military tribunals. (See Oppenheim's *International Law* [6th ed., by Lauterpacht], Vol. II, pp. 451 et seq.) The chief type of war crime that concerns us is the violation of recognized rules of legitimate warfare committed by members of the armed forces. However, because of the Nazi conception of "total war," we also include acts by military, political and industrial leaders which normally constitute crimes in the penal codes of the civilized world. The two types of war crimes may well require different types of domestic tribunals, but could be coped with by a single International Criminal Court. See Chaps. V, VI.

3. *Commission Report*, pp. 95, 120.

4. But see Levy: "The Law and Procedure of War Crime Trials," 37 *Am. Pol. Sci. Rev.* (1943), 1052, 1077. Frangulis, "Responsables de la Guerre," in II *Dictionnaire Diplomatique*, 581, 585, takes it for granted that "the ratification of the Briand-Kellogg Pact has proclaimed war to be a crime and it has been recognized as such by a large number of States. Hence, in our time penal sanctions are possible, although this was not the case in respect to the war of 1914 and its authors."

5. It will be recalled that Art. 227 of the Treaty of Versailles "publicly arraigned William II of Hohenzollern, formerly German

Emperor," for a "supreme offense against international morality and the sanctity of treaties," to be tried before a specially constituted tribunal.

6. *Cf.* "Instructions Given to the German Plenipotentiaries," XI, in Luckau: *The German Delegation at the Paris Peace Conference,* pp. 199 et seq.

7. Kelsen: "Collective and Individual Responsibility in International Law with Particular Regard to the Punishment of War Criminals," 31 *Cal. L. Rev.* (1943), 531, 532, correctly concludes that Germany has violated the principle of a "just war" under international law. But most modern authorities do not accept this principle. Were the German Government's guilt of starting an unjust war to be taken for granted, however, it might be reasoned that *all* the acts of the German troops — whether or not they were violative of the laws and customs of warfare — were unlawful; they were all "fruits of the poisoned tree." But a surer basis of liability is to deal only with individual acts clearly contrary to the laws and customs of warfare once a war has been embarked upon.

8. There have been many other pronouncements by United Nations' statesmen on the subject of war criminals, among them the Declaration of January 13, 1942, at St. James's Palace, London, of nine of the governments in exile, President Roosevelt's warnings of August 21 and October 7, 1942, the statement in the House of Parliament by the Lord Chancellor, October 7, 1942, the statement of October 2, 1942 by Commissar Molotov, the British and United Nations Declarations of October 25, 1941, the Soviet and Chinese notes of November 27, 1941 and January 9, 1942, the statement by Foreign Secretary Eden on March 10, 1944 to the House of Commons on Japanese atrocities against British prisoners of war. On March 24, 1944 both Roosevelt and Churchill again proclaimed punishment; Churchill included not only the "miscreants" but also their agents, and Roosevelt promised that "those having a part in such acts — *leaders, subordinates and functionaries* — would all be punished." On September 26, 1944, in the House of Commons, Churchill once more promised punishment, stating that the British Government insists that German war criminals should find no haven in neutral countries. On March 9, 1943 the United States Senate unanimously adopted the concurrent resolution presented by Senator Barkley to the effect that "the dictates of humanity and honorable conduct in war demand that this inexcusable slaughter and mistreatment shall cease

and that it is the sense of this Congress that those guilty, *directly or indirectly*, of these criminal acts shall be held accountable and punished in a manner commensurate with the offenses for which they are responsible." *Congressional Record* — Senate, March 9, 1943, 1773. On July 14, 1944, Secretary of State Hull condemned the puppet Hungarian Government for participating in the Nazi extermination of Jews and warned them that "they cannot escape inexorable punishment which will be meted out to them when the power of the evil men now in control of Hungary has been broken." At the same time he promised that justice would "certainly be meted out to those responsible" for "the cold-blooded murder of the population of the Greek village of Distomo," another Lidice. On July 15, 1944, the French Provisional Government proposed to the Allies that a new and solemn warning be delivered to Hitler's Government that eleventh-hour massacres of the French would be punished. Various influential private organizations in America (and doubtless also in England), such as the American Federation of Labor, the Congress of Industrial Organizations, the Institute of Jewish Affairs of the American and World Jewish Congresses, the National Catholic Welfare Conference and others, have likewise called for trial and punishment of individual malefactors.

9. Although the *Schutzstaffel* and other Nazi private armies were established as a private guard to keep the Nazi party in power or, euphemistically, to "protect the Third Reich against the enemies within," they have sometimes been thrown into battle against external enemies and are therefore part of the military forces of the Reich.

10. See, for example, Norden: "The History of the Mannesmann Concern," *Free World* (1944), Vol. VII, pp. 223 et seq.

11. The first systematic statement of the rules of legitimate warfare was the famous "Instructions for the Government of the Armies of the United States in the Field," drafted by Dr. Francis Lieber, revised by a board of Army officers, and published, upon approval of President Lincoln, in G.O.100 of the War Department, April 24, 1863. This code was the foundation for similar provisions in the Hague conventions. But even earlier, treaties were entered into in 1785 between the youthful United States of America, represented by John Adams, Thomas Jefferson and Benjamin Franklin, and the Kingdom of Prussia, expressing remarkably humane provisions in case of war between the contracting parties; similar provisions being

incorporated in the treaties of 1799 (signed by John Quincy Adams) and 1828 (signed by Henry Clay). See Bartlett: "Liability for Official War Crimes," 35 *L.Q.R.* (1919), 177, 183–4.

12. Considering only major belligerents, States which have ratified or adhered to the 1907 Hague Convention (IV) respecting the laws and customs of war on land include China, Great Britain, Russia (with reservations) and the United States of America, on the one hand; and Germany (with reservations), and Japan (with reservations) on the other. Italy had ratified the 1899 convention but not the 1907 one.

Belligerent States which have ratified the Geneva Convention of 1929 regarding the treatment of prisoners of war (an expansion of Chap. II of the Hague Conventions of 1899 and 1907) are China, Great Britain, and the United States of America; and, among the Axis powers, Germany and Italy. When war broke out between the United States and Japan, our Government confirmed its intention to observe the Geneva prisoners of war convention not only in respect to prisoners of war but, so far as adaptable to them, to civilian internees. The Japanese Government thereupon notified the United States Government that it would do likewise in respect to American prisoners of war and civilian internees. *U.S. Dept. of State Bull.,* Vol. X (January 15, 1944), p. 78.

The Hague Convention of 1899, although superseded by the Hague Convention IV of 1907 as between those nations that are parties to the 1907 agreement, is still in force between the United States and such other belligerent parties to the 1899 agreement as have not yet ratified or adhered to the 1907 convention. So also the Red Cross convention of 1929, Chapter 5, supersedes the Red Cross conventions of 1864 and 1906 as between parties to the 1929 agreement, but the former continue in force between our country and such other contracting parties to the 1864 and 1906 agreements as have not yet ratified or adhered to the 1929 agreement.

Technically, the Hague Convention of 1907 was rendered legally not binding during the first world war, when Montenegro and Servia, which had not ratified that convention, entered the war; since Art. 2 provided that it should be effective only if *all* belligerents were parties to the convention. However, it must be emphasized that to the extent that the Hague regulations are merely declaratory of existing *customary* international law, they were and are binding on all belligerents. For a discussion of the American practice during the first world war, see Flory: *Prisoners of War* (1942), p. 22. See also note 15 below.

13. The traditional view is that even after conversion of international law into domestic law enemy nationals are not immediately punishable. This view (based, however, on normal peacetime intercourse of nations) is that the injured State can demand a reparation from the offenders' State, which might include an obligation to punish them or to surrender them for trial, only in case of a refusal by that State to punish them. However, by Art. 228 of the Treaty of Versailles the Germans recognized the "right of the Allied and Associated Powers to bring before military tribunals persons accused of having committed acts in violation of the laws and customs of war"; and the American *Rules of Land Warfare* (Par. 346c) include among remedies of the injured belligerent "punishment of captured individual offenders," without reference to a prior demand for reparations in the nature of the enemy's obligation to punish its own war criminals.

14. The "written rules . . . are in large part but formal and specific applications of general principles of the unwritten rules. While solemnly obligatory as between the signatory powers, they may be said also to represent the consensus of modern international public opinion as to how belligerents and neutrals should conduct themselves in the particulars indicated. As a general rule they will be strictly observed and enforced by United States forces in the field, as far as applicable there, without regard to whether they are legally binding upon all the powers immediately concerned." *Rules of Land Warfare,* Sec. 5, p. 2.

15. Phillipson: *International Law and the Great War* (1915), p. 142. International "legislation" often only reinforces pre-existing common law:

"The fundamental elements, the guiding principles of the law of war, fortified as they have been by modern international Conventions and declarations, are by no means of recent growth. They have long possessed the force of law, and they have been repeatedly observed in earlier wars and in the wars of our own time. To allege that the non-ratification by a State of this or that treaty or of this or that article renders it inoperative — especially when the treaty or article formulates rules that had already been accepted by civilized States — is a vain pretension." Id. The provisions of the customary law of nations are occasionally more specific than those of the conventional law of warfare.

16. The Germans in both the last and the present wars have attempted to justify a great many atrocities on the ground of "military necessity." See J. H. Morgan: *The War Book of the German General Staff* (*Kriegsbrauch im Land Kriege*), (1915). However, "military necessity does not admit of cruelty — that is, the infliction of suffering merely for spite or revenge; nor of maiming or wounding except in combat; nor of torture to extort confessions. It does not admit of the use of poison in any way, nor of wanton devastation of a district. It admits of deception, but disclaims acts of perfidy. . . ." *Rules of Land Warfare*, Sec. 25, p. 7. For the views of an American apologist, see C. A. Anderson: "The Utility of the Proposed Trial and Punishment of Enemy Leaders," 37 *Am. Pol. Sc. Rev.* (1943), 1081, 1090, 1092. "Waiving the question of the expediency of trying to define the limits of military authority within another nation, it is word-chopping to try to decide when departure from the chivalric code of battle is justifiable. How can we evaluate the direness of the situation from the enemy's point of view?" It is necessary to warn the reader that this great concern for Germany's "direness of the situation," which by no stretch of the imagination could possibly justify the cold-blooded murder of countless innocent civilians by the most diabolical instruments of torture, does not emanate from Herr Joseph Goebbels but from an American "sociologist."

17. FM 27–10, 1940, Art. 5, p. 2.

18. This is true even of the German *Kriegsbrauch im Land Kriege.* See also Carpentier: *Les Lois de la Guerre Continentale,* (1913); Scott and Garner: *The German War Code Contrasted with the War Manuals of the United States, Great Britain, and France,* War Information Series No. 11, February, 1918.

19. The contention of the defense in the Saboteurs' Case (*Ex parte Quirin,* 317 U.S. 1, 1942) was that "once Congress made an act a criminal offense, the same act could not constitute an offense against the law of war and, *ipso facto,* the military commission lost jurisdiction. . . . The fallacy of this argument seems to be demonstrated by such a case as *U.S.* v. *Greene et al.* (146 Fed. 803, S.D. Ga., 1906), where the two civilian conspirators were tried by a district court, the military conspirator having already been tried by a general court-martial. The contention of the military offender that he was entitled to a civil trial has never been successfully main-

tained before courts or committees of Congress, although insisted upon down to the present day. One cannot select his own tribunal for trial nor insist on trial by the tribunal which can impose the lighter penalty." Munson: "The Arguments in the Saboteur Trial," 91 *Pa. L. Rev.* (1943), 239, 248–9.

20. Thus, for example, on August 23, 1865, a special military commission constituted in Washington, D.C., by the President, tried and convicted Captain Henry Wirz, Commandant of the Confederate military prison at Andersonville, Georgia, upon several charges, including "*murder in violation of the laws and customs of war*"; and he was hanged. Trial of Henry Wirz, Letter from Secretary of War ad Interim, House of Representatives, Ex. Doc. No. 23, 40th Cong., 2d Sess., 1868, p. 5.

21. See *State* v. *Gut.*, 13 Minn. (1868), 341, 357; 1 Hale, *Pleas of the Crown*, 59, 433; *Commonwealth* v. *Holland*, 62 Ky. (1 Duvall) 182. "The act being belligerent in the legal import of that comprehensive term, it was not robbery in the technical sense" (183). Bishop: *Criminal Law* (9th ed., 1923), Vol. I, Sec. 131, p. 86; id., Vol. II, Sec. 631 (1, 3), pp. 477–8.

22. See *State* v. *Cook,* Phillips (N.C., 1868), 535, 537. See also *State* v. *Blalock,* id., 242. While these decisions interpret a statute, their reasoning would apply generally.

23. See page 152.

24. The American *Rules of Land Warfare* (Par. 355) contain a special provision for "crimes punishable by all penal codes, such as arson, murder, maiming, assault, highway robbery, theft, burglary, fraud, forgery, and rape," and provide that "if committed by an American soldier in a hostile country against its inhabitants, [they] are not only punishable as at home, but a more severe punishment, if legally imposable, shall be preferred in cases in which the death penalty is not inflicted." But "offenses by armed forces" (Par. 347), which include bombardment of hospitals and other privileged buildings, poisoning of wells, and ill-treatment of inhabitants in occupied territory," may also be punished by death. And both the crimes mentioned in Par. 355 and offenses mentioned in Par. 347 are included in Chapter 11 under the general heading, "Penalties for Violations of the Laws of War," and by Par. 357 are made subject to the death penalty.

25. Viscount Maugham in the House of Lords, October 7, 1942, Parliamentary Debates, Vol. 124, p. 561.

26. "International law is a law grounded on the general assent of the nations of the world. . . . No rule can be abolished, or amplified or restricted in its operation, by a single nation or by a few nations or by private individuals acting in conjunction with a Government." Dissent of Nielsen, Commissioner, in *United States of America on behalf of International Fisheries Company* v. *United Mexican States,* Claims Commission United States and Mexico, 1931, 207. It shows to what a condition of blindness some publicists have been reduced when it is necessary to argue that a State cannot get away with mass murder by "legalizing" it under its own law and then clamoring for the "rule of law" when it is proposed to try its own mass murders. Compare the article by Anderson (note 16) with the following statements by a modern writer and a sixteenth-century authority: ". . . We judge men not by some special code that they create for themselves, but by the sense of right and wrong that is implanted in the breast of every rational being." Healy: "Rules of War," 91 *Law Journal* (1941), 76. "It is also a privilege of soldiers that their ignorance of the law is condoned, inasmuch as it is more properly their business to understand arms. But this does not apply to crimes; for nature herself admonishes them that what you would not like done to yourself, you should not do to others." Belli: *De Re Militari et Bello Tractatus,* Part VII, Chap. III.

27. Borchard: "Political Theory and International Law," in Merriam and Barnes: *A History of Political Theories* (1924), pp. 120, 130. (Italics supplied.)

28. "A ruler drunk with the consciousness of overwhelming power might venture to defy the moral sentiments of mankind. . . . He could not ride off on the plea of military necessity; for, as Professor Westlake has been careful to point out, we have evidence in the preamble of the Hague Conventions on the subject that 'military necessity has been taken into account in framing the Regulations, and has not been left outside to control and limit their application.' The powers distinctly say that the wording of the rules which they have drawn up 'has been inspired by the desire to diminish the evils of war as far as military necessities permit.' Those, therefore, who imagine that a state is free to ignore because of the exigencies of the moment any rule to which it has subscribed its signature are as erroneous in their reasoning as they are anarchical in their sentiments. The laws of war are made to be obeyed, not to be set aside

at pleasure." Lawrence: *The Principles of International Law* (7th ed., 1923), p. 374.

29. On pp. 111–113 a brief summary of the underlying general principles of the criminal law of civilized States is presented, to illustrate the sources of the law applicable by an International Criminal Court.

30. Pp. 70–76.

31. In fairness, it should be mentioned that the conduct of the Japanese armies during the Russo-Japanese War is generally regarded as having been above reproach from the point of view of the laws and customs of warfare. The same cannot be said of the behavior of German troops during the first World War.

32. The Polish Ministry of Information, 1942.

33. *German Occupation of Poland,* Republic of Poland, Ministry of Foreign Affairs, 1942. See also *The German Invasion of Poland,* Published by Authority of the Centre for Information and Documentation of the Polish Government, 1940.

34. Notes of November 25, 1941 and January 6, 1942, addressed by Commissar of Foreign Affairs V. M. Molotov to all ambassadors and ministers of the countries with which the USSR maintains diplomatic relations, in *Soviet War Documents,* Information Bulletin, Special Supplement, December 1943, Embassy of the Union of Soviet Socialist Republics, Washington, D.C.

35. *U.S. Dept. of State Bull.,* Vol. X, No. 242 (Feb. 12, 1944), pp. 168–75. See also Anthony Eden's statement in the House of Lords on March 10, 1942, regarding eyewitness reports of Japanese atrocities at Hong Kong; and Hsü: *The War Conduct of the Japanese* (1938), and *A New Digest of Japanese War Conduct* (1941).

36. The published reports of German atrocities in Belgium, France and inside Germany in World War I are too numerous to list. Germany has, of course, published counter-charges. The difference between the two points of view is that German atrocities and violations of the laws and customs of war and civilized criminal law were and are *official policies* of the government and military leaders (as evidenced by official legislation, orders and decrees) and therefore both premeditated and on a wholesale scale; atrocities by Allied soldiers were the occasional lawless acts of individual soldiers — something that occurs in any army or large gathering of men from all walks of life.

37. See *U.S. Dept. of State Bull.,* Vol. IX, No. 210 (July 3, 1943),

p. 1, announcing appointment of Hon. Herbert C. Pell as the representative of the United States on the United Nations Commission for the Investigation of War Crimes.

38. *U.S. Dept. of State Bull.*, Vol. IX, No. 214 (July 31, 1943), p. 62.

39. Annex to Hague Convention No. IV of 1907, which embodies Regulations respecting the laws and customs of war on land covered by that convention, Art. 23, Par. (c). This provision forms Par. 32 of the American *Rules of Land Warfare*, FM 27–10, 1940. (Hereinafter cited as *Rules.*)

40. Hague Convention, Art. 23, Par. (d); *Rules,* Par. 33. "As the right to kill an enemy in war is applicable only to such public enemies as make forcible resistance, this right necessarily ceases so soon as the enemy lays down his arms and surrenders his person or asks for quarter. 'Qui merci prie, merci doit avoir,' is an old maxim. After such surrender, the opposing belligerent has no power over his life, unless new rights are given by some new attempt at resistance. By the present rules of international law, quarter can be refused the enemy only in cases where those asking it have forfeited their lives by some crime against the conqueror under the laws and usages of war." Halleck's *International Law* (4th ed., 1908), Vol. II, p. 23.

41. Geneva Convention of July 27, 1929, relative to the treatment of prisoners of war, Art. 2; this forms Par. 73 of the American *Rules.*

42. Geneva (Red Cross) Convention of July 27, 1929, for the amelioration of the condition of the wounded and sick of armies in the field, Art. 1; *Rules,* Par. 174.

43. Geneva Convention of July 27, 1929, relative to the treatment of prisoners of war, Arts. 13, 14, 15; *Rules,* Pars. 86, 87, 88.

44. Id., Art. 46; *Rules,* Par. 119.

45. Id., Art. 16; *Rules,* Par. 89.

46. Annex to Hague Convention No. IV, October 18, 1907, embodying the Regulations respecting the laws and customs of war on land adopted by that convention, Art. 50; *Rules,* Par. 343.

47. *Rules,* Par. 359, p. 90. See also Par. 76 h, p. 18. (Italics supplied.) Par. 358 d of the *Rules,* provides that "Hostages taken and held for the declared purpose of insuring against unlawful acts by the enemy forces or people may be punished or put to death if the unlawful acts are nevertheless committed." But it goes on to say that "Reprisals against prisoners of war are expressly forbidden by

the Geneva convention of 1929. (See par. 73.)" But both Pars. 76 h and 359 state that "when a hostage is accepted he is treated as a prisoner of war."

48. Grotius: *De Jure Belli ac Pacis,* Chap. XI, Art. XVIII, Sec. 1. For an illuminative analysis of the status of law and practice on the taking of hostages in modern war, see Hammer and Salvin: "The Taking of Hostages in Theory and Practice," 38 *Am. J. Int. L.* (1944), 20–33.

49. Polish Ministry of Information, *Polish Fortnightly Review,* London, July 15, 1942, No. 48.

50. Official German announcement by Prague Wireless regarding the extermination of the village of Lidice, June 10, 1942, in Schwarzenberger: *International Law and Totalitarian Lawlessness* (1943), p. 153.

51. Official German announcement in *Der Neue Tag,* June 25, 1942, regarding the extermination of the village of Ležáky, in Schwarzenberger, op. cit., p. 154.

52. Hague Regulations, 1907, Art. 46; *Rules,* Par. 299.

53. *Netherlands News,* Vol. IX (1944), pp. 173–4.

54. *Hitler's Ten Year War on the Jews,* Institute of Jewish Affairs, New York (1943), pp. 300, 301.

55. Summarized by Daniel J. Brigham in telephonic report from Berne, Switzerland to *New York Times,* July 5, 1944.

56. *Information Bulletin,* Embassy of the Union of Soviet Socialist Republics, No. 143 (December 28, 1943), p. 2. I should have preferred to cite the official report of the Kharkov trial, but this was not available.

57. *Information Bulletin,* etc., No. 144 (December 30, 1943), p. 2.

58. From report signed by N. Derzhavin, chairman of the Soviet Scientists' Anti-Fascist Committee; Nikolai Burdenko, Academician and member of the Extraordinary State Commission for the Establishment and Investigation of the Crimes of the German-Fascist Invaders, and forty-three other members of the Soviet Academy of Sciences, *New York Times,* May 28, 1944.

59. *Soviet War Documents,* op. cit., pp. 125–6.

60. Id., p. 125.

61. Id.

62. See Anderson in note 16.

63. *Report of the Committee on Alleged German Outrages,* presided over by Viscount Bryce (1915), pp. 39, 40, 43–4, 61.

CHAPTER IV

1. We may profitably contrast the callous German-Japanese ignoring of United Nations' protests regarding the mistreatment of prisoners of war and civilians with General Washington's courteous and sincere reply to General Clinton in 1780 regarding the treatment of British prisoners of war: "I am exceedingly obliged by the favorable sentiments you are pleased to entertain of my disposition towards prisoners; and I beg leave to assure you, Sir, that I am sensible of the treatment which those under your direction have generally experienced. There is nothing more contrary to my wishes, than that men in captivity should suffer the least unnecessary severity or want; and I shall take immediate action to transmit a copy of the report you enclose . . . to the commandant at Charlottesville, with orders to inquire into the facts, and to redress grievances wherever they may exist." George Washington: *Writings* (coll. and ed. by W. C. Ford, 1889–91), Vol. VIII, pp. 360–1. Compare the correspondence in the *Baralong* case, 10 *Am. J. Int. L.* (Supp., 1916), 79 et seq.

2. Oppenheim: *International Law* (6th ed. by Lauterpacht, 1940), p. 448. The German abuse of the instrument of reprisal during the present war as well as the last is notorious.

3. It has been argued that "collective responsibility" (i.e., the State's responsibility) "as a rule" excludes the responsibility of individual violators of the laws and customs of warfare. Kelsen: "Collective and Individual Responsibility in International Law with Particular Regard to the Punishment of War Criminals," 31 *Cal. L.R.* (1943), 530, 550. But this is not necessarily so; the individual can be criminally responsible; the State, at least civilly. Even if demand for satisfaction must first be made upon the State whose nationals have violated the laws and customs of warfare, before the injured State can punish such violators as fall into its hands, this condition has abundantly been fulfilled in the case of the German and the Japanese governments.

4. E.g., the trial of war offenders after the close of the American Civil War and the British-Boer War, as well as the trial of war offenders by France during the first World War, and the Versailles Peace Treaty provision for the postwar trial of Germans in Allied military tribunals.

5. See, for example, the articles by Manner: "The Legal Nature

and Punishment of Criminal Acts of Violence Contrary to the Laws of War," 37 *Am. J. Int. L.* (1943), 407, 420 et seq.; and Kelsen, op. cit.

6. See *Coleman* v. *Tennessee,* 97 U.S. 509 (1878), and Finch: "Jurisdiction of Local Courts to Try Enemy Persons for War Crimes," 14 *Am. J. Int. L.* (1920), 218–23; Manner: op. cit., p. 420, note 58.

7. For example, Hall: *A Treatise on International Law* (8th ed., 1924), Sec. 135, pp. 495–6.

8. Schwarzenberger: *International Law and Totalitarian Lawlessness* (1943), p. 61. In this scholarly work the author correctly points out that the fact that the privilege of exclusive trial in the courts of the occupying power does not extend to illegal acts of warfare was not sufficiently taken into account in the well-known case of *Coleman* v. *Tennessee,* 97 U.S. 509 (1878). In appraising this famous decision it must also be borne in mind that it was a Southern (Confederate) State that sought to subject a Northern (Union) officer to trial. One wonders whether the reasoning of the Supreme Court would have been the same if the case had involved the attempted trial by a Northern State court of a former officer of the Confederacy. See also Mérignhac: "De la Sanction des Infractions au Droit des Gens," 24 *Rev. Gen. de Droit Int. Public* (1917), 5, 33 et seq.

9. See Chap. III, note 13, and note 4 of present chapter; Mérignhac, op. cit., pp. 35–6.

10. See Chap. III, note 19.

11. An illustration is furnished by the "Terms of Surrender of the Boer Forces in the Field" at the close of the South African War, where, although it was guaranteed that no civil or criminal measures would be taken against any of the ordinary burghers who surrendered under the terms, "the benefit of this clause will not extend to certain acts contrary to the usages of war which have been notified by the Commander-in-Chief to the Boer generals, and which shall be tried by court martial immediately after the close of hostilities." See Parl. Papers, South Africa (1902), Comd. 1096. However, since the Boer War was terminated through *subjugation,* the Terms of Surrender did not, technically, constitute a treaty of peace.

12. *Commission Report,* p. 123.

13. "The German Government recognizes the right of the Allied and Associated Powers to bring before military tribunals persons accused of having committed acts in violation of the laws and cus-

toms of war. Such persons shall, if found guilty, be sentenced to punishments laid down by law. This provision will apply notwithstanding any proceedings or prosecution before a tribunal in Germany or in the territory of her Allies. . . ." "Treaty of Peace with Germany," Art. 228 13 *Am. J. Int. L.* (Supp.), (1919), 151, 250–1.

14. Viewed from the standpoint of ordinary criminal law, the acts that violate the prohibitions of the laws and customs of warfare are also (with a few exceptions such as abusing a flag of truce) the familiar domestic crimes of murder, theft, arson, rape, kidnapping, etc. They could therefore be prosecuted as ordinary crimes, even though committed during wartime.

15. Manner, op. cit., p. 425, argues that because the Allies assented to the trial of German war criminals in German national courts, the precedent for their trial by the Allies was destroyed. However, the Allies gave this consent merely as a matter of grace and expediency, and retained the right to retry the accused, if not satisfied with the outcome, although they never exercised that right. Nor did the Declaration of Amnesty appended to the Treaty of Lausanne of July 24, 1923, which abolished the penal clauses of the unratified Treaty of Sèvres of August 10, 1920 (which had provided for postwar trials in foreign military tribunals or in an international court of Turkish violators of the law of war and of humanity) necessarily vacate the position taken by the Allies at the Peace Conference. Moreover, if a precedent could be established at Versailles it can also be established in the forthcoming peace treaty. Precedents must have some beginning.

16. The armistice agreement and the treaty can also eliminate any question of whether war criminals found among *surrendered* Axis troops fall within the category of captured prisoners of war who are subject to trial for war crimes. The Lord Chancellor of England has made the suggestion in the House of Lords (October 8, 1942) that surrender of the war criminals for trial "before the conclusion of peace" should be one of the conditions of the armistice agreement.

CHAPTER V

1. See note 8, Chap. VII.

2. Grotius: *De Jure Belli ac Pacis*, Book III, Chaps. XI, XVI, by strong implication; Spaight: *War Rights on Land* (1911), 462, and authorities therein cited.

3. Geneva Convention of July 27, 1929, relative to treatment of prisoners of war, Treaty Series No. 846, 47 Stat. 233, Arts. 47, 60, 61, 62, 63, 64. The Department of State protested violations by the Japanese of these and related articles in the case of captured American aviators.

4. The status of "prisonership" may, under customary international law, be forfeited by the commission of war crimes. Flory: *Prisoners of War* (1942), 37. "There appears to be sufficient evidence to conclude that, at least in Anglo-American law, prisoners of war have received for several hundred years national treatment when accused of crimes cognizable by civil courts. Until the latter part of the nineteenth century, prisoners of war had no guarantees against less than national treatment from military courts or in cases punishable by summary procedure, except in so far as the general principles of humanity tended to protect them. The offenses to which the detaining state's ordinary military rules could not apply tended by the end of the nineteenth century to have penalties fixed by international law. Since the beginning of the twentieth century there has been a trend in treaty law to establish, in conjunction with the rule of national treatment, a minimum international standard." Id., 93.

5. "Report of the Subcommittee on the Trial and Punishment of War Criminals," 37 *Am. J. Int. L.* (1943), 663, 666.

6. *U.S. Dept. of State Bull.*, Vol. VII, No. 165 (August 22, 1942), pp. 709, 710.

7. *New York Times,* September 9, 1942, p. 4.

8. *U.S. Dept. of State Bull.*, Vol. IV, No. 228 (November 6, 1943), pp. 310–11.

9. Information Bulletin Embassy of the U.S.S.R., Washington, Nos. 143, 144 (December 28, 30, 1943).

10. See Glueck: "By What Courts Shall War Offenders be Tried?" LVI *Harv. L. Rev.* (1943), 1059, 1063 et seq. Cf. Manner: "The Legal Nature and Punishment of Criminal Acts of Violence Contrary to the Laws of War," 37 *Am. J. Int. L.* (1943), 407, 422–5.

11. Glueck, op. cit., 1061.

12. ". . . At present, we have no power to try Germans for the murders of any British people, or other people not being Germans, in Germany or in German-occupied territory. I want to make this perfectly clear. A German who has committed the crime of murdering one or more Englishmen in a German prison camp, or otherwise

in Germany, may come here, after the war, and live in luxury in a Mayfair hotel, disporting himself in this city without anybody having the right to touch him. Our Courts have no jurisdiction to try him for that offence. That is so in other countries. I believe it is the case in the United States of America, *mutatis mutandis.*" Viscount Maugham in the House of Lords, October 7, 1942, Parliamentary Debates, Lords, Vol. 124, 555, 564. Cf. statement of Lord Chancellor Simon: ". . . I take it to be perfectly well-established International Law that the laws of war permit a belligerent commander to punish by means of his Military Courts any hostile offender against the laws and customs of war who may fall into his hands wherever be the place where the crime was committed." Id., 578–9. See the excellent studies, "Jurisdiction with Respect to Crime," E. D. Dickinson, Reporter, *Research in International Law* under the Auspices of the Faculty of the Harvard Law School, M. O. Hudson, Director, Supp. to *Am. J. Int. L.*, Vol. XXIX, (1935); and G. Hackworth: *Digest of International Law,* Vol. II (1941), pp. 179 et seq.

13. Chap. IX.

14. For instance, Congress has enacted legislation giving jurisdiction to American courts for such crimes as perjury before an American diplomatic or consular officer, counterfeiting of American currency, stamps, passports, etc., perjury or fraud in applications for immigration, etc. See e.g., 11 Stat. 61 (1856); 43 Stat. 165 (1924), 8 U.S.C. Sec. 220 (1940). Cf. *United States* v. *Bowman,* 260 U.S. 94, 98 (1922); *United States ex rel. Majka* v. *Palmer,* 67 F. (2d) 147 (C.C.A. 7th, 1933). Other nations have also taken it upon themselves to modify in respect to various crimes the traditionally fundamental theory of the strict territoriality of jurisdiction.

15. German law in respect to the trial of foreigners provides that, irrespective of the law of the State where the act was committed, German criminal law is applicable to those who have *abroad* committed one of several types of crime, including offenses committed against a German official, soldier, or member of the Empire's Work Service (*Reichsarbeitsdienst*) during or in respect to the execution of their duties; capital or high treason against Germany; crimes committed by means of explosives; disclosure of trade or manufacturing secrets of a German enterprise; counterfeiting coins; illicit drug traffic, etc. Decree of May 6, 1940, *Reichsgesetzbuch* 1. I, 754, Secs. 4, 5.

16. Practically all, if not all, judicial decisions and treaties adher-

ing to the territorial principle deal with normal, peacetime relations of friendly sovereigns.

17. Digest of the Opinions of the Judge Advocate General of the Army, 1912 (1917), 511 (VIII B).

18. Glueck, op. cit., 1059, 1065–6.

19. Decree of the Reichspräsident (March 21, 1933), laws of August 7, 1934 (after Hindenburg's death), of February 28, 1935 (after return of the "Saarland"), April 23, 1936 and April 30, 1938 (after reunion of Austria with Germany). In justification of the "blood purge" in which Röhm and others within the Nazi party were liquidated by Hitler, in a law of July 3, 1943 (RGB 1. I, 529) the Nazi Government declared all acts committed during June 30, July 1 and July 2, 1934 to suppress alleged treasonable attacks to be "lawful as self-defense of the State."

20. There is one class of crimes in connection with which the validity of United Nations' jurisdiction must be in doubt: *i.e.*, crimes by German, Hungarian, Italian, Japanese or other Axis nationals against their fellow-nationals, particularly in the earliest stages of Axis governments. Such offenses may be regarded as domestic crimes, the affair, therefore, of the respective enemy countries themselves, and subject to trial by their governments when they are permitted by the United Nations' occupying forces to administer their own justice. In such cases both the territorial and the nationality principles of jurisdiction are applicable; and even under our comprehensive definition of war crimes in this era of Germanic "total war," the nationals of Axis lands attacked by their fellow-nationals cannot be regarded as enemy "belligerents" in the sense of international law. In the absence of an "international bill of rights" and a code of international law providing sanctions for violations of such rights, such offenders have to be prosecuted under domestic law by the governments that will succeed the Nazis and Fascists now in power in Axis lands, exactly as Quislings and collaborationists are being dealt with by the French and other peoples restored to independence. The law to be applied would then be a matter of local determination. How the successor governments fulfill their moral and legal obligations to punish Germans, Hungarians, Rumanians, Japanese and other Axis subjects for the crimes against their fellows will be perhaps the most revealing index of the extent of the postwar change of heart the Axis peoples will profess to have

undergone. In the meantime, there are enough other Axis criminals to keep United Nations tribunals busy for many years to come.

21. Compare the statement of Viscount Maugham in the House of Lords, October 7, 1942: ". . . There are offences which cannot, I think, effectively be tried before national Courts. I will mention a few: crimes against persons, and in particular against Jews, who have been deprived of any nationality; cases of mass murder as the consequence of an order, such as the drastic removal of foodstuffs ordered by a German officer or by some sort of German tribunal, necessarily causing death by exposure; orders for the removal of numbers of young women, sometimes to an unknown destination and obviously for the purposes of prostitution; cases where two or more Courts of different Allied States have jurisdiction; cases where it is uncertain which of two or more such Courts have the necessary jurisdiction; and finally, cases where, owing to political unrest in the country where the crime was committed, it may be difficult to hold a proper trial, and that country may request the International Tribunal to accept the duty of trying the case. Those are only examples. In all these cases it seems to be desirable that a special International Tribunal, however cumbrous its machinery may be, should be set up and given the necessary powers, rather than that the criminal should escape for lack of a suitable tribunal. I think that almost all the international jurists in this country at the present time — and there is a great number of them — are at one on this matter." Parliamentary Debates, Lords, Vol. 124, 565–6.

22. The politico-legal justification for the right to prosecute Germans and other Axis nationals in an international tribunal for crimes committed against "stateless" persons or those whose nationality cannot be conclusively established springs from necessity coupled with the duty of the Family of Nations to enforce the laws of warfare when a recalcitrant State has demonstrated its unwillingness or inability to do so. While international law impliedly limits sanctions to punishment for war crimes committed against *belligerents* and their subjects, the status of stateless persons is exceptional; they are not nationals of any particular belligerent State and are, in effect, universal aliens. It is contrary to justice and reason to leave them in a politico-legal vacuum. The same motives of humanity and good sense which brought about the invention of "Nansen passports" in the case of denationalized persons call appropriately for placing the vindication of law and justice in the

case of injuries to stateless persons under the general auspices and jurisdiction of law-abiding nations operating through an international tribunal. The Moscow Statement of November 1, 1943 spoke of "the case of German criminals whose offenses have no particular geographical localization" as being those who are to "be punished by joint decision of the Governments of the Allies." The United Nations can appropriately add to this category offenses that have no particular *nationality* "localization."

23. *Commission Report,* pp. 95, 121–2.

24. Treaty of Peace with Germany, Art. 229, 13 *Am. J. Int. L.* (Supp.) (1919), 151, 251.

25. *Commission Report,* p. 142.

26. *Commission Report,* p. 146: ". . . the various states have declared certain acts violating the laws and customs of war to be crimes, affixing punishments to their commission, and providing military courts or commissions within the respective states possessing jurisdiction over such offences."

27. What is called "military government" in the United States is usually called "martial law" by the British, and is referred to as such by Continental writers.

28. Letter to author from General deBaer, Chairman, Commission I for Questions Concerned with the Liquidation of the War (formerly known as "Commission on War Criminals"), London International Assembly, League of Nations Union. Employment of military courts would run into difficulties not only in Belgium but in other countries of the United Nations as well. Thus Viscount Maugham, the learned former Lord Chancellor of England, who has given much study to this problem, said in the House of Lords: "I see great difficulty in attempting to try the ordinary crimes by Military Courts, as suggested in Articles 228 and 229, unless, indeed, there should be a permanent occupation of Germany. In our law there is no Military Court with such a power. Martial law, of course, is not law at all, and our Military Law does not concern itself with such crimes as we are here considering. It seems to me much better, as regards offences against British subjects, to make provision for the trial of the alleged offenders before our own High Courts with their traditions and their practice and with experienced Judges to decide the matters." Parliamentary Debates, Lords, Vol. 124 (October 7, 1942), 555, 561–2.

29. However, that law would, in essence, be but a domestic-law implementation of the general international laws and customs of warfare or an embodiment of the general principles of criminal law observable by most civilized nations.

30. Root: "The Outlook for International Law," *Proceedings of the American Society of International Law,* 1915, pp. 9–10.

CHAPTER VI

1. A court of this scope would perhaps have to be set up by international convention rather than by executive agreement, especially if it were to function after the war had been concluded. It might therefore entail, for the United States, the problem of obtaining ratification of the treaty by two-thirds of the Senate. The United States could also be engaged, however, by a joint congressional resolution implemented by executive agreement. See McClure: *International Executive Agreements* (1941); Corwin: *The President: Office and Powers* (1941); Holt: *Treaties Defeated by the Senate* (1933); Laski: *The American Presidency, An Interpretation* (1940).

2. One might tentatively include in this class such offenses as acts of political terrorism, threatening a war of aggression in violation of treaty obligations, construction of war materials prohibited by international agreement, crimes against the currency of a member of the family of nations, international white slavery and drug traffic, piracy and acts assimilated thereto, and (envisaging a closer collaboration of nations in the propagation of basic democratic ideas) such crimes against "international public order" as violations of the provisions of an "international bill of rights."

3. For a history of the idea of an International Criminal Court and a brief summary of the literature, see Pella: *"La Cour Pénale Internationale et la répression du terrorisme"* 18 Rev. De Droit Pénal et de Crim. (1938), 409. See also 2 Permanent Court of International Justice, Advisory Committee of Jurists, *Procès-Verbaux of the Proceedings of the Committee,* June 16–July 24, 1920, (1920), 129, 142, 209–12, 498–516, 521, 748; Phillimore: "An International Criminal Court and the Resolutions of the Committee of Jurists," *Brit. Y. B. Int. L.,* 1922–3, pp. 79–85; Bellot: "Draft Statute for the Permanent International Criminal Court," in *Int. Law Assoc., Rep. of 33rd Conference* (1924), p. 75; Pella: *La Criminalité Collective des Etats et le Droit Pénal de L'Avenir* (1925); Politis: *The New Aspects of International Law* (1928); Von Weber: *Internationale*

Strafgerichtsbarkeit (1934); Lévitt: "A Proposed Code of International Criminal Law," 6 *Rev. Int. de Droit Pénal* (1929), 19; "*Procès-Verbaux des travaux de la commission chargée de la rédaction d'un projet de code pénal international,*" 8 *Rev. Int. de Droit Pénal* (1931), 191.

4. In connection with the Turkish massacres, Art. 230 of the Treaty of Sèvres at the close of World War I provided that "In the event of the League of Nations having created in sufficient time a tribunal competent to deal with the said massacres, the Allied Powers reserve . . . the right to bring the accused persons . . . before such tribunal, and the Turkish Government undertakes equally to recognize such tribunal."

5. Permanent Court of International Justice Advisory Committee of Jurists, *Procès-Verbaux of the Proceedings of the Committee* (1920), p. 521 (hereinafter cited as *Proceedings*).

6. Mr. Root differentiated his views as to "jurisdiction over international crimes in time of peace," for which "an exact definition of such offences is indispensable," from "*the application of laws of war to acts of war.*" *Proceedings,* pp. 505–6. (Italics supplied.)

7. League of Nations. The Records of the First Assembly. Plenary Meetings, 1920, p. 764. Compare pp. 110–113 hereof.

8. *Commission Report,* p. 95.

9. Pp. 21, 85 above.

10. *Commission Report,* p. 122. This formulation is part of the preamble to the Hague conventions respecting the laws and customs of war on land.

11. Arts. 2, 3, 13, 14, 15, 16, Convention for the Prevention and Punishment of Terrorism, opened for signature at Geneva, November 16, 1937, in Hudson: *International Legislation* (1941), Vol. VII, pp. 862, 865–6, 869, 870–1.

12. Art. 2, Convention for the Creation of an International Criminal Court, opened for signature at Geneva, November 16, 1937, in Id., pp. 878, 880.

13. Opened to signature on November 16, 1937, the first convention was signed by the representatives of 24 States, the second by those of 13. A ratification of the first was deposited only by India. Mexico, in 1939, wished to accede to it with a reservation regarding extradition for political crimes. Evidently no ratification of the second convention was deposited. Perhaps the gathering clouds of World War II were mainly responsible for the failure of this project.

14. Others have been discussed at various conferences of the International Law Association in Buenos Aires, 1922, Stockholm, 1924, and Vienna, 1926. See Levy: "The Law and Procedure of War Crime Trials," 37 *Am. Pol. Sci. Rev.* (1943), 1052, 1070–6.

15. P. 83 above.

16. See p. 37 above for our definition of war criminals. The usually more general concepts of the customary law permit of greater adaptation to the needs of prosecutions in connection with modern warfare.

17. Schwarzenberger: *International Law and Totalitarian Lawlessness* (1943), p. 79.

18. German Observations, May 29, 1919, Temperley: *A History of the Peace Conference of Paris* (1920), Vol. II, p. 305.

19. *Commission Report,* pp. 145–6.

20. Id., p. 146.

21. In the *Hudson* case the Supreme Court was considering the question whether, as an inherent power, the circuit courts established by Congress could exercise a common-law jurisdiction in a criminal case, in the absence of a specific statute making the act involved a crime. It was held that when Congress creates a court with limited jurisdiction and confines its operations to "certain specific objects," that court cannot with propriety "assume to itself a jurisdiction much more extended, in its nature very indefinite. . . ." If the Constitution *had* empowered the federal circuit courts to take cognizance of common-law offenses, or if the defendant had been tried in a *state* court in the absence of a statute, he could not then have protested that this was a trial for an act that had not previously been prohibited as a crime.

22. The case arose under the Federal Judiciary Act of 1789, Chap. 20, Secs. 9, 11, giving the Federal courts jurisdiction of all "crimes and offenses cognizable under the authority of the United States." The original draft of this Act which was submitted to Congress gave these courts jurisdiction of all "crimes and offences cognizable under the authority of the United States *and defined by the laws of the same,*" but the last eight words of the draft were not approved by Congress and did not therefore appear in the statute. This significant change in the draft of the bill was not known until Charles Warren discovered the original draft in the archives of the United States some twenty years ago. "Had the Supreme Court consulted these Senate Files, it is probable that the decisions in *United*

States v. Hudson, in 1812, and *United States v. Coolidge,* in 1816, might have been otherwise than they were." Warren: "New Light on the History of the Federal Judiciary Act of 1789," 37 *Harv. L. Rev.* (1923), 49, 51, 73. It should also be borne in mind that Madison was President of the United States from 1809 to 1817 and the Jeffersonian party to which he belonged did not wish to enlarge the powers of the Federal Government more than was necessary. See also Bishop: *Criminal Law* (9th ed., 1923), Vol. I, pp. 129–32.

23. Stephen: *A Digest of the Criminal Law* (1877), p. xi.

24. "But where the individuals of any state violate this general law, it is then the interest as well as the duty of the government under which they live, to animadvert upon them with a becoming severity, that the peace of the world may be maintained. For in vain would nations in their collective capacity observe these universal rules, if private subjects were at liberty to break them at their own discretion. . . ." Blackstone: *Commentaries on the Laws of England,* Vol. IV, Ch. V, p. 68.

25. The American Basic Field Manual, *Rules of Land Warfare,* provides specifically that among the remedies open to an injured belligerent "in the event of clearly established violation of the laws of war" is the "punishment of captured individual offenders." In the Treaty of Versailles (Art. 228) the Germans acknowledged the right of an injured State to punish violators of the laws and customs of war.

26. Schätzel: *"Bestrafungen nach Kriegsbrauch," Archiv fur Militärrecht,* Achter Band (1920), pp. 13–24.

27. Verdoss: *"Die völkerrechtswidrige Kriegshandlung und das Strafanspruch der Staaten* (1920), pp. 30–2.

28. It is an "orthodox principle that individuals are not subjects of the law of nations"; there is an "absence of international war crimes chargeable either to the collectivity of persons forming a nation or to its members individually. . . . In the absence of international authority, international conventions on the conduct of warfare as a rule make it the duty of States to transform or incorporate their provisions into national regulations and to enforce the latter against the persons subject to their control." Manner: "The Legal Nature and Punishment of Criminal Acts of Violence Contrary to the Laws of War," 37 *Am. J. Int. L.* (1943), 407–10.

29. The obligations imposed on the High Contracting Parties to issue instructions to the troops in conformity with the Regulations of

the Conventions of 1899 and 1907 by no means constitute a recognition that in the absence of such domestic instructions a State may not legitimately punish violators of the rules of civilized warfare — be they their own subjects or enemy subjects who fall into their hands — regardless of existence or non-existence of legislation. The provisions of the conventions merely stress the fairness of a State's giving notice to its troops. The basis for punishment is a matter of domestic law. See Winthrop: *Military Law and Precedents* (2nd ed., 1920), pp. 291-2 for the effect of ignorance of the military code on the part of soldiers.

30. The law of nations "is in truth common law; or, rather, the common law has appropriated the law of nations, making it a part of itself." Bishop, op. cit., p. 356.

31. A convincing literature in opposition to the majority view has in recent years grown up. See, especially, Politis: *The New Aspects of International Law* (1928), (and references therein); Verdross: *Die völkerrechtswidrige Kriegshandlung und der Strafanspruch der Staaten,* (1920), pp. 33 et seq.; Schwarzenberger: "War Crimes and the Problem of an International Criminal Court," *Czechoslovak Yearbook of International Law* (1942), pp. 67-9; Aufricht: "Personality in International Law," 37 *Am. Pol. Sci. Rev.* (1943), 217, 235-43; Kelsen: "Collective and Individual Responsibility in International Law with Particular Regard to the Punishment of War Criminals," 31 *Cal. L. Rev.* (1943), 531, 534-8. See also intimations to like effect in *Ex parte* Quirin, 317 U.S. 1, 27-28 (1942), the *"Saboteurs' Case."*

32. Politis and Kelsen, in the works cited in the prior note, give various examples, largely, however, from conventional (written) international law. Of course States may agree to make violations of their international covenants by individuals mutually punishable. See the convention mentioned in note 11 above and text thereto.

33. East's *Pleas of the Crown* (1806), Vol. II, pp. 821-2.

34. See Russell: *Crimes and Misdemeanors* (3rd ed., 1843), pp. 246-7; Trial of George Gordon, XXII Howell's *State Trials* (1787), Vol. XXII, p. 214; Trial of John Vint, 1 Blackstone, 510. Blackstone, *Commentaries* (1825 ed.), p. 63, although referring to statutes involving "offenses [by individuals] against the law of nations," stresses the fact that "acts of parliament, which have from time to time been made to enforce this universal law, or to facilitate the execution of its decisions, are not to be considered as introductive

of any new rule, but merely as declaratory of the old fundamental constitutions of the kingdom, without which it would cease to be a part of the civilized world."

35. *Respublica* v. *De Longchamps*, 1 Dallas (1784), 110, 111, 113, 114, 117.

36. Evidently the Supreme Court has never reversed the *Hudson* case. One of its most recent statements approving its doctrine is found in *Donnelly* v. *United States*, 276 U.S. 505, 511 (1928). But see Bishop, op. cit., Sec. 484, p. 356: "Any conduct in one of our citizens, or in a foreigner within our borders is punishable which tends to involve our government in difficulty with a foreign power. The offense, with us, would be against the United States, not the State; and should be indictable in the United States courts without the aid of a statute, but such is not the common professional understanding. Under the English unwritten law it is so . . . libelling a foreign prince or other person in official station abroad, and the like, are offenses against the law of nations, therefore punishable without statutory aid where common law crimes prevail." And again: "In just principle . . . the unwritten law of crime as applied in [localities beyond state limits] by the . . . unwritten law of nations, must, in all places not within State limits, and not within some exceptional rule, constitute a common law of the United States. Accordingly, in reason, the United States tribunals would appear to have common law cognizance of offenses upon the high seas, not defined by statutes; and of all other offenses within the proper cognizance of the criminal courts of a nation, committed beyond the jurisdiction of any particular State." Id., Sec. 201, pp. 131–2. And consider the statement by J. Story in *United States* v. *Coolidge*, 1 Gallis, 488, 495 (1813): "Whatever room . . . there may be for doubt as to what common-law offenses are offenses against the United States, there can be none as to admiralty offenses."

37. *Ex parte Quirin*, 317 U.S. 1 (1942).

38. Id., pp. 29–30. See also Ops. Atty. Gen. (1869) 297, 299–300, 310. Manner, op. cit., p. 415, is in error in claiming that the *Quirin* case holding to the effect that the law of war may sometimes (in the words of Professor Hyde) "address its injunctions to individuals by attaching an internationally illegal quality to particular acts" is a mere dictum. Both the briefs (pp. 7, 13–14) and the opinion (p. 29) recognize the relevancy of the point in question to the major issue presented to the court.

39. Hyde: "Aspects of the Saboteur Cases," 37 *Am. J. Int. L.*
(1943), 88. (Italics supplied.) One of the arguments of the defense
was that there is a "serious question as to whether there was any
such offense as the violation of the law of war." This was probably
based on the theory that inasmuch as Congress has been given specific power by the Constitution (Art. I, Sec. 8) to define offenses
against the law of nations, there can be no offense of this kind in the
absence of a specific statute, in accordance with the *Hudson* case.

40. 16 *Am. J. Int. L.* (1922), 721. (Italics supplied.)

41. *Aktenstück* Nr. 2584, Drucksachen des Reichstags, Wahlperi-
ode 1920 (Bd. 5, 6), 2542, 2568. So, also, on other occasions some of
the decisions of German courts "seem to indicate a willingness on
the part of some German judges, at least, to apply customary international law directly." Masters: *International Law in National
Courts* (1932), p. 46.

42. An interesting instance of the prosecution of a formerly high-
placed official for violations of the laws and customs of warfare grew
out of the revolt led by Arabi Pasha against the Khedive of Egypt
(July 1882), whose authority was supported by the British fleet off
Alexandria. Arabi was prosecuted in an Egyptian court but under
procedure somewhat modified to conform to British standards. He
pleaded guilty to one charge — rebellion — and the death sentence
was commuted to degradation of rank, confiscation of property and
exile; he was found not guilty of the following offense: "Ahmed
Arabi is accused . . . of having, *against the laws of war and in violation of the right of nations,* hoisted the white flag at Alexandria on
the morning of July 12, and of having at the same moment withdrawn his troops, and ordered the pillage and firing of the town of
Alexandria." Halleck's *International Law* (4th ed., 1908), Vol. II,
p. 351, n. 1. See also 75 British and Foreign State Papers (1883–4),
672–5; 74 id. (1882–3), 591; and compare van Bemmelen: *L'Egypte
et l'Europe* (1884), Vol. II, pp. 328 et seq.

43. The idea that violations of the laws and customs of warfare
constitute in effect *international crimes,* subject to the universal jurisdiction of the belligerent Powers and triable in either municipal
courts or an international tribunal set up for the purpose by the
great majority of the belligerents, evidently came to the Versailles
Commission from the Law Officers of the Crown who presented
such an arguments to the Imperial War Cabinet. See Lloyd George:
Memoirs of the Peace Conference (1939), Vol. I, pp. 59 et seq., for

Lord Birkenhead's eloquent argument in support of the trial of the ex-Kaiser, particularly for "responsibility for the invasion of Belgium in breach of International Law and for all the consequent criminal acts which took place," and "in the matter of unrestricted submarine warfare," not only the sinking of the *Lusitania,* but the fact that "since then thousands of women and children, in our clear and frequently expressed view, have been brutally murdered. . . . It is surely vital that if ever there is another war, whether in ten or fifteen years, or however distant it may be, those responsible on both sides for the conduct of that war should be made to feel that unrestricted submarine warfare has been so branded with the punitive censure of the whole civilized world that it has definitely passed into the category of international crime. 'If I do it and fail,' the Tirpitz of the next war must say, 'I too shall pay for it in my own person.'" Id., pp. 63–4.

44. Cohn: "The Problem of War Crimes To-day," 26 *Trans. of the Grotius Society* (1941), 125, 143. See also Schwarzenberger, op. cit., pp. 78–9.

45. For a scholarly analysis of this maxim, see Hall: "Nulla Pœna Sine Lege," 47 *Yale L. J.* (1937), 165. See also *Consistency of Certain Danzig Legislative Decrees with the Constitution of the Free City,* Permanent Court of International Justice, Advisory Opinion, December 4, 1935. Publications of the Court, Series A./B. No. 65.

46. Notice, however, that ignorance of the law cannot usually serve as a defense in a domestic tribunal, whether civil or military. See Winthrop: *Military Law and Precedents* (2nd ed., 1920), p. 291. "Ignorance of these ordinances will not be admitted as a defense." From form of "Ordinances, Army of the United States," to be issued by the Military Government to the people of occupied territory, in *Military Government,* U.S. War Department, Basic Field Manual (FM 27–5, 1940, p. 33).

47. This was taken for granted by the American representatives on the Versailles Commission on Responsibilities.

48. See *Reg.* v. *Leslie,* 8 Cox C. C. 269 (1860); *Barronet's Case,* 1 E. and B. 1; Kenny: *Outlines of Criminal Law* (ed. by Webb., 1907), p. 63.

49. Grotius: *De Jure Belli ac Pacis,* Book III, Chap. XI ("Moderation Concerning the Right of Killing Men in a Just War"), Sec. 16, Cl. 1. Compare the following: "A wrong opinion has been entertained concerning the conduct of *Lord Chief Justice Holt* and the

Court of King's Bench in *England,* in the noted case of the Russian Ambassador. They detained the offenders, after conviction, in prison, from term to term, until the Czar *Peter* was satisfied, without ever proceeding to *judgment;* and from this it has been inferred, that the Court doubted, whether they could inflict *any punishment* for an infraction of the law of nations. But this was not the reason. The court never doubted, that the law of nations formed a part of the law of *England,* and that a violation of this general law could be punished by them; but no punishment less than *death* would have been thought by the Czar an *adequate* reparation for the arrest of his Ambassador: *This* punishment they could not inflict, and *such* a sentence as they could have given, He might have thought a fresh insult. Another expedient was therefore fallen upon. However the princes of the world, at this day, are more enlightened, and do not require impracticable nor unreasonable reparations for injuries of this kind." *Respublica* v. *De Longchamps,* 1 Dallas (1784), 111, 117.

50. Holland: *The Laws and Customs of War on Land as Defined by the Hague Convention of 1899* (1904), p. 45. See also *Institut de Droit International,* "Manuel des lois de la guerre" (1880), Art. 84 and Preamble, 5 *An. de l'Inst. de Droit Internat.* (1881), 156 et seq.; Bartlett: "Liability for Official War Crimes," 35 *L. Q. Rev.* (1919), 177, 186. "A military commission may impose any lawful and appropriate sentence, including death or life imprisonment." *Military Government,* op. cit., pp. 15, 51.

51. A basic alteration was made in the German criminal code Sec. 2 of the law of June 28, 1935 (Reichsgesetzeblatt 1, I, 839), which permits an almost total destruction of the principle: "nullum crimen sine lege," and which has nothing in common with the alleged *ex post facto* quality of application of the common law of nations: "Whoever commits an act which the law declares to be punishable or which *deserves punishment* according to the principles of the criminal law and to the *sound sentiments of the people,* will be punished. If none of the sections is directly applicable, the act will be punished according to that section the principle of which best applies to the act concerned." To this should be added the unanimously approved resolution of the *Reichstag* enabling the Führer, *"without being bound by existing provisions of law,* to be able at any time, if necessary, to urge any German to fulfill his obligations with all means which appear to him appropriate." This latter enables Hitler to "legalize" by a stroke of the pen even the most flag-

rant atrocities and gives a "defense" to every German violator of the laws and customs of war. Law of April 26, 1942, Reichsgesetzblatt, I, No. 44, translated as Document No. 5, in *National Socialism* (prepared by Dept. of State, 1943), p. 183. The authoritative work by Ernst R. Huber: *Verfassungsrecht des Grossdeutschen Reiches* (1939) emphasizes the fact that the *Führer* is the "lawgiver of the German people . . . unites in himself all of the sovereign authority of the Reich," and can do anything he pleases with respect to law, not being "limited by checks and controls, by special autonomous bodies or individual rights" and being "all-inclusive and unlimited." "There are no personal liberties of the individual which fall outside of the realm of the state and which must be respected by the state."

52. *Commission Report*, p. 123. As we have seen, the source of this formula is the preamble to the Hague conventions on land warfare.

53. James Brown Scott unjustifiably heaped ridicule on a similar concept employed in the proposal to try the ex-Kaiser, "a supreme offense against international morality and the sanctity of treaties." Scott: "The Trial of the Kaiser," in House and Seymour: *What Really Happened at Paris* (1921), pp. 231 et seq.

54. For an illuminative account of the application of this Article by the Permanent Court, see Pfankuchen: *Article 38 of the Statute of the Permanent Court of International Justice and International Law* (1931), unpublished doctoral dissertation on file in the Law Library of Harvard University. This Article has been adopted in the draft convention prepared by the Commission on War Crimes of the London International Assembly, League of Nations Union, except that (c) is limited to the general principles of *criminal* law.

55. Publications of the Court, Series D, No. 1 (3rd ed.).

56. In many instances, too, the conventions contain mealy-mouthed statements reflecting uneasy compromises. Although with one hand they purport to impose obligations upon the belligerents, with the other they take them away through such qualifying phrases as "where circumstances permit," "when the exigencies of military necessity permit," etc. "Military necessity" is a particular favorite of the German General Staff, more crimes having been committed in the German version of its name than in the name of any other virtue used to sanctify brutality and injustice. An International Criminal Court is a peculiarly appropriate — because neutral — agency for deciding whether or not general custom which existed among civilized

peoples *before* the acts of which the accused are charged had or had not made such acts, under the circumstances in question, part of legitimate "military necessity" accepted by all or the great majority of nations.

57. *Proceedings,* p. 335.

58. Holland: *Studies in International Law* (1898), p. 152.

59. Italics supplied. Compare the following from Fachiri: *The Permanent Court of International Justice* (1925), p. 91: "It is submitted that the source of law here contemplated embraces those broad rules and maxims whether more particularly associated with the Roman or Anglo-Saxon systems which are common to the good sense and conscience of the *more enlightened portions of mankind,* and therefore, universally recognized among civilized nations." (Italics supplied.)

60. Hudson: *A Treatise on the Permanent Court of International Justice* (1934), p. 528; id. (1943), p. 610.

61. Compare the following from Story: *Conflicts of Laws* (7th ed., 1872), pp. 24–5: "The laws of one nation may be founded upon a narrow selfishness, exclusively adapted to promote its own peculiar policy, or the personal or proprietary interest of its own subjects, to the injury or even the ruin of those of the subjects of all other countries. A particular nation may . . . assume a superiority of powers and prerogatives, for the very purpose of crushing those of its neighbors who are less fortunate or less powerful. In these, and in many other cases which may easily be put without any extravagance of supposition, there would be extreme difficulty in saying that other nations were bound to enforce laws, institutions, or customs of that nation which were subversive of their own morals, justice or polity." If this is true of one nation, it must be true of the family of nations acting through the medium of an international tribunal.

62. Surely an international criminal court would not be bound to ignore a "general principle of law recognized by civilized nations" simply because one or two States have seen fit to enact into basic law the tyrannical principles mentioned in note 51.

63. The defense of "justification" is of course, like the others, a defense under *domestic* law. However, if, in most countries, the defense is canceled by recognizing that such conduct, when committed in violation of the laws and customs of legitimate warfare, is *not* done in "lawful warfare," then it, too, becomes part of the "prin-

ciples of law recognized by civilized nations" and, as such, enforceable by the International Criminal Court.

64. Where there is a difference in standards among the various civilized systems of law as to negligence and other fields (e.g., insanity, infancy, "superior orders," the line drawn between grand and petty larceny, etc.), the International Criminal Court would be justified in either adopting the standard employed by the majority of civilized nations (especially if it were a considerable majority) or that employed in the law of the accused's nation.

65. Other provisions are perhaps not of sufficient generality to be regarded as reflecting "general principles of law recognized by civilized nations." Here may be included, for example, the "indeterminate" sentence and probation, or the extra-mural supervision of more promising types of offenders. It is not generally known that probation, a typically American institution, has made considerable headway abroad. See Trought: *Probation in Europe* (1927).

66. The Treaty of Versailles provided that trial before Allied military tribunals of persons accused of having committed acts in violation of the laws and customs of war shall be had, "notwithstanding any proceedings or prosecution before a tribunal in Germany or in the territory of her allies." *Treaty of Peace with Germany*, Art. 228 (1919), 13 *Am. J. Int. L.* (Supp.), 151, 250–1.

67. Ideally, the proposed International Criminal Court should be established through the collaboration of Germany, Japan and other Axis nations, as well as neutrals. But it by no means follows that if the co-operation of those nations is not sought or obtained in the setting up of the Court, the judges will not be impartial. Any reasonable person, reflecting upon the work of the Leipzig tribunal and of the notorious "people's courts" in Nazi Germany, or the type of court used by the Japanese in going through the form of "trial" of American aviators who bombed legitimate military objectives in Tokio, and comparing this with the attitude and performance of typical Anglo-American courts, must conclude that there is much more likelihood of a German or Japanese war offender receiving an impartial trial in an International Criminal Court set up by the United Nations than of an American, English, or Polish offender, or one of the Jewish faith, receiving a fair trial in an Axis tribunal. Whether Germans and Japanese will admit they have had a fair trial is another question. But *whatever* is done to Germans and Japanese, their future "leaders," given the opportunity and the

means, can readily construct an elaborate fairy tale of "lynch law" applied by the International Criminal Court. It is not the judgment of hate-filled and gullible peoples that is important; it is the judgment of impartial history.

68. E.g., in the employment by the latter of the "*Juge d'Instruction*" (a chief difference between the Continental "inquisitorial" system and the Anglo-American "accusatorial" system), the greater employment of documentary evidence and written statements of witnesses and public investigators, the permission granted the injured party to participate in the prosecution as "*partie civile*" in pressing private claims for damages, etc.

69. See Winthrop: *Military Law and Precedents* (2nd ed., 1920), p. 29.

70. "Notes of a meeting held at President Wilson's house, Paris, June 13, 1919," Miller: *My Diary at the Conference of Paris,* Vol. XVI, pp. 400–2.

71. One draft convention now under consideration by the United Nations Commission provides for the appointment of the original panel of 35 judges by joint decision of the High Contracting Parties, the appointments to be made "regardless of the nationality of the judge"; subsequent appointments are to be by election of the court from nominees of the High Contracting Powers.

72. These include a comprehensive and well-conceived draft by the League of Nations Union's Commission on War Criminals in London, under the chairmanship of General M. de Baer, and another prepared in the United States Department of State.

73. See note 2 above.

74. Senatorial ratification of the appointments may be required as a condition precedent to American ratification of the convention establishing the court.

75. This is, essentially, the provision of Art. 5 of the 1937 Geneva Convention (unratified) for the creation of an International Criminal Court to deal with acts of terrorism. The draft statute under consideration in London includes "acknowledged authorities on criminal law," and requires them to be conversant with English, which is to be the official language of the Court.

76. The draft convention referred to in previous notes provides for the appointment by the court of a "United Nations' Procurator General," with the same qualifications as the judges from nominees of the High Contracting Parties.

77. E.g., insanity, self-defense, compulsion (to be distinguished from "superior orders"), necessity, etc.; killing in "heat of blood," under legally adequate provocation, killing by criminal negligence rather than intentionally, etc. Note the deliberate omission of the defense of "former acquittal or conviction."

78. See Brinton: *The Mixed Courts of Egypt* (1930), Chaps. X, XI, XII.

79. See p. 28 above, where this point is illuminated by experience in connection with the Leipzig trials.

80. *Commission Report*, p. 145.

81. After announcing that mankind is already aware of the ringleaders and organizers of German atrocities, including Hitler, Göering, Hess, Goebbels, Himmler, Ribbentrop, and Rosenberg, Premier Molotov said that "The Soviet Government considers it necessary that any one of the leaders of fascist Germany who in the course of the war already has fallen into the hands of authorities of States fighting against Hitlerite Germany be brought to trial without delay before a *special international tribunal* and punished with all the severity of criminal law." *Inter-Allied Review*, Vol. II, No. 10 (October 15, 1942), p. 236.

CHAPTER VII

1. *Commission Report*, p. 148.

2. Id., pp. 147–8.

3. *Commission Report*, p. 152.

4. Grotius: *De Jure Belli ac Pacis*, Book I, Chap. IV, Sec. IX; Vattel: *Law of Nations*, Book IV, Chap. VII, Sec. 108.

5. 7 Cranch, 116 (1812).

6. Jean Bodin, often referred to as the founder of the doctrine of sovereignty, not only spoke of rules of an "ordinary" or "civil" character which a political ruler makes law by command, but also of customary laws to which every sovereign is subject and which he cannot lawfully change, there being, therefore, limits to a sovereign's power. The more rigid, legalistic notions of sovereignty are of comparatively late (nineteenth-century) origin. "As in the sixteenth century, so again in the nineteenth century practical political considerations influenced the precise formulation of a theory by law." Coker: "Sovereignty," 14 *Encyc. Soc. Sci.* 265, 267. Practical considerations in our time, especially the fact that sovereigns of certain nations have on more than one occasion sought to overrun the terri-

tories of others in violation of solemn treaty obligations, should bring about a reformulation of the theory of sovereignty. The basis of sovereign immunity in the field of *civil* liability has in recent years been breaking down. See Angell: "Sovereign Immunity — The Modern Trend," 35 *Yale L. J.* (1925), 150 et seq.

7. The ship in question, a public armed vessel of France, commissioned by and in the service of Napoleon, came into Philadelphia after rough weather, to make necessary repairs and lay in supplies. She conducted herself in accordance with both municipal and international law. The United States was then at peace with France. As the schooner was about to depart, she was seized on process issued under a libel filed in a U.S. District Court, which alleged that her libellants had been the sole owners when, previously, she had sailed from Baltimore bound for a Spanish port; that while *en route* she had been seized by persons acting under decrees of the French Emperor and been disposed of in violation of the libellant's rights; that a sentence of condemnation had never been pronounced against her by a court of competent jurisdiction; and that she was still the property of libellants. The U.S. attorney informed the court that the schooner was a public armed vessel of a friendly power; told of the circumstances under which she had involuntarily had to enter the port of Philadelphia; pointed out that if she had ever been the property of libellants such property was divested and became vested in Napoleon within a port of his Empire or a country occupied by his arms outside the jurisdiction of the United States, under the laws of France; and moved the dismissal of proceedings and release of the vessel. The District Court sustained the motion; the Circuit Court reversed it; the Supreme Court reversed the judgment of the Circuit Court and held that the libel must be dismissed and the schooner released.

8. On April 11, 1814, a Convention was entered into between Austria, Prussia, Russia and Napoleon, by which he agreed to retire to the island of Elba. There followed the historic and dramatic "100 days" after the Little Corporal had escaped from the island. On March 13, 1815, the Congress of Vienna issued a Declaration, in terms proposed by Metternich, that by having violated his agreement in escaping from Elba and re-entering France with an armed force, Napoleon had "destroyed the sole legal title upon which his existence depended . . . placed himself outside the protection of the law, and manifested to the world that it can have neither peace

nor truce with him." Consequently, the Powers declared that Napoleon had put himself outside "civil and social relations, and that, as Enemy and Perturbator of the World, he has incurred liability to public vengeance." British and Foreign Papers (1814–15), p. 665. See also pp. 727 et seq.

After Napoleon's defeat at Waterloo, the Prussian Field Marshal Blücher proposed that he be shot on sight as one who, under the above Declaration, was an outlaw. In deference to the wish of the Duke of Wellington, however, this proposal was abandoned. It was then proposed that Napoleon should upon capture, be surrendered to the French Government of Louis XVIII for the "crime of rebellion and treason, with a view to usurping the sovereign authority of France." Since the Bourbon monarch was far from secure on his throne and the Little Corporal was still very popular at home, this solution was rejected by the French Government.

On July 15, 1815, Napoleon gave himself up to Captain Maitland on the English ship *Bellerophon*. After some debate among the Allies, it was agreed that a Convention should be entered into by which Bonaparte would be considered as a common prisoner, albeit in British custody; that he should be imprisoned indefinitely at St. Helena, and that he should not be given up or released by the British except by joint consent. Over Napoleon's protest, the Convention was signed in Paris on August 2, 1815, France accepting the invitation to co-operate a few days later.

The Convention provided that Napoleon "is considered by the Powers . . . as their Prisoner"; that "his custody is specially entrusted to the British government," the "choice of the Place and of the measures which can best secure the object of the present stipulation" being "reserved to His Britannic Majesty"; that the Courts of Austria, Russia and Prussia should appoint Commissioners to abide at the place which the British Government would assign for Napoleon's residence without, however, their being responsible for his custody. The French court was "invited" to send a Commissioner. British and Foreign Papers (1815–16), pp. 200 et seq.

Doubts later having arisen in England whether it was competent for the Crown to detain Bonaparte as a prisoner beyond the termination of the war, bills were enacted (56 Geo. III, Chaps. 22, 23; 1816) laying them at rest. The Preamble to Chap. 22 reveals the motive for Napoleon's imprisonment: "Whereas it is necessary for the Preservation of the Tranquillity of Europe, and for the general safety,

that Napoleon Bonaparte should be detained and kept in custody,"
etc. The Act states that Napoleon should be deemed to be and
treated as a prisoner of war. His status was evidently that of a man
awaiting a trial which was never granted, and unable to be released
on bail.

It should be noted that Napoleon was at this time an *ex*-Emperor;
after his return from Elba he was a rebel against the government of
Louis XVIII. He seems to have been regarded by the Allies as a
stateless person, in the position of a pirate. He was, however, never
tried or sentenced as such.

The trial of Jefferson Davis, ex-President of the Confederacy, for
treason was prevented only by the general amnesty provision at the
close of the Civil War. Although the United States did not recognize the Confederacy as a sovereign State, and Davis as a Chief of
State, it did, inconsistently but understandably, treat Confederate
captured troops as entitled to the status of prisoners of war of an
enemy State. See "The Trial of Jefferson Davis," 21 *Law Magazine
and Law Review* (1866) 258; Case of Davis, 7 Fed. 63 (No. 3,621a,
1867–71).

9. "I agree that it would be folly to contend that an irresponsible
sovereign like the German Emperor, having full constitutional authority to declare a defensive war and having declared this to be
such, could be tried because of this essentially sovereign act or on
the charge that in the prosecution of such a war he disregarded
treaty rights. These acts are imputed to the sovereign state. But my
thesis is that, thus authorized, he must not commit murder in violation of the rules and customs of war. To such conduct his authority
does not extend and while it may, for purposes of reparation in damages, be imputed to the state, this does not relieve him from such
penal visitation as the usages of nations warrant." Gregory: "Criminal Responsibility of Sovereigns for Willful Violations of the Laws
of War," 6 *Va. L. R.* (1919–20), 400, 402.

James Brown Scott, the leading opponent of the trial of the ex-
Kaiser on the ground of sovereign immunity, himself limits such
immunity — at least by strong implication — to the *peacetime* relations of sovereigns. If, therefore, the Allies had tried the ex-Kaiser
before the conclusion of a state of peace, some of the lawyers' objections would have been met. See Adams: "The American Peace Commission and the Punishment of Crimes Committed during War," 39
L. Q. Rev. (1923), 245 et seq.

10. See, among many authorities, Bluntschli: *Das moderne Völkerrecht,* 2nd ed., No. 596. Oppenheim: *International Law* (6th ed. by Lauterpacht, 1940), pp. 270, 279.

11. This refers to the provisions for humane treatment, especially those of the Geneva Prisoners of War Convention of 1929.

12. Quoted by Lord Birkenhead, Attorney-General, in the report of the Law Officers of the Crown to the Imperial War Cabinet. Lloyd George: *Memoirs of the Peace Conference* (1939), Vol. I, p. 60.

13. To be responsible as a Chief of State, the accused must be, in fact and in law, supreme under the polity of his country. If he does not have the actual or constitutional power to forbid or prevent the commission of crimes, and has himself not ordered or participated in them, he cannot be held liable for them. This may become important in attempting to assess the liability of King Victor Emmanuel and the heads of Axis satellite nations. Hitler, however, is constitutionally and in fact omnipotent in the Third Reich; he is the fountain-head of responsibility for both the beginning of a war of brutal aggression and the wholesale atrocities committed during its conduct. The Japanese Emperor would, constitutionally, seem to have the same power as Hitler, although it has been announced by the O.W.I. that President Roosevelt's declaration that the American Government will hold personally and officially responsible the officers of the Japanese Government for "acts of barbarity and manifestations of depravity, such as the murder in cold blood of uniformed members of the United States Armed Forces," and will "in due course bring those officers to judgment," did not extend to the Emperor of Japan. Public press, April 22, 1943. However, since under the Japanese constitution (Art. XVI) the Emperor has the power to order amnesties, commutations, etc., the fact that he refused to save the lives of American airmen under circumstances that protected them through the Geneva Convention of 1929, would implicate him in the murder of helpless prisoners of war. On the theory that a limitation of his power is impossible because he received it from the Sun Goddess, the Emperor of Japan is an absolute monarch and, as such, constitutionally master over the lives and property of his subjects. Causton: *Militarism and Foreign Policy in Japan* (1936), p. 48. See also "What to Do with Japan," Round Table No. 22, *Free World* (1944), Vol. VII, pp. 232 et seq.

14. Réforme Sociale, 1915, p. 203, cited by Garner: *International Law and the World War* (1920), Vol. II, pp. 465, 489.

15. Id.

16. Compare the Kaiser's admission of responsibility in the crocodile-tears letter he sent to Emperor Franz Josef early in the first World War: "My soul is torn; it is necessary to put everything to fire and blood; to slaughter men and women, the children and the aged; not to leave standing a tree or a house. By means of these measures of terrorism, the only ones capable of striking a people so degenerate as the French, we may finish the war before two months. If I respect humanitarian considerations, the war may be prolonged for several years. In spite of my repugnance I have therefore chosen the first system, which will spare much blood, although in appearance the contrary may seem to be the case." Quoted by Mérignhac: "*De la Sanction des Infractions au Droit des Gens,*" etc., 24 *Rev. Gen. de Droit Internat. Public* (1917), pp. 5, 52, from No. 318 of the *Bulletin de l'Œuvre des Ecoles d'Orient.* Cf. Hitler's statement in the text above.

17. Rauschning: *Hitler Speaks* (1939), pp. 89–90.

18. Order of the Supreme Command of the German Army, issued in the name of Hitler as Commander-in-Chief, January 14, 1942, quoted by Schwarzenberger: *International Law and Totalitarian Lawlessness* (1943), p. 152, quoting the three "Molotov Notes on German Atrocities," published on behalf of the Embassy of the U.S.S.R. in London by H. M. Stationery Office, 1942.

19. Field Marshal von Reichenau's Order of October 10, 1941, in Schwarzenberger, op. cit., p. 150.

20. Schwarzenberger, op. cit., pp. 16–17, citing Rauschning.

21. With sound instinct, the coroner's jury of Kinsale, England (May 1915), accused William II as well as his officers who sank the *Lusitania* of "wilful and wholesale murder."

22. As part of their diabolical shrewdness the Nazi military authorities are "hedging" against the future by treating certain American and British prisoners of war satisfactorily and then allowing some to escape so they can report on the good treatment they received. The treatment of Russian prisoners of war is a truer indication of the Nazi mentality and guilt.

23. See Chap. III, pp. 37–38.

24. Cf. Garner: *Recent Developments in International Law* (1925), p. 453.

25. Lord Birkenhead, in Lloyd George, op. cit., p. 62.

26. See note 8.

27. "We are prepared, before the bar of history, to take upon ourselves the responsibility of saying that this man [the former Kaiser] has been guilty of high crimes and misdemeanors, that he has broken the peace of the world, and that he ought to either be exiled or otherwise punished in his own person." Lord Birkenhead, in Lloyd George, op. cit., p. 61.

28. Notes of meeting in President Wilson's House, Paris, June 13, 1919, in Miller: *My Diary at the Conference of Paris,* Vol. XVI, pp. 401–2.

29. Cf. Schwarzenberger, op. cit., p. 106: "A State which consistently breaks its pledged word and contravenes fundamental rules of international customary law, automatically ceases to be a member of the international society. In effect, it outlaws itself." This conclusion is supported by a careful examination of precedents.

30. Dispatch of August 2, 1877, to Mr. Foster (Mexico) by Secretary Evarts, in Moore: *Digest of International Law* (1906), Vol. I, p. 6.

31. Grotius, in his "distinction between a people, although acting unjustly, and pirates or brigands," would perhaps have to place the Nazi State in the class of an association of pirates or brigands: "A commonwealth or state does not immediately cease to be such if it commits an injustice, even as a body; and a gathering of pirates and brigands is not a state, even if they do perhaps mutually maintain a sort of equality, without which no association can exist. The reason is that pirates and brigands are banded together for wrongdoing; the members of a state, even if at times they are not free from crime, nevertheless, have been united for the enjoyment of rights, and they do render justice to foreigners. . . ." *De Jure Belli ac Pacis,* Book III, Chap. III, Sec. II.

32. "In former times it was said to be a customary rule of International Law that pirates could at once after seizure be hanged or drowned by the captor. But this cannot now be upheld, although some writers assert that it is still the law. It would seem that the captor may execute pirates on the spot only when he is not able to bring them safely into a port for trial; but Municipal Law may, of course, interdict such execution." Oppenheim: *International Law* (5th ed., 1937), Vol. I, p. 492.

33. James Brown Scott, a strong opponent of the trial of the ex-

Kaiser, comforted those who were disappointed in the claim that Wilhelm II was immune with the suggestion that "in the future the sovereign or chief executive may, by agreement of the nations, be triable for a crime or offense by an international tribunal." Scott: "The Trial of the Kaiser," in House and Seymour: *What Really Happened at Paris* (1921), pp. 231, 238. In the same work, in response to a question asked him at a public lecture on the subject, he says: "If . . . nations should agree that in certain cases in the future, if offenses be committed in the future, the chief of State should then be tried, then, of course, they have agreed to it. Personally, I think that would be unfortunate, and I hope it will never be attempted." Id., p. 479.

34. One cannot be blamed for harboring some skepticism as to whether the guilty Chiefs of State will be treated any more firmly at the close of this war than they were at the end of the first World War. Consider, for example, the press statement of Undersecretary Welles on October 8, 1942, according to which, although the Inter-Allied Commission set up to cope with war crimes "will deal chiefly with people responsible for war atrocities," it remains a question "whether Hitler will be one." On the other hand, Secretary Hull gave assurances on September 18, 1944, that Hitler and the other arch-criminals are on the list of those marked for punishment by the United Nations War Crimes Commission. These promises were echoed by British and Russian officials.

35. Scott: "The Trial of the Kaiser," in House and Seymour: *What Really Happened at Paris* (1921), pp. 231, 245–6, 240, 257–8.

36. Scott, op. cit., pp. 231, 246.

37. In Lloyd George, op. cit., p. 60.

38. The Nazis have done so many fantastic and incredible things that nothing should surprise the world in the deeds they will perform on the way out. They might, to suggest but one bizarre but perfectly possible thing, present the United Nations with the body of one of the doubles Hitler is alleged to have, while he himself is spirited away to remain a legend like *"der alte Barbarossa."*

CHAPTER VIII

1. Text-writers usually ignore the "act of State" problem, merging it, as do Oppenheim, the English Rules and the American *Rules of Land Warfare,* with the defense of obedience to orders of a military superior, which is considered in the next chapter.

2. Kelsen: "Collective and Individual Responsibility in International Law with Particular Regard to the Punishment of War Criminals," 31 *Cal. L. R.* (1943), 530, 549–52.

3. Id., 541.

4. Even where national law intervenes, the acts involved would never have been made crimes under municipal law had they not been first prohibited by international law. The prohibitions of the laws and customs of warfare are the *common denominator* of all municipal legislation on the subject.

5. See Spaight: *War Rights on Land* (1911), p. 462.

6. Kelsen, op. cit., 531.

7. This, by the way, is the hole bigger than a barn-door which Mr. Kellogg's interpretation of the Kellogg-Briand Pact leaves: "There is nothing in the American draft of an antiwar treaty which restricts or impairs in any way the right of self-defense. That right is inherent in every sovereign state and is implicit in every treaty. Every nation is free at all times and regardless of treaty provisions to defend its territory from attack or invasion and *it alone is competent to decide* whether circumstances require recourse to war in self-defense. If it has a good case, the world will applaud and not condemn its action." D. H. Miller: *The Peace Pact of Paris, A Study of the Briand-Kellogg Treaty* (1928), pp. 213–14. (Italics supplied.)

8. See Kelsen's conceptualistic argument. Kelsen, op. cit., 551. It is submitted that the practical reasons in favor of liability outweigh the theoretical ones opposed to it.

9. See Lauterpacht: *The Function of Law in the International Community* (1933), pp. 387–90, and authorities cited therein; Hackworth: *Digest of International Law,* Vol. V (1943), pp. 471 et seq.; Kingsbury: "The 'Act of State' Doctrine," 4 *A.J.I.L.* (1904), 358 et seq.

During an insurrection in Canada in 1837 against the British Government, members of the colonial authorities' military force invaded the American steamer *Caroline* while she was moored on the American side of the Niagara River, attacked passengers believed to be insurgents, burned the steamer and set her adrift over Niagara Falls. An American citizen was killed. In 1840 McLeod, a British subject, was arrested by the New York authorities and held for trial in a State court on arson and murder charges in connection with the attack on the *Caroline.* See *People* v. *McLeod,* 25 Wend. (N.Y.) 481, 566 (1841); 26 Wend., Appendix, 663 (1841). The British minister at Washington demanded McLeod's immediate release on the ground that the destruction of the *Caroline* was a "public act of persons in Her Majesty's service, obeying the order of their superior authorities"; that therefore it could "only be the subject of discussion between the two national Governments," and could "not justly be made the ground of legal proceedings in the United States against the persons concerned." Secretary of State Webster, while declaring that the Federal Government was then unable to comply with the demand, acknowledged the validity of the British argument: "That an individual, forming part of a public force, and acting under the authority of his Government, is not to be held answerable as a private trespasser or malefactor, is a principle of public law sanctioned by the usages of all civilized nations, and which the Government of the United States has no inclination to dispute." The New York court refused to release McLeod at the intervention of the Federal Government, and he was tried but acquitted on proof of an alibi. The episode was followed by enactment by Congress, on August 29, 1842 (5 Stat. at L. 539, Chap. 257, Sec. 1) of the provision authorizing courts of the United States to issue a writ of *habeas corpus* where a subject of a foreign State is in custody for an act done or omitted under an alleged right or privilege claimed under the sanction of a foreign State, "the validity and effect whereof depend upon the law of nations." Cf. *Underhill* v. *Fernandez,* 65 Fed. Rep. 577 (1895).

In agreeing with Webster, Hall points out that "When a state in the exercise of its right of self-preservation does acts of violence within the territory of a foreign state, *while remaining at peace with it,* its agents cannot be tried for murder of persons killed by them. . . ." The *Caroline* case involved a murder committed on the territory of a *neutral,* the United States. Calhoun, in the Senate, contraverted the position of the British "that where a government authorizes or approves of the act of an individual, it makes it the act of the government, and thereby exempts the individual from all responsibility to the injured country." He argued that "the laws of nations are but the laws of morals, as applicable to individuals, so far modified, and no further, as reason may make necessary in their application to nations. Now, there can be no doubt that the analogous rule, when applied to individuals, is, that both principal and agents, or . . . instruments, are responsible in criminal cases; directly the reverse of the rule on which the demand for the release of McLeod is made. . . . Suppose, then, that the British, or any other government, in contemplation of war, should send out emissaries to blow up the fortifications erected, at such expense, for the defense of our great commercial marts . . . would the production of the most authentic papers, signed by all the authorities of the British Government, make it a public transaction, and exempt the villains from all responsibility to our laws and tribunals?" Moore: *A Digest of International Law* (1906), Vol. II, pp. 23–30, 409–14.

It will be noted that the above transaction involved the action of a government on *neutral* territory in *peacetime;* and the British and Webster's views of the act-of-State exemption are not therefore applicable to the relations of belligerents in wartime, especially when the alleged offenses are violations of the laws and customs of legitimate warfare.

10. Only the sporadic ordinary crime committed by a soldier on his own initiative and not as part of the official politico-military policy of the Nazi and Japanese governments or those of their satellites could, under the above theory, be legitimately punished.

11. Whether or not an act done even under color of office is an "act of State" is a question justiciable within the courts of the State in question; and while its quality depends on action within the State's constitutional limitations, the constitution of the Third Reich could easily be interpreted by German courts to make all the violations of the laws and customs of warfare "acts of State" for the sole purpose of shielding individual malefactors. Such American jurists as Marshall long ago held that an act which is otherwise a trespass upon private rights cannot be "legalized" by governmental authorization, whether executive or legislative, acting beyond constitutional powers. *Little* v. *Barreme*, 2. Cranch (1804) 170. But the Germans would not at all be embarrassed by such a doctrine.

12. Lauterpacht (editor) revising Oppenheim's views in the sixth edition (1940) of the latter's *International Law*, pp. 453–4. It should be noted, however, that the statement in Lauterpacht's Oppenheim seemingly merges the concept of superior orders with that of acts of State.

13. Wright: *A Study of War* (1942), Vol. II, p. 912.

14. "From a practical point of view the first step in making sanctions effective is to divide the delinquent government from its people, and this would be facilitated by a legal theory which held that if a government has resorted to violence, contrary to the interna-

tional obligations of the state, it should be considered to have violated not only international law but also the state's constitution, which, owing its authority to recognition by the family of nations, cannot be assumed to permit violations of the fundamental laws of that society. Such an act of the government should not therefore impose responsibility upon the state as such but should render the government itself liable not only to international sanctions but also to such constitutional sanctions as are provided in case of a betrayal of the state's fundamental laws. A government guilty of aggression should be guilty also of treason. With this theory, the sanctions against a delinquent government might be supported not only by public opinion in foreign countries anxious to sustain international law but also by patriotic opinion in the state which has been betrayed by the delinquent government. Such a theory would be parallel to the common practice of dealing with corporations whose acts have violated criminal law by proceeding not against the corporation as such but against its officers." Wright, op. cit., pp. 913–14.

15. Even the Leipzig court did not resort to the act-of-State argument. It exempted the defendant in the *Dover Castle* submarine case not on the ground that the German Reich had ordered or subsequently ratified lawless submarine warfare, but on the ground of the defendant having sunk the British hospital ship in obedience to the orders of the German admiralty; i.e., "in obedience to the service order of his highest superiors, an order which he considered to be binding."

16. The Draft Convention for the Creation of an International Criminal Court prepared by the London International Assembly, League of Nations Union, and now among those being considered by the United Nations Commission, does not specifically provide for this. It might, however, be covered under the general defense of "superior orders," although the principles involved are not identical.

CHAPTER IX

1. See, for example, Hall: *International Law* (6th ed., 1909), p. 410; Holland: *The Laws and Customs of War on Land* (1904), Arts. 97, 98, p. 45; Phillipson: *International Law and the Great War* (1915), p. 259; Oppenheim, through whose influence the British and American *Rules* provide immunity, maintained this position throughout the five editions of his *International Law,* without dis-

tinction between the government and a military superior as the
source of the order. In the sixth edition, by Lauterpacht (1940),
Vol. II, p. 453, this position is abandoned.

2. The source of the provision is evidently Oppenheim's *International Law* (1st ed., 1906), Vol. II, pp. 264–6. It seems to have
entered therefrom originally into the 1914 edition of the U.S. Army's
Rules of Land Warfare through the official *British Land Warfare,
An Exposition of the Laws and Usages of War on Land for the
Guidance of Officers of His Majesty's Army,* by Col. J. E. Edmonds
and L. Oppenheim (1913).

3. FM 27–10 Basic Field Manual, 1940, p. 87. Oppenheim makes
no distinction between commanders and ordinary troops; he clearly
would exempt all who violate the laws and customs of warfare as
long as they do so upon a governmental order: "Violations of rules
regarding warfare are war crimes only when committed without an
order of the belligerent government concerned. If members of the
armed forces commit violations *by order of their government* they
are not war criminals, and may not be punished by the enemy."
Oppenheim: *International Law* (1st ed., 1906) Vol. II, pp. 264–6.
See note 47 for Oppenheim's argument in support of his view, which
can seriously bedevil the administration of criminal justice in the
case of violators of the laws and customs of warfare.

4. See Chap. VII.

5. Members of the *Gestapo* and other civilian political terror-
istic groups, and the criminalistic industrialists, would not be protected, unless they could be treated as part of the military forces.
Justice requires, however, that the various private revolutionary
forces established by the Nazis and then "legalized" by them (e.g.,
the S.S. "Elite Guards" and the S.A. "Storm Troopers") should not
be afforded the privilege of the defense of superior orders at all.
Even if it should turn out that they have been made part of the
army by German legislation or decree, they originated as private
organizations and their members are volunteers who entered these
organizations for their own aggrandizement; their offenses are ordinary crimes. On the other hand, a decision of the *Reichsgericht* in
the case of "defendant H. Obertruppfuehrer of the S.A.," who was
prosecuted for the consequence of obeying an illegal command of
his superior, M, commander of an S.A. (Storm Troopers') *Sturm-
bann,* "to bring F. into the police station," takes it for granted that,
by virtue of the "Law for the Protection of the Party and State"

(December 1, 1933, R. G. B. 1. I. 1016) a member of the S.A. is in the same position with respect to obedience of orders of a superior as is an ordinary soldier of the *Wehrmacht*. "In doubtful cases, the rules applicable to the *Wehrmacht* may be applied in reaching a decision, taking into account, of course, all the differences between the two services." Case No. 5 D 339/37, *Reichsgericht, 5 Strafsenat,* July 12, 1937, in *Reichsgericht, Strafsachen* 71, p. 284.

6. See note 2 above.

7. "Instructions for the Government of Armies of the United States in the Field," G.O. 100 of A.G.O. of April 24, 1863. This code is generally conceded to be a chief basis not only of subsequent American army rules of warfare but of the international conventions governing legitimate warfare.

8. The sole question is whether there is always liability if the order turns out to have been in fact unlawful, regardless of the accused's knowledge.

9. Winthrop: *Military Law and Precedents* (2nd ed., 1920), p. 296.

10. Id., p. 297.

11. Soviet Russia's military law greatly emphasizes the duty of instant, unquestioning obedience, yet also permits the soldier to lodge complaints when ordered to do something unlawful. See "Disciplinary Code of the Red Army," in *Courts Martial Law* (Library of Congress Law Library, 1943), pp. 5, 17–18.

12. In Germany both the *Reichsgericht* and the *Reichsmilitär- gericht* have adopted the principle that only lawful orders are binding on the subordinate. Cf. decision of the *Reichsgericht* of July 21, 1925, 59 *Entscheidungen des Reichsgerichts in Strafsachen,* 330, 333 et seq., and decisions of the *Reichsmilitärgericht* therein cited. See also the decision of the *Reichsmilitärgericht of* December 30, 1915, 7 *Archiv für Militärrecht,* 106, 381 (c), 21 Deutsche Juristenzeitung (1916), 902. However, there is controversy as to the line between "lawful" and unlawful. Schmidt: *Militärstrafrecht* (1936), p. 58, note 4; Rittau: *Militärstrafgesetzbuch* (No. 196 *Guttentagsche Sammlung*), (2nd ed., 1935), p. 50 et seq. It should be noted that in extreme cases of pressing danger a superior may enforce obedience by physical coercion (i.e., at the point of a gun) without rendering himself punishable. German Military Penal Code, Sec. 124.

13. Winthrop, op. cit., p. 297.

14. It should be remembered that ignorance of the law is normally no excuse in domestic criminal courts; for otherwise too many offenders would be excused and there would be no inducement to know the common prohibitions of ordinary penal codes. But while ignorance of law is no defense in itself, it may throw light on the applicability of the defense of superior orders in borderline cases involving reasonable grounds for belief that an order that was in fact illegal was seemingly lawful. Not only is ignorance of law in itself no defense, but it is also no valid justification or excuse that in the country from which an alien defendant came the act for which he is being prosecuted in his place of temporary residence is no crime. *Rex* v. *Esop*, 7 Car. & Payne, 456 (1836). See Bruce: *The Institutions of Military Law, Ancient and Modern* (Edinburgh, 1717), p. 207: "The general Presumption is, That all who live under any State or Government, are acquainted with its Laws; yet as Ignorance of the Laws is generally presumed to Soldiers, so there wants not Abundance of Instances of their being restored against Deeds, which probably were the Effects of such Ignorance. Yet the Ground of this Restitution is not properly their *Ignorance* of the Laws, (for then, many others might for the same Reason lay Claim to it) but the main Cause is, That their Time being wholly ingrossed by military Imployments, it can scarce be expected they will have Leisure to advise with those whose Profession obliges them to be thoroughly acquainted with Law. And therefore it hath of late been decided in some foreign Courts, That if a Soldier be quartered where he has Opportunity of consulting Lawyers, and himself not being upon actual Duty, he is to forfeit the Privilege; his Error in that Case being rather the Effect of *Negligence* than *Ignorance*. . . . Yet here we are to consider, that this Privilege is only to be understood with Respect to *positive Law*, but nowise to be extended to the *Law of Nature or Nations*. If therefore a Soldier do an Action, which all civilized People reckon a Crime, or which natural Instinct dictates to be such, he is certainly unworthy of the Privilege." See also Chap. VI, note 46.

15. In ordinary military law, he must of course first be given an opportunity to defend his action at a court-martial; but Germany, for instance, permits the use of physical force to obtain instant obedience in certain situations. See note 12.

16. Renault: "*Faits de Guerre Contraire au Droit des Gens*," 39 *Rev. Pénitentiaire* (1915), 427. Compare the attitude of an Ameri-

can (Confederate) officer when ordered to burn Chambersburg during the Civil War (1865): "This act of his subordinate was a great shock to General Lee's sensibilities. Although the destruction of Chambersburg was wholly in the nature of a reprisal for the wholesale destruction of the Virginia valleys and the burning of Southern cities, yet it was so directly in contravention of General Lee's orders, and so abhorrent to the ideas and maxims with which he imbued his army, that a high-spirited Virginia soldier flatly refused to obey the order when directed by his superior officer to apply the torch to the city. That soldier, whose disobedience was prompted by the highest dictates of humanity, deserves a place of honor in history. He was . . . a fit representative of that noblest type of soldier who will inflict every legitimate damage on the enemy in arms against his people, but who scorns, even as a retaliatory measure, to wage war upon defenseless citizens and upon women and children. This knightly Southern soldier was Colonel William E. Peters, of the Twenty-First Virginia Cavalry, who has for forty-six years been a professor in the University of Virginia and at Emory and Henry College. He obeyed the order to move into Chambersburg with his troops and occupy the town, as he was not apprised of the purpose of its occupancy; but when the next order reached him to move his men to the courthouse, arm them with torches, and fire the town, his spirit rose in righteous revolt. He calmly but resolutely refused obedience, preferring to risk any consequences that disobedience might involve, rather than be instrumental in devoting defenseless inhabitants to so dire a fate. . . . Colonel Peters was promptly placed under arrest for disobedience to orders; but, prudently and wisely, he was never brought to trial." Gordon: *Reminiscences of the Civil War* (1903), pp. 305–6.

17. 2 Cranch 170 (U.S., 1804).

18. See cases collected in Winthrop, op. cit., note 52, p. 887.

19. Buchanan: *Reports of Remarkable Trials,* Part II (1813), pp. 3, 58. This case was complicated by the probability that Maxwell had *exceeded* his orders.

20. The report of the trial would seem to indicate that the orders under which Maxwell acted—probably oral rather than written— were confused.

21. 26 Fed. Cas. 653, 657–58. No. 15,494 (C.C.D. Pa., 1813). (Italics supplied.) In *United States* v. *Carr,* 25 Fed. Cas. 306, No. 14,732 (C.C.S.D. Ga., 1872), a sergeant at a United States fort was

prosecuted for having shot to death a soldier who had used disrespectful language. The accused's defense that he had acted under orders of his military superior, the ranking sergeant (and in order to suppress a mutiny or disorder), was waived aside by the circuit court judge in charging the jury, the court stating that a soldier is bound to obey only the lawful commands of his superior and that an order to shoot for use of disrespectful words would, if executed, be murder in both the giver and the executor of the order. (There was also an instruction regarding belief and reasonable grounds to believe that killing was necessary to suppress a mutiny.) A similar result was reached by Justice Story in a case in which a sentry on board a ship carried out the orders of a naval officer to run through the body any man who abused him by words. *United States* v. *Bevans*, 24 Fed. Cas. 1138, No. 14,589 (C.C.D. Mass., 1816); reversed on other grounds, 3 Wheat. 336 (U.S. 1817). "Such an order would be illegal and void, and not binding upon any person; and the party who should give the order, equally with the party who should execute it, would be involved in the guilt of murder." Id., 1140.

22. 13 Howard (1851), 115, 137. (Italics supplied.) The rule in civil suits might well be different from that in criminal prosecutions, since the consequences to the defendant are less serious.

23. Cf. *United States* v. *Bright*, 24 Fed. Cas. 1232, 1238, No. 14,647 (C.C.D. Pa., 1809): "This is said to be a hard case upon the defendants, because, if they had refused obedience to the order of the governor, they would have been punished by the state. I acknowledge it is a hard case; but with this you [the jury] have nothing to do if the law is against the defendants. It may, however, be observed that, had the defendants refused obedience, and been prosecuted before a military or state court, they ought to have been acquitted, upon the ground that the orders themselves were unlawful and void, and we ought, of course, to suppose that they would have been acquitted."

24. See note 21. See also *Commonwealth* v. *Blodgett*, 12 Metc. (Mass.), 56 (1846). For subsequent decisions, see *State* v. *Sparks*, 27 Texas 627 (1864); *Jones* v. *Commonwealth*, 34 Ky. 34 (1866); *Manley* v. *State*, 137 S.W. 1137 (1911). Cf. *In re Fair*, 100 Fed. (C.C.D. Neb., 1900), 149.

25. In a suit involving an alleged trespass by an officer in seizing whiskey under orders of his superior, Mr. Justice Miller stated: "It

is a sufficient answer to the plea, that the defendants were subordinate officers acting under orders of a superior, to say that *whatever may be the rule in time of war, and in presence of actual hostilities,* military officers can no more protect themselves than civilians in time of peace by orders emanating from a source which is itself without authority." *Bates* v. *Clark,* 95 U.S. 204, 209 (1877) (Italics supplied.)

26. Winthrop, op. cit., p. 296.

27. 15 Fed. Cas. 1235, No. 8673 (C.C.D. Cal. 1867). In this case, an action for false imprisonment, it is said that the order may legitimately be deemed unlawful only where "at first blush it is apparent and palpable to the commonest understanding that the order is illegal." 1240.

28. *In re Fair,* 100 Fed. 149, 155 (C.C.A. 9th, 1900). See also *Commonwealth ex rel. Wadsworth* v. *Shortall,* 206 Pa. St. 165 (1903). In such cases it can often be seen that the court in fact found the order to have been *lawful* and need not therefore have enunciated the principle respecting palpably unlawful orders. See also the recent case of *Neu* v. *McCarthy,* 309 Mass. 17 (1941): "Failure of instant obedience leads to military punishment, which may be severe. Recognition of the peculiar necessity of discipline in the military service . . . has led courts in well considered cases to regard obedience to a military order as a justification for conduct which would otherwise give rise to . . . criminal liability, unless the order is so palpably unlawful that a reasonable man in the position of the [soldier] obeying it would perceive its unlawful quality." Id., 22–3. (The illegal order was given by a commanding officer to a private to drive through an intersection regardless of traffic lights.) See also 55 *Harv. L. Rev.* (1942), 651, 653–4, for a discussion of the test of "palpable illegality" in connection with the tort liability of soldiers; and *Restatement: Torts,* Sec. 146, American Law Institute.

29. Harshness of the result was sometimes avoided by pardon after conviction, as in *United States* v. *Bright,* 24 Fed. Cas. 14,647 (1809).

30. Act of Parliament No. 6–1900, 3 Stats. of the Cape of Good Hope, 1652–1905 (1906), 4251.

31. 17 Cape Repts. 56, 58 (1900). (Italics supplied.) The pre-existing English rule is exemplified in *Rex* v. *Thomas,* 4 Maule & Selwyn, 414 (1816). Defendant, a sentinel on a man-of-war, was ordered to keep boats away while the ship was paying off, and given

a musket with blank and ball ammunition. He called repeatedly to certain boats to keep off, and when one persisted in getting close to the ship, he fired and killed an occupant. The jury found that it was the defendant's mistaken impression that it was his duty to fire; but the judges unanimously declared it to be murder, though a proper case for pardon.

32. This part of the test would seem to rule out only the rare and extreme instances where the soldier obeyed an officer whom he knew to be intoxicated, insane, or not in pursuit of strictly military business, but engaged on some independent enterprise of looting, murder, rape, etc.

33. Different evidential rules might legitimately be adopted, on the basis of experience, to govern ease of proof. For instance, "when an officer has a commission to the rank of captain it will be some evidence he was a 'commander'; when he has a commission to the rank of colonel, it will be a presumption that he was a 'commander'; and when he has any commission over the rank of colonel, it will be assumed as a matter of law that he was a commander. Adoption of such arbitrary rules . . . will aid judicial administration and insure prosecution of the framers of policy." Jacobs: "Superior Orders in Wartime," unpublished class paper in author's Seminar on War Criminals, Harvard Law School, 1943, pp. 21–2.

34. *British Manual of Military Law*, Art. 443.

35. Taken from *Izvestia*, December 21, 1943, No. 300 (8293). I have unfortunately been unable to obtain a copy of either the instrument of accusation or the official opinion of the Kharkov court.

36. Notice the resemblance of this to Sec. 347 of the American *Rules* and its English progenitor.

37. Judgment in the cases of Lieutenants Dithmar and Boldt, 16 *Am. J. Int. L.* (1922), 674, 708, 721–2. (Italics supplied.)

38. Id., p. 721. (Italics supplied.) Notice that the German Supreme Court had no hesitancy in applying *international* law directly to individuals.

39. In a recent diatribe reeking with that foul hypocrisy which the Nazis have added to their heartless crimes, Goebbels, in virtually inviting Germans to lynch American aviators for alleged attacks on non-military objectives, warned that pilots "could not invoke the fact that they were obeying orders from higher ups for, completely forgetting what the Germans did to Warsaw, Rotterdam and Belgrade, he went on 'there is no article of war that stipulates

that a soldier, guilty of a vile action, is guiltless by the simple fact he was obeying his superior. Our century has seen the introduction among enemies of certain limits separating war from crime. It would be too much, however, to ask of our victims of this nameless barbarism to stay within such limits without protest. It has always been our wish . . . that war should be conducted within limits of chivalry. Our adversary, however, does not seem capable of such limitation, as the entire world can now bear witness. But the world will also soon see that if this intolerable condition is prolonged we will find means of defending ourselves against such crimes. We owe it to our people, which is defending itself with so much honesty and courage, that it be not allowed to become human game to be hunted down by the enemy.'" Brigham, in *New York Times,* May 27, 1944, from Berne.

40. This conclusion is arrived at from examination of interpretations of Sec. 47 of the Military Penal Law, which provides: "Where the execution of an order in a military matter violates a penal law, the superior who gave the order is alone responsible therefor. However, the subordinate who obeyed the order shall be punished as a participant (i.e., as an accomplice (*Mittäter*), instigator (*Anstifter*) or accessory (*Gehilfe*) . . . if he knew that the order concerned an act which aimed at a civil or military crime or offense (*Verbrechen oder Vergehen*). German decisions have interpreted this to require a finding (a) that the superior's order was *aimed* at the commission of a crime, and (b) that the subordinate *knew* such was the superior's intention when he issued the order; mere doubt as to the superior's aim is not enough to make the subordinate responsible. 13 *Entscheidungen des Reichsmilitärgerichts,* 180. See Rittau: *Militärstrafgesetzbuch (Guttentagsche Sammlung,* No. 196) (2nd ed., 1935), p. 54, note 6. Cf. Keil: *"Zur Auslegung der Ziffer 2 des § 47 Militärstrafgesetzbuch, Archiv für Militärrecht* (1913–14), pp. 26–39.

41. 16 *Am. J. Int. L.* (1922), 707. A German court-martial refused to consider a like defense by Captain Charles Fryatt, and executed him, claiming he was not a member of a combatant force. See II Grotius Society, 54–5; 10 *A. J. I. L.* (1916), 865.

42. Schwarzenberger: *International Law and Totalitarian Lawlessness* (1942), p. 63, points out that "with the Treaty of Washington Act, 1922, this provision became part of British criminal law." See Treaties of Washington Act, 1922, 12 & 13 Geo. 5, c. 21, s. 4,

and McNair: "When Do British Treaties Involve Legislation?"
B. Y. I. L., 1928, pp. 65–6.

43. Schwarzenberger, *op. cit.*, p. 72.

44. Evidently French military law as applied during the last
World War refused to recognize any defense of superior orders. The
fact of obedience by a subordinate of a superior's order under particularly unavoidable circumstances was, however, sometimes made
the basis of recommendation for clemency after conviction. Mérignhac: *"De la Sanction des Infractions au Droit des Gens,"* XXIV *Rev.
Gen. de Droit Internat. Public* (1917), 5, 53.

45. This time element, together with the fact that the "superior
orders" defense deals only with *military* orders, most nearly dis-
tinguishes the defense of "compulsion" from that of superior orders.
Stephen (*A Digest of the Criminal Law*, 1877, Art. 31) states the
law of compulsion as follows: "An act which, if done willingly,
would make a person a principal in the second degree or an aider
and abettor in a crime, *may* be innocent if the crime is committed
by a number of offenders, and if the act is done only because, during
the whole of the time in which it is being done, the person who does
it is compelled to do it by threats on the part of the offenders in-
stantly to kill him or do him grievous bodily harm, if he refuses;
but *threats of future injury* do not excuse any offense." (Italics supplied.) The threatened grievous injury to the actor must be immediately present and the fear must be well grounded. See *State* v.
Nargashian, 26 R.I. (1904), 299, and cases therein cited. Statutory
provisions clarify the issue by either permitting compulsion as a
defense under carefully guarded circumstances or only for certain
crimes, or prohibiting it altogether. See, e.g., N.Y. Pen. Law, Sec.
859; N.D. Comp. Laws (1913), Sec. 9212; Cal. Pen. Code (Deering,
1937), Sec. 26; and cf. Hawaii Rev. Laws (1935), Sec. 5324: ". . .
No one shall be able to justify himself against a charge of his doing
an injury to another by showing the threat of an imminent danger of
an equal or less injury to himself."

It is clear that if and when coercion is a justification the reason
lies in the recognition of the strength of the instinct of self-preservation; i.e., a recognition of human frailty; but a soldier's entire
work involves the suppression of the instinct of self-preservation.

46. As to the defense of "compulsion," see prior note.

47. The *rationale* of Oppenheim's rule of complete exemption is
stated to be that "the law cannot require an individual to be pun-

ished for an act which he was compelled by law to commit." *International Law*, 1st to 5th editions, Vol. II, Sec. 253, note. It has been correctly pointed out that under the Oppenheim theory of "compulsion by law," the Nazi "'law' would not permit punishment of those who were engaged in exterminating helpless Nazi-conquered peoples in accordance with its commands. But does it follow that the Polish law, for example, cannot require punishment of those who murdered priests and women in Poland, because the Nazi 'law' compelled them to commit these murders? The question whether a given killing is a legitimate act of warfare or a war crime is determinable by International Law, which requires punishment for war crimes in the interest of the entire community of civilized States, and, of course, not by the 'law' of the lawless belligerent government which authorized or ordered it." Sack: "Punishment of War Criminals and the Defence of Superior Order," 60 *L. Q. Rev.* (1944), 63, 67. "Professor Verdross claims that a prisoner of war can claim as a right to be tried in accordance with his own criminal law, whenever this happens to be more lenient, as, e.g., when, under it an excuse unknown to the law of the captor State is provided. Though the captor State may apply this principle, it is not prescribed by International Law. To interpret in this manner the principle of reciprocity on which Professor Verdross bases his argument, would amount to a reduction of the responsibility for war crimes to the lowest possible denominator. . . . This doctrine would offer too easy a means of evading the risks involved in the commission of war crimes and it would open the door to an immunity, unlimited for all practical purposes, of war criminals." Schwarzenberger, op. cit., p. 64.

48. A great deal of *ex post facto* punishment has been provided for in Nazi Germany: "Whoever commits an act which the law declares punishable or which deserves punishment according to the principle of criminal law and to the *sound feelings of the people,* will be punished." Sec. 2 of the law concerning alteration of the criminal code, June 28, 1935, R.G.B.1. I, 839. (Italics supplied.) The Nazis have also tried and punished many nationals of the countries they have occupied, for alleged crimes committed before the year 1939, the acts of which, by *the laws of those countries,* were not crimes at that time. In addition, a resolution "unanimously approved" by the Robot *Reichstag* provides that the "Führer must without being bound by existing provisions of law, be able at any

time, if necessary, to urge any German to fulfill his obligations with all means which appear to him appropriate," thereby enabling Chancellor Hitler to "legalize" in advance the most flagrant atrocities and giving a "defense" of superior orders to every German violator of the laws and customs of war. Law of April 26, 1942, in Doc. No. 5, *National Socialism*, prepared by the Department of State, 1943, p. 183. The word "urge" is perhaps inaccurately translated ("zur Erfüllung seiner Pflichten *anzuhalten*") unless one bears in mind the Nazi methods of "urging."

49. I have not discussed the defense of "ignorance or mistake of fact," which is of course also available to soldiers, and might indeed be used often as a device for mitigating the rigors of the superior-orders defense, by using the fact of obedience to orders as a stepping-stone to proof of ignorance or mistake of fact. Stephen stresses this device: ". . . the fact that he did so act, and the fact that the order was apparently lawful, are in all cases relevant to the question whether he believed, in good faith and on reasonable grounds, in the existence of a state of facts which would have justified what he did apart from such orders." Stephen: *Digest of the Criminal Law* (1877), Art. 202. It has been suggested that such an order not only should be of evidential value on the issue of ignorance or mistake of fact, but should go farther and raise a presumption that the soldier honestly and reasonably believed in a state of facts which, had they been actual, would have relieved him of responsibility. Brown: "Military Orders as a Defense in Civil Courts," 8 *J. Crim. L. and Crimin.* (1917–18), 190, 207. "Thus a soldier ordered by a superior officer to shoot a group of civilians might perhaps at his trial successfully defend on the grounds that it is to be presumed he believed they were guerillas who under the laws of war may be executed as illegal belligerents and were not hostages being executed for the acts of others of the civil population for which there is, as the soldier should know, no justification under the rules of war. Under the test previously indicated, the order would not be 'clearly illegal.' But an order to shoot a group of captured enemy soldiers in uniform, after an argument between them and the superior giving the order, would not raise such a presumption of fact and would not even be relevant to his defense. Such an order would be 'clearly illegal' under the previous test." Goldman: "Availability of the Defense of 'Superior Orders' to Enemy War Criminals Tried by United States

Military Tribunals," student's class paper in author's Seminar on War Criminals, Harvard Law School, 1943.

CHAPTER X

1. At the present writing (August 1944) the Argentine Government has broken diplomatic relations with Germany and Japan, but has passed through a "colonels' revolution" showing its continued sympathy for Fascism. Turkey has broken diplomatic relations with the Axis. The position of Eire is peculiar; it is a neutral, yet a member of the British Commonwealth of Nations. See also notes 5, 23, 24.

2. Although prisoners of war are triable for violations of the laws of warfare, they must ordinarily be released at the end of the war. There is some doubt whether officers and soldiers surrendered or "extradited" by the defeated belligerent in accordance with terms of an armistice convention can be technically deemed "prisoners of war," in the light of the Geneva Convention of 1929(Art. 1, Sec. 2) applying its terms to ". . . persons belonging to the armed forces of belligerents who are captured by the enemy *in the course of military operations.*" However, the Versailles Commission (only the Japanese members dissenting) concluded that "every belligerent has, according to international law, the power and authority to try the individuals alleged to be guilty of . . . violations of the Laws and Customs of War," not only "if such persons have been taken prisoners," but also if they *"have otherwise fallen into its power."* *Commission Report,* p. 121 (italics supplied). The armistice as well as the treaty of peace can readily provide a lawful basis of postwar trial of war criminals, as was done by Art. 228 of the Treaty of Versailles: "The German Government recognizes the right of the Allied and Associated Powers to bring before military tribunals persons accused of having committed acts in violation of the laws and customs of war."

3. See *Soviet War Documents,* Special Supp. to Information Bulletin, Embassy of U.S.S.R., 1943. The instrument of accusation, naming seven of the highest German political and military officials as responsible for the mass murders at Lidice, Czechoslovakia, was laid before the United Nations Commission on June 10, 1944.

4. DeBaer: "Report of the Commission on some Questions Connected with the Handing Over of War Criminals for Trial,"

October 1943, in London International Assembly, *Reports on Punishment of War Crimes* (limited, mimeographed edition), pp. 372, 375.

5. IX *U.S. Dept. of State Bull.* (1943), 62. Similar warnings were made indirectly, through the press, on August 30, 1944, by the American Secretary of State, Cordell Hull, and by Sir Cecil Hurst, Chairman of the United Nations War Crimes Commission. One recent official declaration as this goes to press was Churchill's statement of September 26, 1944, in reply to a question in the House of Commons, that some neutrals had already made satisfactory statements but that he had not "noticed any particular pronouncement" from Spain. (Perhaps Franco is uneasy about the precedent this would set.) Churchill added: "The governments are resolved to do their utmost to provent Nazi criminals finding a refuge in neutral territories from the consequences of their crimes. . . . It is not our intention to allow the escape of these men to be effected without exerting almost every resource which a civilized power can contemplate." One wonders whether this will include economic sanctions against such countries as Fascist Spain and Argentina. On September 28, 1944, Secretary of State Hull revealed that in August another warning had been given, this seemingly directed especially to Argentina and possibly also to Portugal, and couched in the strong language that the relations of neutrals with the United States "would be adversely affected for years to come" if they should provide sanctuary for Hitler and other war criminals.

6. Statement of July 31, 1943, by the National Socialist Information Service.

7. *Danziger Vorposten*, July 23, 1942. Quoted in 24 "Jewish Comment," December 1, 1943. Observe the psychopathologic phenomenon of "projection," the throwing upon his innocent victims of the blame, the motivation, and the misconduct of the person who is himself black with guilt.

8. How badly the Allies misjudged the probable action of the Netherlands may be shown by the following extract from the minutes of the Interallied Conference to Prepare for the Peace Congress and of the remarks of Lord Birkenhead to the Imperial War Cabinet: "Baron Sonino asked what would be done if Holland declined to give up the ex-Kaiser, basing herself on her tradition of Liberal views. Mr. Lloyd George said that Holland would then be put outside the League of Nations. M. Clemenceau agreed. . . .

He said that there would be no question of Holland standing against
the opinion of all the Allied Powers." Lloyd George: *Memoirs of
the Peace Conference* (1939), Vol. I, p. 84. (Hereinafter cited as
Memoirs.) How Hitler repaid the Dutch for their kindness to
Wilhelm II is well known.

9. This is the method evidently envisioned by Lord Birkenhead
in his report to the Imperial War Cabinet: "Infinite vistas of litigious
disputations are opened by an argument whether according to the
law of Holland he can be extradited or not. And if, contrary to my
opinion, he could be extradited, he could only be charged for the
very offense (possibly a limited one) which had been successfully
alleged as the ground in law of his extradition. I think it is unnecessary to ask whether in law we can extradite him, because it seems to
me that Holland must, in effect, give him up. The League of Nations
or the Conference of the Allies which will precede the formation of
the League of Nations has, or will have, powerful arguments to address to Holland, and the internal condition of Holland seems to
me to be such that it would be very difficult for her to reject arguments of the kind indicated. This is not a point of law, but my own
conclusion is that the difficulty of obtaining control of the person
of the ex-Kaiser from Holland will not be an insuperable one."
Memoirs, p. 61.

10. Some of the Allied statesmen breathed a sigh of relief at Holland's stand, for it seemed to them desirable to "let sleeping dogs
lie." Extradition of other leading war criminals (e.g., the Crown
Prince, also in Holland; Crown Prince Rupprecht of Bavaria, who
evidently found asylum in Switzerland — both of them chargeable
with atrocities and ordinary theft by looting) was never even requested by the Allies. In fact some notorious criminals who were in
the power of the Allies at the time of the Armistice were not even
tried by them, but returned to Germany. U-boat Lieutenant Kiese-
wetter, for instance, who had sunk the hospital ship *Glenart Castle,*
and against whom ample evidence of guilt was at hand, was, after
detention in the Tower of London for trial, returned to Kiel, un-
scathed, in 1919. Will this regard for the "delicacies of the situation"
and letting "bygones be bygones" so far as high-placed malefactors
are concerned be repeated by the United Nations statesmen at the
close of the present war? Rudolf Hess has not yet been tried.

11. See note 1.

12. For an illustration of the denial of an extradition request, on

the ground that the offenses for which the demanding State (Republic of Salvador) wanted to put the refugee on trial were of a political nature, see *Re Ezeta*, 62 Fed. (N.D. Cal. 1894), 972.

13. Thus, "in the treaties signed by Belgium, extradition for false imprisonment is allowed only when it has been committed by a private person; deportations of civilians done by a person in authority (which has consistently been the case) are not covered. On the other hand all treaties provide extradition for abduction: in some cases this might possibly cover the deportation of minors, and that of females for the purpose of prostitution, but not of male adults." DeBaer, op. cit., p. 377.

14. A few statutes and draft conventions provide by implication or directly that acts otherwise political in character may none the less be extraditable if committed with unusual cruelty or barbarity or if, in case of civil war, they violated the laws of legitimate warfare. Thus Field's *Outlines of an International Code* (1876) provides that "any offense committed in furthering civil war, insurrection or political commotion, which, if committed between belligerents, would not be a crime" is non-extraditable; implying, of course, that if the offense did not meet such test the offender could be extradited. The Resolution adopted by the Institute of International Law at Oxford in 1880 (*Annuaire de l'Institut de Droit International*, 1880, V. No. 14 (b), p. 127, provides that "in passing upon acts committed during a political rebellion, an insurrection or a civil war, it is necessary to inquire whether or not they are excused by the usages of war." See also Beauchet: *Traité de l'Extradition* (1899), p. 227, who states that if the acts are against the law of nations, even in an international war, such acts shall not be deemed anything but ordinary common-law crimes and shall be subject to extradition.

15. This claim will probably be put forth by Nazi-Fascist lawyers, those very *"Herren Professoren"* whom Hitler has treated with contempt. They will claim that the killings of the innocent civilians were part of their "legal" policy — an argument to be expected from that amalgam of hypocrisy and arrogance that typifies Nazi *"Weltanschauung,"* which regards the world as Germany's oyster, to be generously opened for the "good" of the rest of benighted mankind.

16. DeBaer, op. cit., p. 378.

17. *Dagens Nyheter*, August 1, 1943.

18. *Handelstidningen*, August 18, 1943.

19. *Berner Tagwacht,* August 9, 1943.

20. The fallen dictator did not flee to Switzerland (up to May 1944, when the above quotation was included in this work); but his daughter, Edda, the widow of the little bereaved Count Ciano, did; and it may well be that some of the German financial "wizards" and trickster economists, who are accessories to the lootings which are part of the official German program of conquest, have already purchased villas in Switzerland or other neutral countries.

21. *Arbeiter Zeitung,* August 3, 1943.

22. Pertinax, in *New York Times,* August 1, 1944.

23. *New York Times,* September 6, 1944. On September 29, 1944, the Argentine Government claimed to have closed its doors to Axis war criminals and to have prohibited their making deposits or purchases in Argentina, the Foreign Office stating that it was "unconceivable" that informed quarters could have believed press reports to the effect that Axis war criminals would be granted asylum in the Argentine. This was however followed shortly by President Roosevelt's charge that the Argentine Government had repudiated its "solemn inter-American obligations" and his statement of "increasing concern" over the development of Nazi-Fascist influence in that country. The exact position of Eire, Portugal, and Vatican City has as yet not been made public. Spain has recently denied that there was any basis for the view that Axis leaders might find refuge there.

24. At a press conference held in London on August 30, 1944, Sir Cecil Hurst, Chairman of the United Nations War Crimes Commission, announced that considerable pressure will be put on any neutral countries giving refuge to war criminals: "If any substantial movement took place under which the authors of war crimes began to take refuge in neutral countries, I have no doubt that if the United Nations found that existing extradition measures were inappropriate, some arrangement would be made forthwith. After the last war Holland dug herself in over the question of the ex-Kaiser at Doorn. You may be sure the United Nations governments are alive to that danger on this occasion."

CHAPTER XI

1. The numbers will be large absolutely though small relatively. "The number of persons eventually found guilty will undoubtedly be extremely small compared to the total enemy populations. It is

not the intention of this Government or of the Governments associated with us to resort to mass reprisals. It is our intention that just and sure punishment shall be meted out to the ringleaders responsible for the organized murder of thousands of innocent persons and the commission of atrocities which have violated every tenet of the Christian faith." President Roosevelt, in White House press release, 7 *U.S. Dept. of State Bull.* (1942), 797.

2. See pp. 21, 85.

INDEX

INDEX

INDEX

iii

iv

INDEX

INDEX

INDEX

xi

INDEX

xii

A NOTE ON THE TYPE IN WHICH
THIS BOOK IS SET

The text of this book is set in Caledonia, a Linotype face designed by W. A. Dwiggins, the man responsible for so much that is good in contemporary book design and typography. Caledonia belongs to the family of printing types called "modern face" by printers — a term used to mark the change in style of type-letters that occurred about 1800. It has all the hard-working feet-on-the-ground qualities of the Scotch Modern face plus the liveliness and grace that is integral in every Dwiggins "product" whether it be a simple catalogue cover or an almost human puppet.

The book was composed, printed, and bound
by Kingsport Press, Kingsport, Tennessee.